Aid to Armenia

Manchester University Press

SERIES EDITOR: BERTRAND TAITHE

This series offers a new interdisciplinary reflection on one of the most important and yet understudied areas in history, politics and cultural practices: humanitarian aid and its responses to crises and conflicts. The series seeks to define afresh the boundaries and methodologies applied to the study of humanitarian relief and so-called 'humanitarian events'. The series includes monographs and carefully selected thematic edited collections which cross disciplinary boundaries and bring fresh perspectives to the historical, political and cultural understanding of the rationale and impact of humanitarian relief work.

Islamic charities and Islamic humanism in troubled times
    Jonathan Benthall

Humanitarian aid, genocide and mass killings: Médecins Sans Frontières, the Rwandan experience, 1982–97
    Jean-Hervé Bradol and Marc Le Pape

Calculating compassion: Humanity and relief in war, Britain 1870–1914
    Rebecca Gill

Humanitarian intervention in the long nineteenth century
    Alexis Heraclides and Ada Dialla

The military–humanitarian complex in Afghanistan
    Eric James and Tim Jacoby

Global humanitarianism and media culture
    Michael Lawrence and Rachel Tavernor (eds)

A history of humanitarianism, 1775–1989: In the name of others
    Silvia Salvatici

Donors, technical assistance and public administration in Kosovo
    Mary Venner

The NGO CARE and food aid from America 1945–80: 'Showered with kindness'?
    Heike Wieters

The Red Cross movement: Myths, practices and turning points
    Neville Wylie, James Crossland, Melanie Oppenheimer (eds)

Aid to Armenia
Humanitarianism and intervention from the 1890s to the present

Edited by Jo Laycock and Francesca Piana

Manchester University Press

Copyright © Manchester University Press 2020

While copyright in the volume as a whole is vested in Manchester University Press, copyright in individual chapters belongs to their respective authors, and no chapter may be reproduced wholly or in part without the express permission in writing of both author and publisher.

Published by Manchester University Press
Oxford Road, Manchester M13 9PL
www.manchesteruniversitypress.co.uk

British Library Cataloguing-in-Publication Data
A catalogue record for this book is available from the British Library

ISBN 978 1 5261 4220 7 hardback
ISBN 978 1 5261 7905 0 paperback

First published 2020

The publisher has no responsibility for the persistence or accuracy of URLs for any external or third-party internet websites referred to in this book, and does not guarantee that any content on such websites is, or will remain, accurate or appropriate.

Typeset by
Servis Filmsetting Ltd, Stockport, Cheshire

Contents

List of illustrations	vii
List of contributors	viii
Acknowledgements	x
Figures	xiii
Maps	xv

Introduction   1
Jo Laycock and Francesca Piana

1. Humanitarian accountability: Anglo-American relief during the Hamidian massacres, 1894–98   17
Stéphanie Prévost

2. Pragmatism and personalities: Etienne Brasil and Brazilian engagement with Armenia, 1912–22   34
Heitor Loureiro

3. 'An appeal from afar': The challenges of compassion and the Australian humanitarian campaigns for Armenian relief, 1900–30   50
Joy Damousi

4. Humanitarian crisis at the Ottoman–Russian border: Russian imperial responses to Armenian refugees of war and genocide, 1914–15   66
Asya Darbinyan

5. 'Making good' in the Near East: The Smith College Relief Unit, Near East Relief and visions of Armenian reconstruction, 1919–21   83
Rebecca Jinks

6   Care and connections: Orphans, refugees and Norwegian relief in the
    Soviet Armenian Republic, 1922–25   100
    Inger Marie Okkenhaug

7   Humanitarian diaspora? The AGBU in Soviet Armenia, 1920–30s   115
    Vahé Tachjian

8   Tremor and change: Humanitarian interventions after the 1988
    earthquake in Armenia   131
    Katja Doose

9   Humanitarian intervention meets a de facto state: International
    peacebuilding consortiums in Nagorny Karabakh, 2003–16   147
    Laurence Broers

10 Refuge in the 'homeland': The Syrians in Armenia   164
    Sossie Kasbarian

    Afterword: Displacement and the humanitarian response to suffering:
    reflections on aiding Armenia   181
    Peter Gatrell

    Epilogue   187
    Ronald Grigor Suny

    Index   190

Illustrations

Figures

1 American Committee for Armenian and Syrian Relief aid map, 1918. MRL 2: Near East Relief Committee Records, series 1, box 5, folder 1–2, The Burke Library at Union Theological Seminary, Columbia University in the City of New York.   xiii
2 American Committee for Armenian and Syrian Relief map of Armenian deportations. MRL 2: Near East Relief Committee Records, series 1, box 4, folder 5, The Burke Library at Union Theological Seminary, Columbia University in the City of New York.   xiv

Maps

1 The Ottoman Empire in 1914   xv
2 The Ottoman/Russian Borderlands 1914–23   xvi
3 Armenia and Nagorny Karabakh   xvii

Contributors

Laurence Broers is an Associate Fellow at the Royal Institute for International Affairs at Chatham House and co-editor-in-chief of the triannual journal *Caucasus Survey*. He is the author of *Armenia and Azerbaijan: Anatomy of a Rivalry* (Edinburgh University Press, 2019).

Joy Damousi is Director of the Institute of Humanities and Social Sciences, Australian Catholic University. She has published on the aftermaths of war and the history of migration and refugees. Her current research is on histories of child refugees and Australian humanitarianism during the twentieth century.

Asya Darbinyan is a Postdoctoral Fellow in Holocaust and Genocide Studies at Stockton University. She holds a PhD in History from the Strassler Center for Holocaust and Genocide Studies, Clark University (2019). Previously, she was the Deputy Director of the Armenian Genocide Museum-Institute, Yerevan.

Katja Doose is a Postdoctoral Fellow at the Ecole des Hautes Etudes en Sciences Sociales (EHESS) and a part-time lecturer at the Graduate Institute in Geneva. She focuses on Soviet and Russian environmental history.

Peter Gatrell teaches History at the University of Manchester where he is also affiliated to the Humanitarian and Conflict Response Institute. His latest book is *The Unsettling of Europe: The Great Migration, 1945 to the Present* (Allen Lane, 2019).

Rebecca Jinks is Lecturer in Modern History at Royal Holloway, University of London. Her research and teaching interests include histories of comparative genocide, humanitarianism, gender and photography.

List of contributors

Sossie Kasbarian is Senior Lecturer in Comparative Politics at the University of Stirling. She specialises in Middle East Politics and Diaspora Studies. She is co-editor of *Diaspora: A Journal of Transnational Studies*.

Jo Laycock is Senior Lecturer in Migration and Diaspora History at the University of Manchester. She is the author of *Imagining Armenia: Orientalism, Ambiguity and Intervention, 1879–1925* (Manchester University Press, 2009). Her current research focuses on refugee relief and resettlement in Soviet Armenia.

Heitor Loureiro is Professor of Brazilian Foreign Policy at Faculdades Metropolitanas Unidas (FMU), São Paulo, Brazil. He received his PhD in History at São Paulo State University (Unesp). During the doctorate, he was visiting scholar at the Matenadaran in Yerevan, Armenia.

Inger Marie Okkenhaug (PhD, University of Bergen 1999) is a Professor of History at Volda University College, Norway. Her current research deals with Scandinavian relief and welfare in Palestine and among Armenians in Syria and Armenia after the First World War.

Francesca Piana is a Visiting Lecturer at the Global Studies Institute of the University of Geneva. She holds a PhD in International History and Politics from the Graduate Institute of International and Development Studies in Geneva (2013). Her research includes the history of internationalism, humanitarian aid, migration, and gender in twentieth-century European and international history.

Stéphanie Prévost is Senior Lecturer in nineteenth-century British History at the Université de Paris. She holds a PhD on 'Britain and the Eastern Question, 1875–1898' (Tours University, 2010). Her current research includes British relief to Ottoman Armenian victims and refugees before the Genocide.

Ronald Grigor Suny is William H. Sewell, Jr. Distinguished University Professor of History at the University of Michigan and Emeritus Professor of Political Science and History at the University of Chicago. He has finished a biography of the young Stalin – *Stalin: Passage to Revolution* – for Princeton University Press and a series of historiographical essays on Stalinism and Soviet history – *Red Flag Wounded: Stalinism and the Fate of the Soviet Experiment* – for Verso Books.

Vahé Tachjian was born in Lebanon and he earned his PhD at the Ecole des Hautes Etudes en Sciences Sociales (EHESS), Paris. He is the chief editor of the *Houshamadyan* website (based in Berlin), a project to reconstruct the Ottoman Armenians' local history and memory.

Acknowledgements

This volume has been several years in the making. We thank all of our contributors for their hard work and for persisting with this volume even when the going was slow. This is not an easy time to work in academia, especially as an early career researcher, and we are grateful for your dedication.

A one-day workshop 'Aid to Armenia' held at Birkbeck College, University of London in summer 2016 began the conversations and collaborations which resulted in this volume. Although our focus has shifted somewhat from the workshop to this volume, we are grateful to all of those who presented their research, acted as discussants and participated in a final roundtable – Anna Aleksanyan, Dawn Chatty, Katja Doose, Peter Gatrell, Rebecca Gill, Philippa Hetherington, Armine Ishkanian, Becky Jinks, Sossie Kasbarian, Inger Marie Okkenhaug, James Perkins, Stéphanie Prévost, Maria Rizou and Anahit Shirinyan. All of you have played an important role in shaping this collection. We would also like to thank the Humanities Research Centre at Sheffield Hallam University, the Reluctant Internationalists research project at Birkbeck College and the Pierre du Bois Foundation in Geneva for supporting this workshop. A credit for the title, 'Aid to Armenia', should go to Johanna Conterio of the Reluctant Internationalists project.

In putting this volume together we have consciously tried to capture the diversity of scholars working on Armenia and humanitarianism, and have included contributions from scholars from Armenia, from the diaspora and from a range of other regions. The volume is intended to provide a platform for new and developing research; bringing the work of postgraduates and early career scholars together with that of more senior scholars. We thank Bertrand Taithe for his encouragement in developing this edited volume and for his support and helpful comments along the way. Thanks to all of the team at Manchester University Press for their support and especially for their patience with this project. Anonymous readers from the press provided helpful comments on our initial proposal and on a later draft of the manuscript, we thank them for helping refine our approach. Laure Humbert and Davide Rodogno kindly read the introduction and helped us think through some revisions.

Acknowledgements

Jo Laycock: I thank former colleagues in History at Sheffield Hallam University for their support and friendship. In particular, Robbie Aitken, Laura Evans and Merv Lewis helped keep me going through difficult times. Chris Hopkins of the Humanities Research Centre provided vital support for this project and for my research in general. Since moving to the History department at the University of Manchester, Sasha Handley, Sarah Roddy and Charlie Wildman-Tarrozi have been invaluable sources of support and encouragement with my research, as well as good friends. Many of the dilemmas I have faced while putting this book together have been resolved over a bottle (or two) of wine with Ulrike Ziemer and Laurence Broers. You have both helped me to look outside my own discipline and better understand the modern South Caucasus. In Armenia, I would like to thank Shushan Ghazaryan for incredible research assistance, insight and friendship. From Michigan, Jeremy Johnson has helped me keep my sense of humour through the challenges of research and writing. Closer to home, Ben Hill should be thanked for his patience during all the times I got 'lost' in this project, and for untangling some of the hideous sentences I managed to come up with. I am also grateful to Emma Laycock for bringing me back down to earth with her periodic reminders to stop 'going on about everything', and to Stella and Bill Laycock for always being there.

Francesca Piana: I am indebted to many people and institutions. Davide Rodogno, Professor at the Graduate Institute of International and Development Studies, introduced me to the history of humanitarianism as a PhD student and research assistant, while he also has been a continuous support ever since.[1] The Swiss National Science Foundation generously awarded me with postdoctoral fellowships, which gave time for reading, researching, and writing.[2] I am thankful to the Armenian Genocide Museum-Institute in Yerevan for awarding me with the Raphael Lemkin scholarship in 2013. At Birkbeck College, Jessica Reinisch and the Reluctant Internationalists project provided an energetic environment for the organisation of the workshop from which this book originated. Being a Postdoctoral Fellow in Women's and Gender History at the Department of History of the University of Binghamton and *Journal of Women's History* created further time for dedicated thinking and writing. More recently, my time at the University of Geneva has been enriching and productive. Over the years, many colleagues have been a source of support and friendship. I am grateful to Anna Aleksanyan, Pamela Ballinger, Elisa Camiscioli, Heather Dehaan, Shaloma Gauthier, Tom McDonough, Jean Quartaet, Pierre-Yves Saunier, and Melanie Tanielian in North America; Jane Cowan, Peter Gatrell, Rebecca Gill, and Benjamin Thomas White in the UK; Julie Billaud, Riccardo Bocco, Valentina Calzolari Bouvier, Irène Herrmann, Andre Liebich, Jacques Oberson, Daniel Palmieri, Amalia Ribi Forclaz, Matthias Schulz and Özcan Yilmaz in Geneva. My friends have been source of deep conversations and joyful laughs. Francesca Alfieri, Davide Piana and Niccolò have offered much needed breaks from thinking and writing about the past. My parents, Donatella Bonfiglio and Attilio Piana, have been loving and encouraging all the way through and for that I am truly grateful. Jo, I am glad that we bumped into each other at the British Library some years ago. This book is also the outcome of an incredible amount of emails and Skype conversation, as well as some deserved lunch and dinner breaks in Manchester and Geneva.

Notes

1 'Histoire des associations internationales et des organisations internationales non-gouvernementales humanitaires en Europe occidentale au 19ème et 20ème siècle (1800–1945)', under the supervision of Professor Davide Rodogno and financed by the Swiss National Science Foundation (PP0011_118875), 2008–2012.
2 '"Parallel Lives": Women, Imperialism, and Humanitarianism, ca. 1880–1950', financed by the Swiss National Science Foundation (P2GEP1_148355, P300P1_158445, P3P3P1_167696), 2013–2017.

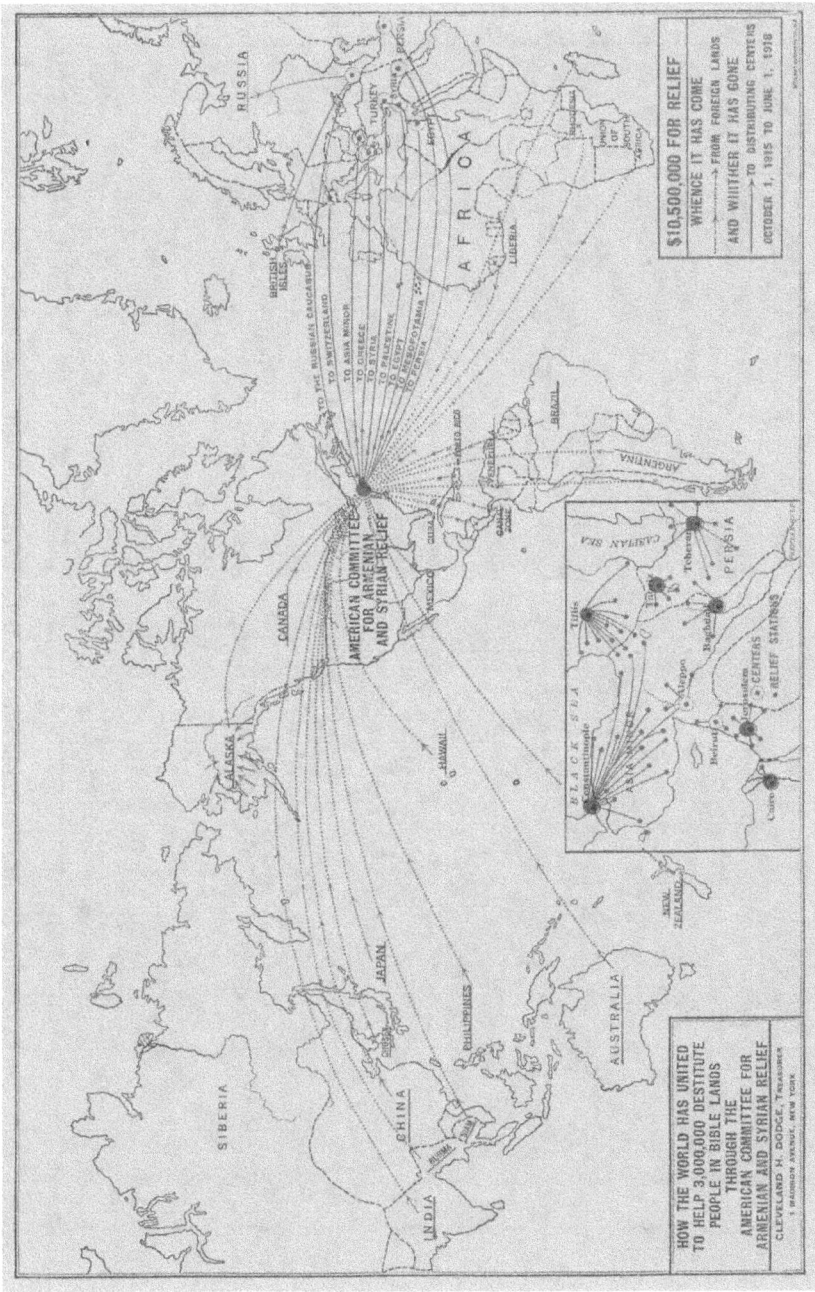

Figure 1 American Committee for Armenian and Syrian Relief aid map, 1918

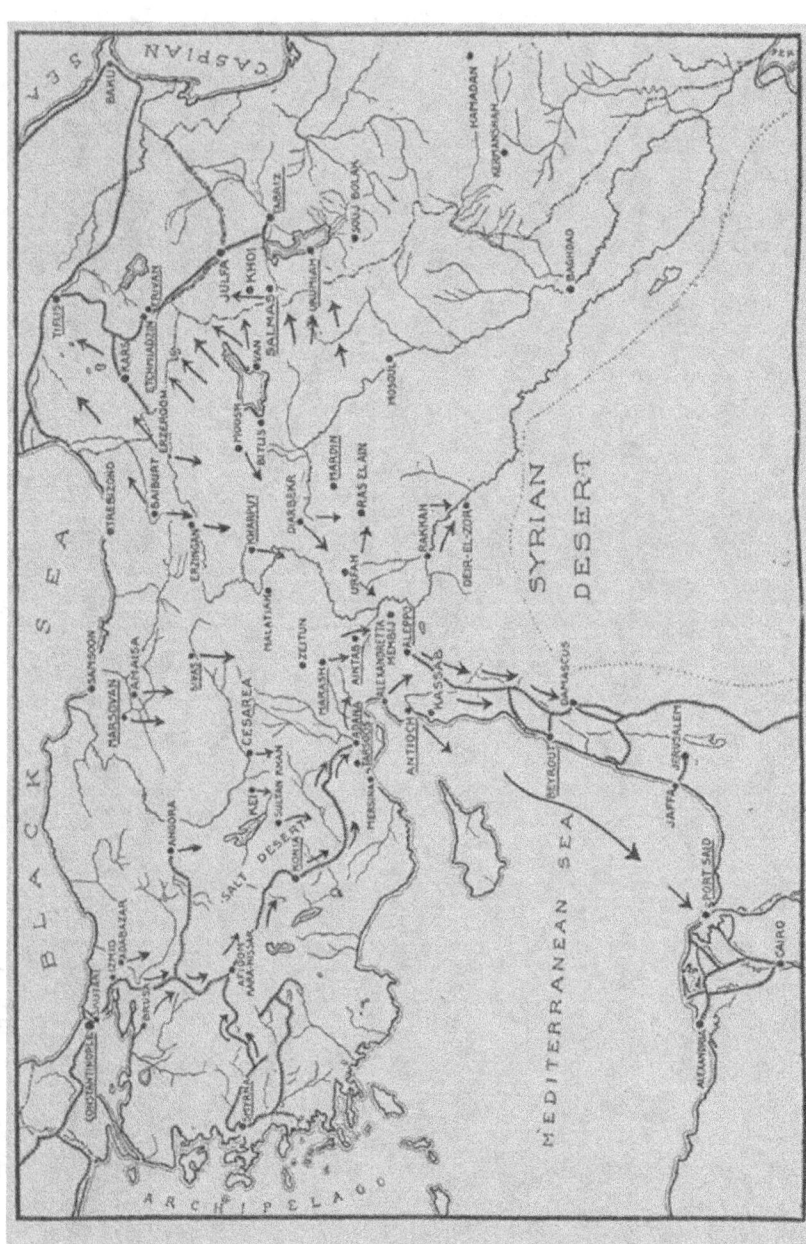

Figure 2 American Committee for Armenian and Syrian Relief map of Armenian deportations

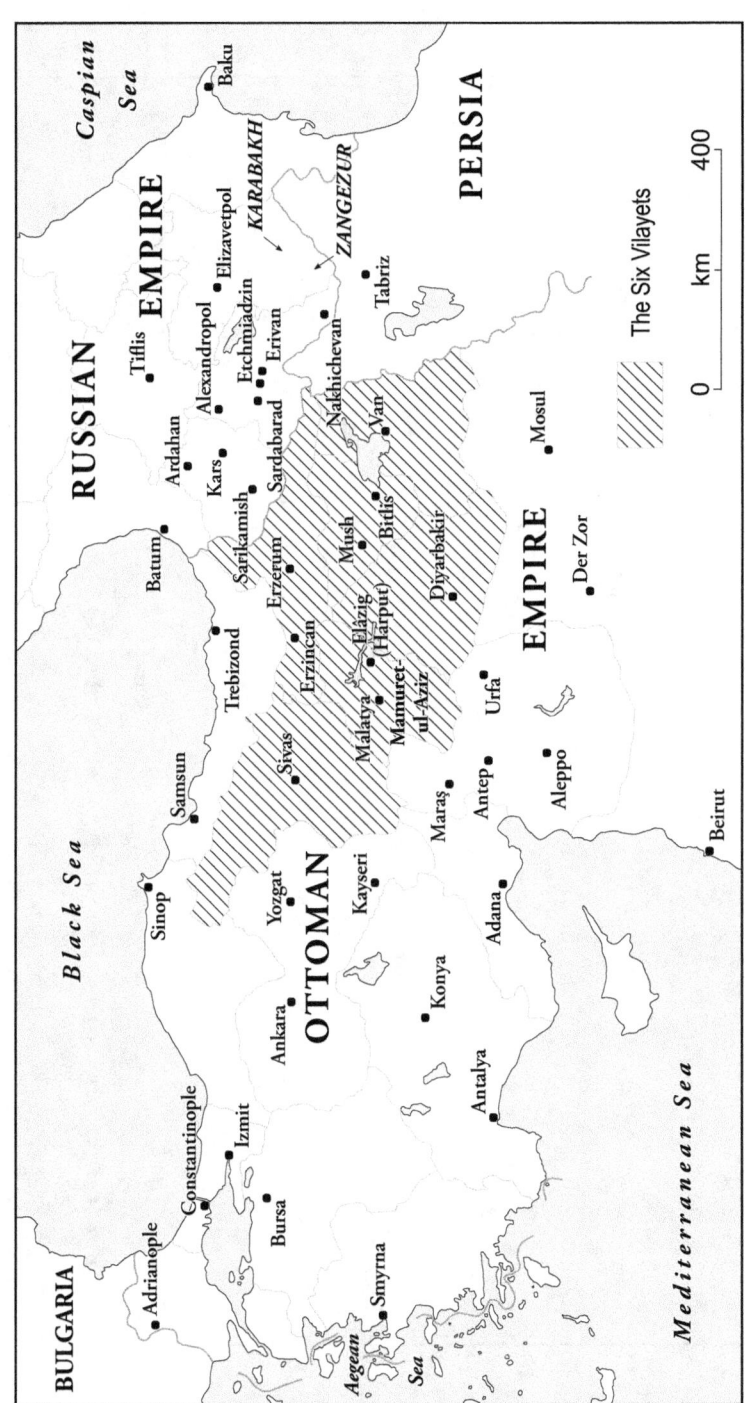

Map 1 The Ottoman Empire in 1914

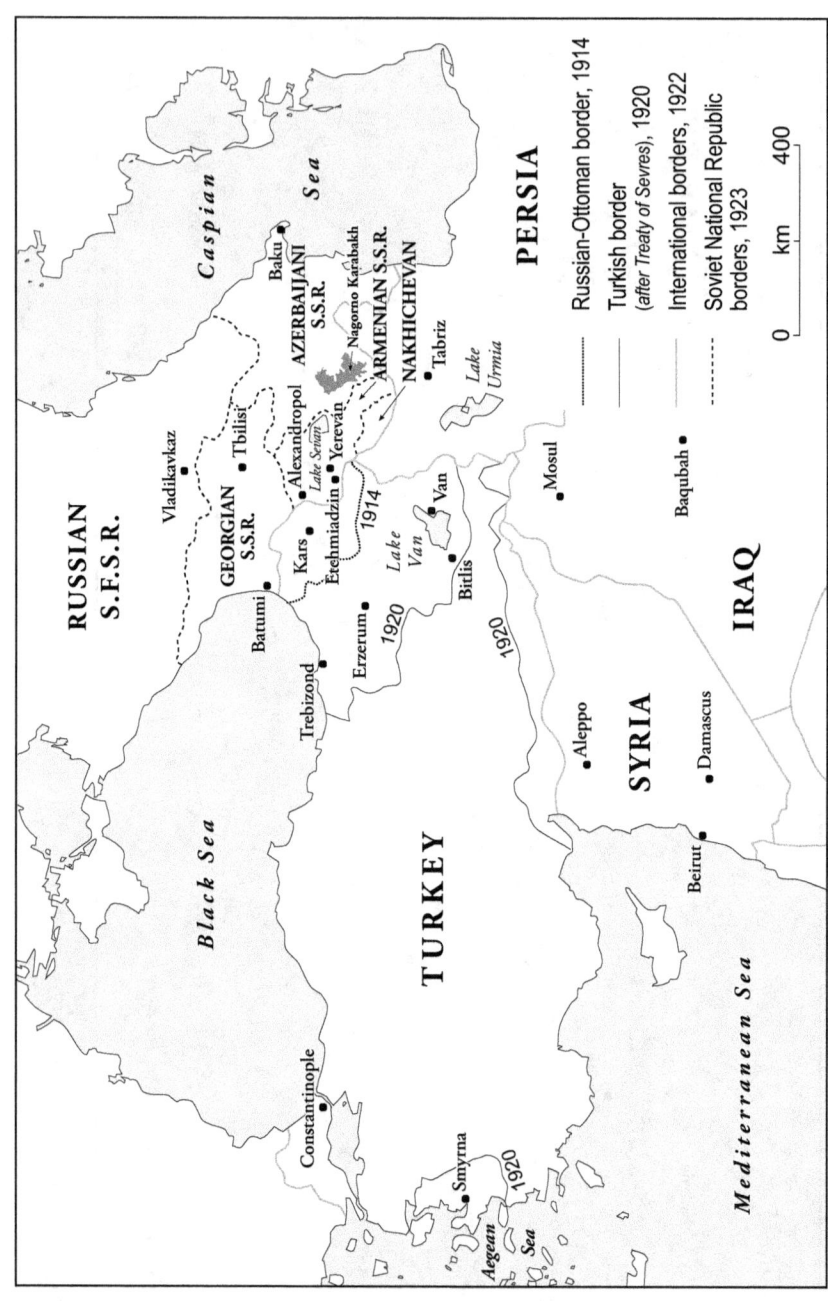

Map 2 The Ottoman/Russian Borderlands 1914–23

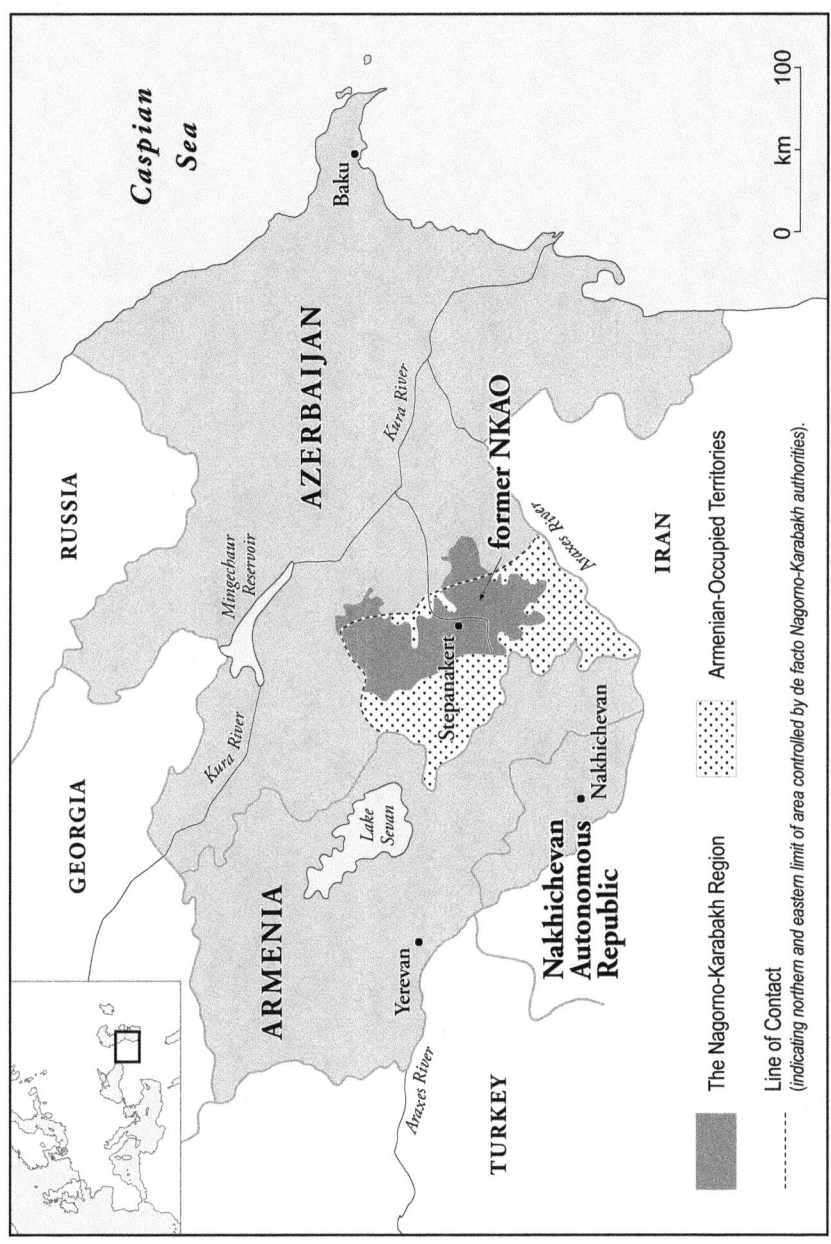

Map 3 Armenia and Nagorny Karabakh

Introduction

Jo Laycock and Francesca Piana

Recognising humanitarianism: Armenia and the Aurora Prize

In April 2016, one year after the centennial of the Armenian Genocide, the Aurora Prize for Awakening Humanity was inaugurated in Yerevan, capital of the Republic of Armenia. Initiated by Armenian-American and Russian philanthropists Vartan Gregorian, Noubar Afeyan and Ruben Vardanyan, the prize recognises 'any individual or group that commits an extraordinary act of humanity'.[1] The first prize was awarded to Marguerite Barankitse for her long-term engagement in saving, sheltering and educating orphans and refugees in the 'Maison Shalom' in the aftermath of civil war in Burundi.[2] Aurora Laureates like Barankitse are awarded a $100,000 grant and are given the opportunity to donate a further $1 million to other humanitarian organisations or initiatives of their choice.[3]

Judged by a panel of leading international figures in the worlds of humanitarian aid, human rights and genocide prevention, the launch of the Aurora Prize garnered a great deal of international attention, not least because of its celebrity co-chair of judges, the American actor George Clooney.[4] Alongside the prize, the Aurora Humanitarian Initiative created the online '100 Lives' project which charted the stories of 100 Armenians descended from genocide survivors. It also founded the 'Aurora Dialogues', which bring together leading figures from the worlds of aid, philanthropy, business and media in order to discuss urgent challenges facing contemporary humanitarianism. Since the initial prize the Aurora Initiative has broadened the scope of its work. In 2017, it established the Aurora Humanitarian Index, an international study of public attitudes towards humanitarian actions, along with funding a number of Aurora 'Gratitude Projects', which provide scholarships for students from the Greater Middle East and North Africa.[5]

The work of the Aurora Humanitarian Initiative reflects much about the nature and dynamics of contemporary humanitarianism. The publicity for the prize demonstrates the growing importance of an online presence for humanitarian organisations, in particular social media-based fundraising. This has been connected to more longstanding practices such as the forging of connections with highly visible celebrity advocates.[6] It also mirrors a wider trend towards bringing to the fore the voices of individuals, both humanitarians and the recipients of aid, who have been crowded out of historical writing and public discourse by the narratives of a few major humanitarian organisations. The creation of the Humanitarian Index meanwhile echoes an increasing focus on visibility, accountability and transparency across the sector, with particular emphasis placed on the measurement and communication of humanitarian 'effectiveness'. Finally, the Aurora dialogues embody an emerging willingness of humanitarian actors to critically, and sometimes publicly, reflect on their aims, motivations, effectiveness and shortcomings.

Other aspects of the Aurora Humanitarian Initiative connect with more problematic aspects of humanitarianism and its history. For example, the name of the initiative is inspired by two female figures, the Roman Goddess of Dawn (Aurora), and, as is perhaps more well known, an Armenian survivor, Aurora Mardiganian.[7] Mardiganian was orphaned during the genocide of the Ottoman Armenians when, between 1915 and 1923, more than a million Armenians were systematically exterminated by the Ottoman authorities against the backdrop of the First World War and Ottoman and Russian imperial collapse.[8] Against the odds Mardiganian survived this ordeal and fled through Russia to the USA. After her arrival in America, Mardiganian's story was turned into a 'memoir', *Ravished Armenia*. The young woman later starred in a fundraising film based on her experiences, *Auction of Souls*. The film recounted the experiences of Aurora Mardiganian in graphic detail, emphasising themes of sexual violence, abduction and the suffering of young women.[9]

Aurora Mardiganian is presented in publicity materials associated with the prize as the embodiment of Armenian bravery and survival, bearing witness to the horrors of the Genocide to the world. Some scholars have, in contrast, approached her experience in a more critical manner, suggesting that it could be better characterised as the exploitation of a vulnerable young woman.[10] The use of her image prompts wider questions regarding the ethics of the graphic visual representation of female victimhood in humanitarian campaigns.[11] Moreover, the Aurora Prize's focus on identifying humanitarian 'heroes' or 'heroines', while unquestionably drawing attention to acts of outstanding personal bravery, risks obscuring the structural and political factors that not only lead to 'humanitarian disasters' but also determine the conditions behind the nature and effectiveness of aid.

Awarded 'on behalf of the survivors of the Armenian Genocide and in gratitude to their saviours', the Aurora Prize reflects an emerging trend of connecting the aftermaths of the Armenian Genocide to the ideals and practice of humanitarianism past and present.[12] The emergence of the Aurora Initiative also reflects a desire on the part of some sectors of the Armenian community to shift the terms of contemporary debates on the Armenian Genocide and its recognition (or lack of thereof by Turkey). Initiatives like the Aurora Prize frame the Genocide and its aftermaths not simply as an Armenian *national* cause. Instead they connect it to pressing global questions of humanitarianism, rights and genocide prevention. In the words of its founders, the Aurora Initiative represents 'a continuing effort to transform the Armenian experience from that of "victim" to dignified, active global citizen'.[13]

We suggest that just as considering the activities of the Aurora Humanitarian Initiative can reveal much about humanitarianism's present, examining the history of interventions on behalf of Armenians can shed light on its past. Research addressing humanitarian responses to the Armenian Genocide and its aftermath has now been developing for more than a decade.[14] Building on these developments, this volume broadens the chronological and geographical scope in order to reflect on a range of actors and interventions aimed at aiding Armenia and Armenians, from the late nineteenth century to the present day. *Aid to Armenia*, we suggest, provides a vantage point from which it is possible to reflect critically on four main areas: definitions, chronologies, geographies and actors, which we develop in more depth below.

Definitions

'Humanitarianism' has proved notoriously difficult to define. This difficulty extends from practitioners, who have periodically tried to reflect on their activities, to academics, who, especially since the end of the Cold War, have increasingly turned their attention to humanitarianism's history.[15]

Scholars from various disciplines have seemed preoccupied with providing a definition of humanitarianism and, while recognising the challenges of such an exercise, determining what types of ideas, actions, daily practices and interventions may be considered 'humanitarian'. Anthropologist Didier Fassin defines humanity as 'the generality of human beings who share a similar condition (mankind) [and] … and affective movement drawing humans towards their fellows (humaneness)'.[16] To him, 'humanitarianism has become a language that inextricably links values and affects, and serves both to define and to justify discourses and practices of the government of human beings'.[17] Political scientist Michael Barnett meanwhile 'treat[s] humanitarianism as a morally complicated creature, a flawed hero defined by the passions, politics, and power of its times even as it tries to rise above them'.[18] Historian Johannes Paulmann does not provide 'clear-cut definitions of humanitarianism' but rather tries to disentangle and historicise 'a complex constellation of terms and concepts' by focusing on what he calls 'conjunctures', which he understands as turning points or moments of change.[19] More recently, Fabian Klose has stressed the importance of disentangling between different types of action that have been described as 'humanitarian', arguing for the need to distinguish military and diplomatic 'humanitarian intervention' from other forms of relief and assistance.[20]

Over the past few years Armenia, and in particular the post-genocide relief of Armenians in the Middle East, has come to be accorded an almost iconic place in examinations of the origins and nature of humanitarianism. In part, this reflects the sheer scale of the Armenian Genocide and the relief effort that followed in its wake. Growing interest in the case of Armenia is also perhaps a product of the centenaries of both the Genocide and the First World War in 2015, which were accompanied by a wave of publications on humanitarian responses to these disasters.[21] For example, in his examination of humanitarianism after the First World War, through a set of juxtaposed biographies of exceptional men and women, among them figures such as Fridtjof Nansen, who were closely engaged in post-genocide relief, historian Bruno Cabanes has argued that the concepts and practices of human rights and humanitarianism share a common genealogy.[22] Michelle Tusan and Keith Watenpaugh have similarly turned to the examination of interventions in the aftermath of the Armenian Genocide in attempts to illuminate the intersection of humanitarianism, human rights and state-building processes in the Middle East. However, they have drawn rather different conclusions, with Watenpaugh convincingly arguing against conflating British interventions on behalf of the Armenians with the 'human rights regime' that emerged later in the twentieth century.[23]

While our volume is informed by these and other efforts to establish the 'boundaries' of humanitarianism, our aim is not to provide another, or a narrower definition of this term. Rather, through the case study of Armenia and Armenians, we emphasise the diversity, complexity and contradictions of discourses and forms of aid and intervention in the aftermath of different crises. The volume pays particular attention to how different actors, both institutions and individuals, defined their own work, and the different ends that they sought to achieve through projects that appear to fall into the broad category of 'humanitarianism'.

By bringing together scholarship on different kinds of interventions and paying attention to interactions between individuals and organisations over the course of more than a century, this book highlights the blurred boundaries and tensions between 'relief', 'rehabilitation', 'development' and 'reconstruction', as well as 'charity', 'philanthropy' and 'peacebuilding'. Rebecca Jinks, for example, examines the humanitarian activities undertaken by five students of Smith College, hired by the American relief organisation, Near East Relief (NER) in the aftermath of the Genocide. Her chapter unpacks the different meanings of 'making good' in the Middle East for particular individuals working for the organisation.[24] Laurence Broers, meanwhile, through looking at the much more recent question of Nagorny Karabakh from 2003 to 2016, reflects on how in the very different context of post-Soviet 'de facto statehood' international responses to conflict and displacement have been transformed and have assumed new practices and priorities. Here 'peacebuilding' has emerged as the principle means of carving out a neutral space for international intervention – no easy task in what continues to be a highly charged political context.

As a whole, this volume demonstrates the importance of carefully contextualising humanitarian interventions within specific political, social, economic, ideological and gendered contexts. The case of Armenia provides a framework through which to analyse the often-contested relationship between ideas and practice and to examine how understandings of key concepts such as reconstruction and rehabilitation have changed over time. It does not lead us to a clearer definition of what humanitarianism 'is' but rather restates the extent to which humanitarianism is plural and fragmented, depending on the contexts and the actors involved. What seems clear from the various case studies we present is that, now as then, the majority of organisations and associations that have intervened in Armenia have been keen to frame their activities as being apolitical, often in order to have access to delicate situations. However, humanitarianism is and was a highly political project. An in-depth examination of the case of Armenia reveals the multiple ways in which practices of relief and reconstruction may be implicated in overlapping and sometimes contradictory imperial, national and diasporic projects.

Historiographies and chronologies

Humanitarian interventions on behalf of Armenians have coincided with, and in some cases are understood as characteristic of, moments identified by practitioners and in the historiography as 'watersheds' in the history of humanitarianism, namely the end of the First World War and the end of the Cold War.[25] The emphasis placed on such 'turning points' in the Armenian case is, in part at least, a product of a broader preoccupation in histories of humanitarianism with periodisation and origin stories. Michael Barnett, the first scholar who has attempted to periodise the long-term history of humanitarianism, identifies three ages: the 'imperial', extending from the beginning of the nineteenth century to 1945; the 'neo-humanitarian', extending from the end of the Second World War to the end of the Cold War; and the 'liberal', which started with the end of the Cold War in 1989.[26] From her end, historian Silvia Salvatici rather suggests a more fluid understanding, stressing elements of change and continuity between one period to another and in relation to the different institutions and contexts studied.[27]

Recently, Bruno Cabanes has seen in the First World War and its aftermath the beginning of a new era, when humanitarianism was transformed into a modern, technical, transnational and secular endeavour.[28] Along similar lines, Keith Watenpaugh has argued for the exceptionality of Western humanitarian interventions on behalf of post-genocide Armenians in the Middle East, stressing the extent to which a process of transformation in humanitarian practices took place.[29] Both Cabanes' and Watenpaugh's arguments claim a significant shift from wartime to post-war humanitarian operations. However, such an emphasis on this period as a 'break' tend to obscure significant elements of continuity in practices and agents from the pre-war into the inter-war period. In this volume, we recognise the importance of paying attention to relief efforts and interventions on behalf of the Armenians during and in the aftermath of Genocide for understanding the evolution of humanitarian discourses and practices in the twentieth century. In their chapters, Asya Darbinyan, Rebecca Jinks, Inger Marie Okkenhaug and Joy Damousi provide, in very different ways, fresh perspectives on this critical period.

By adopting a longer chronology and simultaneously expanding the range of institutions, agents and spaces under scrutiny, we demonstrate the problems inherent in attempts to provide a single comprehensive chronology of humanitarianism's history. Together, the chapters speak to the challenge of adopting such a general chronology: they instead highlight the significant ways in which patterns of continuity and change varied according to the contexts, institutions and actors analysed. For instance, the periodisation that sees the end of the First World War as a caesura leading to modern and secular post-war humanitarian aid is challenged by Okkenhaug's examination of the work of Scandinavian women in the Ottoman Empire, who relied on pre-genocide networks to organise their post-genocide humanitarian work.[30] Not only had some of these Scandinavian missionary women started working on behalf of Armenians at the turn of the century, they also continued to pursue their activities in wartime and for several years afterwards, in both inter-war mandate Syria and Lebanon and the Soviet Republic of Armenia.

While existing analyses of the place of the Armenians in humanitarianism's history have focused on the aftermaths of genocide, interventions on their behalf can also reveal much about earlier and later periods. Our longer-term approach offers the opportunity to nuance 'grand narratives' regarding the history of humanitarianism. We challenge a teleological approach according to which humanitarianism has experienced a linear progressive process, from religious, hence supposedly unprofessional, aid practices to non-religious, truly 'scientific' forms.

Moving the gaze backward, the 'Hamidian' massacres of Ottoman Armenians during the 1890s have usually been approached from a political/diplomatic history perspective as a facet of the 'Eastern Question' or by focusing on the evolution of a specific tradition of 'humanitarian intervention'.[31] Chapter 1, by Stéphanie Prévost, offers a new approach, providing a comparative transatlantic analysis of the intersection of fundraising practices of American and British organisations, which are usually addressed in isolation. Her analysis also troubles assumed boundaries between relief 'in the field' and political diplomacy. Moving the gaze forward, despite the common assumption that the international response to the Armenian earthquake in 1988 represented another 'turning point' in the history of relief, little work has been carried out on post-Soviet humanitarian interventions on behalf of Armenians. By spanning the end of the Cold War, the fall of the Soviet Union and beyond, this volume provides insights into longer-term dynamics of continuity and change. Sossie Kasbarian's analysis of responses to Syrian Armenian refugees resettled within the Republic of Armenia demonstrates that even in the context of a very different international 'refugee regime' important continuities with the practices of the post-genocide period may be traced. As Peter Gatrell has shown, history matters for refugees, and the consequences of displacements a century ago continue to shape the paths taken by Syrian Armenian refugees, as well as the response of the Armenian authorities to their fate.[32]

Geographies

The history of Armenia and the Armenians has been written from an almost overwhelmingly 'national' perspective. This national focus is a consequence of genocide and its denial, which have profoundly shaped not only the experiences of Armenia and the Armenians but also the ways that the history of these experiences has been remembered and narrated. In the aftermath of the Genocide, surviving Armenians were divided between new diaspora communities in the Middle East, Europe, the USA and beyond and a new Soviet Republic of Armenia in the South Caucasus. In the diaspora history writing has often functioned as a means of 'national preservation', of countering 'white massacre' (the loss of Armenian identity through assimilation into 'host' societies). This has frequently led to the framing of the Armenian past in narrowly national terms, despite a long and rich history of Armenians as a dispersed and mobile group, which forged connections across and between empires well before the cataclysmic events of 1915.[33] In the face of systematic state-sponsored denial of the Genocide on the part of the Turkish Republic, the focus of many Armenian historians, from the 1960s at least, has unsurprisingly been providing 'evidence' that genocide occurred.[34] This has ranged from the quest to find a 'smoking gun' (proving intent of genocide on the part of the Committee of Union and Progress) to the gathering of testimonies of eyewitnesses and survivors.[35]

In the Soviet Republic of Armenia meanwhile, the writing of Armenian history was dictated by the principles of Soviet nationalities policy.[36] Histories of the Genocide and its aftermaths were woven into a narrative of the Soviet Union as the 'saviours' of Armenians not only from Ottoman violence but also from the self-interested policies of the other European imperial powers. During the last decades of the Soviet Union's existence history writing in Armenia became increasingly dominated by primordialist national narratives.[37] With the outbreak of conflict with Azerbaijan over the territory of Nagorny Karabakh in 1988 such narratives flourished as a means of defining and defending Armenian 'national interests' and they continue to do so. History writing has become increasingly politicised, focused on justifying claims to territory by tracing the unbroken presence of the Armenian nation back through the mists of time.[38]

The trends described above, though understandable in the context of denial, have isolated the history of Armenia and the Armenians from broader and comparative historical contexts. The historiography of humanitarianism is, in contrast, by nature transnational, mapping connections and relationships between places, institutions and peoples that are often distant from one another.[39] This volume navigates these quite different narratives, connecting local, national, regional, imperial and international frames and considering how an ostensibly narrow case study can open up a wide range of geographies and global connections. Many of the international and Armenian actors that are addressed in this volume framed their actions in explicitly national terms or engaged in interventions which claimed particular territories as Armenian 'national' space. We are therefore particularly informed by the work of historians who have emphasised that paying attention to the nation state does not 'stand in opposition' to a transnational or international approach.[40]

For the most part, research on humanitarian connections with Armenia has echoed broader trends in the history of humanitarianism, focusing primarily on Anglo-American and European interventions.[41] This volume has a more ambitious geographical scope, encompassing the South Caucasus, the Russian Empire, Western Europe, South America and Australia as well as the Middle East. We engage with recent research that has begun to challenge normative visions of humanitarian relief as a straightforward transfer from the 'west' to the 'global south', by drawing attention to different sets of connections and encounters.[42] In particular, by bringing to the fore 'donors' from parts of the world other than Europe and the United States, this volume helps challenge both the geographical frameworks that continue to underpin most histories of humanitarianism and the assumptions and hierarchies which they perpetuate. For example, aside from the notable example of Peter Gatrell's *A Whole Empire Walking*, the humanitarian ideals and practices of imperial Russia are conspicuous by their absence from wider histories of humanitarianism.[43] Asya Darbinyan's chapter begins to redress the balance by examining local responses to Armenian refugees at the edge of the Russian Empire.

The case of Australia also remains somewhat marginalised in the current literature on the history of humanitarianism. Joy Damousi's chapter not only draws our attention to another, different national player on the field of humanitarian action, but also demonstrates to the importance of trans-imperial connections and networks (in this case across the British Empire) in shaping the nature of humanitarian engagements. Heitor Loureiro's chapter on the Brazilian government's engagement with the Armenian Question around the time of the First World War meanwhile highlights the extent to which Brazil instrumentalised humanitarian aid to strengthen its diplomatic position both in the Americas and globally. It draws attention to the important role played by diasporas and the significance of individual personalities in shaping which kinds of crises 'mattered'.

Institutions and agents

From the late nineteenth century onwards Armenia and the Armenians became the concern of a number of what are now recognised to be major missionary and humanitarian agencies, not least the American Board of Commissioners for Foreign Missions, the American Red Cross and, after the First World War, the Save the Children Fund. Examining the Armenian case also requires us to turn our attention to humanitarian actors and agencies that are now publicly less well known but were historically no less significant. Near East Relief (now the Near East Foundation), for example, responded to the needs of displaced Armenians in the aftermath of the Genocide on an enormous scale. The fate of displaced Armenians also preoccupied the League of Nations and the International Labour Organisation, which responded by extending the 'Nansen passport' system of providing travel documents to stateless Armenians in 1924 and by developing (with limited success) schemes for agricultural colonies of refugees in the Middle East and the Soviet Republic of Armenia.

It is impossible to write the history of aid to Armenia without engaging with the story of such a large constellation of international organisations and relief agencies. What sets the volume apart from existing literature is that the chapters are grounded in extensive archival research in a large number of repositories of governments and international organisations, as well as on extended fieldwork and professional experience in the South Caucasus. By drawing on this range of evidence, this volume shifts the focus from stories of familiar international agencies to look at other actors, less frequently addressed in narratives of humanitarianism's history. In order to do so, our chapters draw on perspectives from a variety of disciplines, not least anthropologies of displacement and diaspora, and politics and international relations theory. They also draw on sources from a range of hitherto unexplored or under-explored international archives – the archives of diaspora organisations and Russian imperial archives, the records of smaller campaigning groups such as the National Armenian Relief Committee and the Armenian Relief Fund. The later chapters bring a different set of sources and methods to bear on the subject – oral history and ethnographic interviews.

The issue of archives and actors brings us quickly back to the question of humanitarian boundaries. Can we, for example, speak of the transnational Armenian diaspora philanthropic agency, the Armenian General Benevolent Union (AGBU) in the same terms as Save the Children or the International Committee of the Red Cross?[44] When does missionary work become humanitarianism, and when does humanitarianism foster missionary goals? How do we understand the distinction between 'non-state' or 'private' and 'state' actors, especially when the boundaries between them were blurred and they engaged in joint projects of relief or reconstruction? What does it mean when, as in the case of Katja Doose's chapter on responses to the Soviet Armenian earthquake, a state regarded as authoritarian or repressive engages in practices of relief and cooperates with international agencies that define themselves as non-political? As a whole these chapters reinforce claims that there was never a golden era of 'humanitarian space'. Politics, state-building and relief have, for the last one hundred and fifty years at least, been interconnected or even interdependent.

The chapters in this volume suggest the need to go beyond understanding the character or actions of particular agencies and to consider the functioning of networks of concern and action that spanned a range of different agencies and the processes by which, despite their differences, they were able to come to a consensus over ends if not means.[45] They also point to the need to consider more fully the different actors and motives within institutions. Jinks' chapter on the 'Smith Girls', who were employed by the Near East Relief, for example, demonstrates how different motivations could exist within one organisation, revealing the often-contested relationships between organisations and individuals who engaged in relief work on their behalf. More generally, the chapters in this volume address tensions between principles and practice, showing how different actors, both institutions and individual relief workers, made decisions in particular social and political settings according to unexpected circumstances and day-to-day encounters.

Existing scholarship on interventions on behalf of Armenians has focused on 'Western' organisations and mostly those associated with a particular 'liberal' protestant tradition.[46] Considering how and why Armenia and the Armenians came to be considered worthy recipients of 'Western' aid, we suggest, can reveal a great deal about the ways in which religious and orientalist discourses, as well as imperial geopolitics, shaped humanitarianism(s).[47] However, some of these perspectives have tended to take for granted the place of the Armenians as recipients of aid, rather than acknowledging that it was often Armenians themselves who provided aid to Armenia. Building on emerging research on Armenians as humanitarian actors, and examining the neglected role of a range of Armenian actors (Soviet Armenian as well as diasporic) in responding to crisis and conflict, this volume complicates established images of donors and recipients.[48] Vahé Tachjian and Sossie Kasbarian's chapters explore the different ways in diasporic actors responded to displacement and engaged in reconstruction projects in Soviet and post-Soviet Armenia. These chapters demonstrate how these interventions were shaped by particular articulations of Armenian identity and belonging. They also underscore the importance of philanthropy, disaster relief and other forms of aid in the construction of diasporic identities and the maintenance of connections with homelands.

By focusing on the roles of Armenians as actors this volume challenges reductive images of Armenians as simply victims of violence. Building on recent perspectives which have highlighted the ambivalent and sometimes hostile responses that recent 'civil society building' interventions in contemporary Armenia have provoked and the alternative visions of activism they have generated, the chapters in this volume highlight humanitarian interventions as sites of complex and shifting power relations.[49] They pay attention to the capacity of the displaced, and victims of violence and disaster to shape their own lives, by contesting or renegotiating the decisions made on their behalf, albeit in circumstances of extreme hardship.[50] In doing so the chapters not only frame Armenia as a place of conflict and crisis, but rather examine how particular spaces defined as 'Armenian' became the site

Introduction

for multiple and sometimes contested visions and projects for the reconstruction of individual lives, families, communities and states, from within and outside the Armenian community.

Structure

The volume follows a broadly chronological structure. It is not intended to provide a comprehensive history of modern Armenia or of humanitarianism. Instead the chapters focus on a series of moments of crisis when the fate of Armenia and Armenians became an international concern. During the late nineteenth century, the vast majority of Armenians lived in the borderlands of the Russian and Ottoman Empires. For those living under Ottoman rule in particular, this was a period of increasing hardship and vulnerability. During this period two interconnected processes were underway, first, the development of Armenian nationalist movements and second, the emergence of the Armenian Question as an international concern. The First World War and the Armenian Genocide were periods of even greater calamity for Armenians, which led to the death of more than a million Ottoman Armenians and the displacement of thousands more.[51] During the inter-war years, in the aftermath of war, revolution and imperial collapse, thousands of Armenians remained displaced across the Middle East and beyond. As a new Turkish Republic emerged in former Ottoman territories, these refugees were unable to return to their former homes and over the course of the century developed into diverse and dynamic diaspora communities. In the former Russian Empire, meanwhile, a short-lived independent Armenian Republic was established in 1918. By 1920 it had been replaced by a Soviet Republic. The core chapters of this volume address responses to these events, ranging from the initial response to mass displacement on the Caucasus front in 1915, to the question of refugee resettlement, which persisted into the 1930s.

There is then a 'gap' of several decades between chapters on the inter-war period and those addressing the last decade of the Soviet Union. This is not accidental, but rather reflects the way that Armenia and Armenians faded from the international humanitarian imagination during this period. In part this 'gap' reflects the increasing stability and security enjoyed by many (but by no means all) Armenians, in both the Soviet Union and the diaspora during this period. But it also says much about the nature of humanitarianism and the way that international engagement with particular 'causes' did not spring from some eternal well of compassion but rather was shaped by changing social and geopolitical dynamics and priorities.

The final chapters this volume begin with another episode regarded as a turning point in the history of humanitarianism and international intervention, the fall of the Soviet Union and the end of the Cold War. The Soviet Republic of Armenia endured until 1991, when the Soviet Union collapsed, and the independent Republic of Armenia emerged in its wake. Despite serious economic, social and political challenges, not least the conflict with neighbouring Azerbaijan over the territory of Nagorny Karabakh, in 2020 the third Republic continues to survive. This last group of chapters addresses perhaps less familiar ground for historians of humanitarianism, examining new forms of intervention that have emerged during the last years of Soviet rule and the formative years of independence. The final chapter brings us up to the present day, examining the provision of aid to Syrian Armenian refugees in the Republic of Armenia. In lieu of a conclusion, an afterword by Peter Gatrell and an epilogue by Ronald Suny reflect on the broader implications of the volume for histories of refugees and humanitarianism and the history of Armenia and Armenians respectively.

Notes

1 'Selection Process', https://auroraprize.com/en/aurora-prize/2017/selection_process (accessed 14 September 2017).
2 The institution, which was oriented towards reintegrating the children back to their communities, was closed down by the Burundi government in 2015, for Marguerite Barankitse and some of her colleagues denounced the violent repressions undertaken by the police against the opponents of the current president Pierre Nkurunziza. Since 2017, 'Maison Shalom' has been reopened in Kigali and has been working towards relieving and rehabilitating Burundian refugees in Rwanda, preparing for their repatriation. '24 ans d'existence, 2 ans d'exile', www.maisonshalom.org/news/24-ans-dexistence-2-ans-en-exil (accessed 29 May 2019).
3 'Finalists Nominate Organizations for the $1 Million Prize', https://auroraprize.com/en/aurora/detail/9521/finalists-nominate-organizations-for-the-1million-prize (accessed 29 May 2019).
4 For example, R. Revesz, 'George Clooney gives $1.1 million award to Burundi woman who sheltered orphans during civil war', *The Independent*, 24 April, www.independent.co.uk/news/people/george-clooney-gives-11-million-award-to-burundi-woman-who-sheltered-orphans-during-civil-war-a6999086.html (accessed 29 May 2019).
5 The Aurora Prize website includes comprehensive information about their various projects, https://auroraprize.com/en/ (accessed 27 September 2017).
6 On the former set of issues, I. Kapoor, *Celebrity Humanitarianism: The Ideology of Global Charity* (Abingdon: Routledge, 2013).
7 'Inspiration', https://auroraprize.com/en/prize/detail/inspiration (accessed 25 September 2017).
8 While the Turkish state continues a campaign of denial, there is a consensus among mainstream academic historians that the fate of the Ottoman Armenians constituted Genocide. This volume takes the latter position as its starting point and is therefore not concerned with finding 'proof' that Genocide occurred. For the wider debates on this subject, see R. G. Suny, F. M. Göçek, and N. M. Naimark (eds), *A Question of Genocide: Armenians and Turks at the End of the Ottoman Empire* (Oxford: Oxford University Press, 2011).
9 The Genocide's survivors were, for a large part, women who, like Mardiganian, were forced into death marches in the Mesopotamian desert. Armenian women also experienced abduction and forced incorporation into Kurdish and Turkish families; others were raped, tortured

and starved to death. For the book version, Aurora Mardiganian, *The Auction of Souls: The Story of Aurora Mardiganian, the Christian Girl Who Survived the Great Massacres*, interpreted by H. L. Gates (London: Odhams Press, 1919). As noted in Damousi's chapter, the film had a wide circulation, and was shown in Australia.

10 A. Slide, *Ravished Armenia and the Story of Aurora Mardiganian* (Lanham MD: Scarecrow Press, 1997). V. Calzolari-Bouvier, 'L'American Committee for Armenian and Syrian Relief et l'instrumentalisation du témoignage d'Aurora Mardiganian (1918–1919)', *Relations internationales* 171:3 (2017), 17–30. M. Tusan situates the Mardiganian's case in the wider history of humanitarian film during and after the First World War, 'Genocide, Refugees and Famine on Film: Humanitarianism and the First World War', *Past and Present* 237:1 (2017), 197–235.

11 On humanitarian representations, especially photography, H. Fehrenbach and D. Rodogno (eds), *Humanitarian Photography* (Cambridge: Cambridge University Press, 2015). See also J. Paulmann (ed.), *Humanitarianism and Media: 1900 to the Present* (New York: Berghahn Books, 2019).

12 'About the Aurora Humanitarian Initiative', https://auroraprize.com/en/prize/detail/about (accessed 14 September 2017).

13 'Aurora Prize 2017', https://auroraprize.com/en/aurora/detail/10531/aurora-prize-2017- (accessed 14 September 2017).

14 For example, J. Laycock, *Imagining Armenia: Orientalism, Ambiguity and Intervention, 1879–1925* (Manchester: Manchester University Press, 2009); D. Kévonian, *Réfugiés et diplomatie humanitaire: Les acteurs européens et la scène proche-orientale pendant l'entre-deux-guerres* (Paris: Publications de la Sorbonne, 2004); M. Tusan, *Smyrna's Ashes: Humanitarianism, Genocide, and the Birth of the Middle East* (Berkeley, CA: University of California Press, 2012); L. Ekmekçioğlu, *Recovering Armenia: The Limits of Belonging in Post-Genocide Turkey* (Stanford, CA: Stanford University Press, 2016).

15 Practitioners have been producing a large literature on their activities, in the form of memoirs or essays. See for instance, F. Terry, *Condemned to Repeat? The Paradox of Humanitarian Action* (Ithaca, NY: Cornell University Press, 2002). Historians have reflected about what history can offer to the current practice of humanitarianism. For 'humanitarian aid in the archives', see the special issue of *Disasters* edited by Eleanor Davey and Kim Scriven. E. Davey and K. Scriven, 'Humanitarian Aid in the Archives: Introduction', *Disasters* 39:2 (2015), 113–28.

16 D. Fassin, *Humanitarian Reason: A Moral History of the Present Times* (Berkeley, CA: University of California Press, 2012), p. 2.

17 *Ibid*.

18 M. Barnett, *Empire of Humanity: A History of Humanitarianism* (Ithaca, NY: Cornell University Press, 2011), pp. 6–7.

19 J. Paulmann, 'Conjunctures in the History of International Humanitarian Aid during the Twentieth Century', *Humanity: An International Journal of Human Rights, Humanitarianism, and Development* 4:2 (2013), 215–38, 215.

20 F. Klose (ed.), *The Emergence of Humanitarian Intervention: Ideas and Practice from the Nineteenth Century to the Present* (Cambridge: Cambridge University Press, 2015), Introduction.

21 See notes below and, on the First World War and humanitarianism more generally, B. Little, 'An Explosion of New Endeavours: Global Humanitarian Responses to Industrialized Warfare in the First World War Era', *First World War Studies* 5:1 (2014), 1–16 as well as the entries in the 19141918 online International Encyclopedia of the First World War, www.1914-1918-online.net/ (accessed 6 November 2019).

22 B. Cabanes, *The Great War and the Origins of Humanitarianism, 1918–1924* (Cambridge: Cambridge University Press, 2014).
23 M. Tusan, '"Crimes against Humanity": Human Rights, the British Empire, and the Origins of the Response to the Armenian Genocide', *The American Historical Review* 119:1 (2014), 47–77; K. D. Watenpaugh, *Bread from Stones: The Middle East and the Making of Modern Humanitarianism* (Oakland, CA: University of California Press, 2015), pp. 20–2.
24 NER began its life as the American Committee for Armenian and Syrian Relief (ACASR), its name was changed to the Armenian Committee for Relief in the Near East (ACRNE) and then, in 1920, to Near East Relief. The scope of NER's work is documented in J. L. Barton, *The Near East Relief, 1915–1930* [Russell Sage Foundation, New York] Administration of Relief Abroad, a Series of Occasional Papers, 2 ([New York]: Russell Sage Foundation, 1943).
25 For a critical perspective on this approach see B. Taithe 'The "Making" of the Origins of Humanitarianism', *Contemporanea* 18:3 (2015), 489–96.
26 Barnett, *Empire of Humanity*.
27 S. Salvatici, *A History of Humanitarianism, 1755–1989: In the Name of Others* (Manchester: Manchester University Press, 2019).
28 Cabanes, *The Great War and the Origins of Humanitarianism*.
29 K. D. Watenpaugh, 'The League of Nations' Rescue of Armenian Genocide Survivors and the Making of Modern Humanitarianism, 1920–1927', *The American Historical Review* 115:5 (2010), 1315–39. Watenpaugh, *Bread from Stones*.
30 I. M. Okkenhaug, 'Gender and Missions in the Middle East', *Social Sciences and Missions* 23:1 (March 1, 2010), 1–6.
31 A. M. Wilson, 'In the Name of God, Civilization, and Humanity: The United States and the Armenian Massacres of the 1890s', *Le Mouvement Social* 227:1 (2009): 27–44; D. Rodogno, *Against Massacre: Humanitarian Interventions in the Ottoman Empire, 1815–1914: The Emergence of a European Concept and International Practice*, Human Rights and Crimes against Humanity (Princeton, NJ: Princeton University Press, 2012). See two special issues of the journal *Études Arméniennes Contemporaines*: 'The Massacres of the Hamidian Period (I): Global Narratives and Local Approaches', 10 (2018) and 'The Massacres of the Hamidian Period (II): Perceptions and Perspectives', 11 (2018).
32 Peter Gatrell, 'Refugees: What's Wrong with History?', *Journal of Refugee Studies* 30:2 (2017), 170–89.
33 S. D. Aslanian, 'The Marble of Armenian History: Or Armenian History as World History', *Études Arméniennes Contemporaines* 4 (2014), 129–42.
34 R. G. Suny, 'Truth in Telling: Reconciling Realities in the Genocide of the Ottoman Armenians', *The American Historical Review* 114:4 (2009), 930–46.
35 V. Svazlian and Académie des sciences d'Arménie, *The Armenian Genocide: Testimonies of the Eyewitness Survivors* (Yerevan: Gitutiun, 2011). For a critical perspective on Genocide testimonies, M. Nichanian, *The Historiographic Perversion* (New York: Columbia University Press, 2009).
36 On nationalities policy in Soviet Armenia see R. G. Suny, *Looking Toward Ararat: Armenia in Modern History* (Bloomington, IN: Indiana University Press, 1993). For a general survey see J. Smith, *Red Nations: The Nationalities Experience in and after the USSR* (Cambridge: Cambridge University Press, 2013).
37 V. A. Shnirelman, *The Value of the Past: Myths, Identity and Politics in Transcaucasia* (Osaka: National Museum of Ethnology, 2001).

38 R. G. Suny, 'Constructing Primordialism: Old Histories for New Nations', *The Journal of Modern History* 73:4 (2001), 862–96.
39 P. Clavin, 'Defining Transnationalism', *Contemporary European History* 14:4 (2005), 421–39; S. Kott, 'Les organisations internationales, terrains d'étude de la globalisation. Jalons pour une approche socio-historique', *Critique internationale* 52 (2011): 9–16; P.-Y. Saunier, 'Circulations, connexions et espaces transnationaux', *Genèses* 57:4 (2004), 110–26.
40 P. Clavin, 'Conceptualising Internationalism between the Two World Wars', in D. Laqua (ed.), *Internationalism Reconfigured: Transnational Ideas and Movements between the World Wars* (New York: I.B. Tauris, 2011), 1–14, 3.
41 Examples are: Kévonian, *Réfugiés et diplomatie humanitaire*; D. Rodogno, 'Beyond Relief: A Sketch of the Near East Relief's Humanitarian Operations, 1918–1929', *Monde(S)* 6 (2014), 45–64; Watenpaugh, *Bread from Stones*; Tusan, '"Crimes against Humanity"'.
42 For example: E. Fidian Quasmiyeh's examination of 'South–South humanitarianisms', *South–South Educational Migration, Humanitarianism and Development: Views from Cuba, North Africa and the Middle East* (Oxford: Routledge, 2015); M. Hirono, 'Three Legacies of Humanitarianism in China', *Disasters* 37 (2013), 202–20; M. Tanielian, 'Politics of Wartime Relief in Ottoman Beirut (1914–1918)', *First World War Studies* 5:1 (2014), 69–82.
43 P. Gatrell, *A Whole Empire Walking: Refugees in Russia during World War I* (Bloomington, IN: Indiana University Press, 2005). A recent exception is S. Finkel, 'The "Political Red Cross" and the Genealogy of Rights Discourse in Revolutionary Russia', *The Journal of Modern History* 89:1 (2017): 79–118. There is, in contrast, a growing literature on international provision of relief in Russia. See B. M. Patenaude, *The Big Show in Bololand: The American Relief Expedition to Soviet Russia in the Famine of 1921* (Stanford, CA: Stanford University Press, 2002); K. A. Lowe, 'Humanitarianism and National Sovereignty: Red Cross Intervention on Behalf of Political Prisoners in Soviet Russia, 1921–3', *Journal of Contemporary History* 49:4 (2014), 652–74; T. Sasson, 'From Empire to Humanity: The Russian Famine and the Imperial Origins of International Humanitarianism', *Journal of British Studies* 55:3 (2016): 519–37; F. Piana, 'The Dangers of "Going Native": George Montandon in Siberia and the International Committee of the Red Cross, 1919–1922', *Contemporary European History* 25, Special Issue 2 (2016), 253–74.
44 The AGBU was founded by diaspora Armenians in Egypt in 1908. On its history see R. H. Kévorkian and V. Tachjian, *The Armenian General Benevolent Union: One Hundred Years of History* 2 (Cairo: AGBU Central Board, 2006).
45 Thanks to Rebecca Gill for her insights on this issue.
46 On the need to not take this for granted as 'the' history of humanitarianism see A. Green, 'Humanitarianism in the Nineteenth-Century Context: Religious, Gendered, National', *The Historical Journal* 57:4 (2014), 1157–75.
47 Laycock, *Imagining Armenia*. M. Tusan, 'The Business of Relief Work: A Victorian Quaker in Constantinople and Her Circle', *Victorian Studies* 51:4 (2009), 633–61.
48 On Armenians as humanitarian actors during the Genocide see K. Mouradian, 'Genocide and Humanitarian Resistance in Ottoman Syria', *Etudes Armeniennes contemporaines* 7 (2016), 87–103.
49 A. Ishkanian, 'Self-Determined Citizens? New Forms of Civic Activism and Citizenship in Armenia', *Europe-Asia Studies* 67:8 (2015), 1203–27.
50 P. Gatrell, *The Making of the Modern Refugee* (Oxford: Oxford University Press, 2013).
51 Significant recent scholarship on the causes and dynamics of the Armenian Genocide includes: U. Ü. Üngör, *The Making of Modern Turkey: Nation and State in Eastern Anatolia, 1913–1950* (Oxford: Oxford University Press); T. Akçam, *A Shameful Act: The Armenian Genocide and*

the Question of Turkish Responsibility (New York: Metropolitan Books, 2006); R. G. Suny, *'They Can Live in the Desert But Nowhere Else': A History of the Armenian Genocide* (Princeton, NJ: Princeton University Press, 2015); D. Bloxham, *The Great Game of Genocide: Imperialism, Nationalism, and the Destruction of the Ottoman Armenians* (Oxford: Oxford University Press, 2005); J. Laycock, 'Beyond National Narratives? Centenary Histories, the First World War and the Armenian Genocide', *Revolutionary Russia* 28:2 (2015), 93–117.

1

Humanitarian accountability: Anglo-American relief during the Hamidian massacres, 1894–98

Stéphanie Prévost

'Help Armenia! A Happy New Year [1897]!' Through a mass printed New Year card produced on behalf of the Armenian Relief Fund (ARF), British Anglican honorary chaplain H. D. Rawnsley invited its recipients to continue contributing relief for Armenians in the aftermath of a series of massacres that occurred between 1894 and 1896 in the Ottoman Empire.[1] These massacres were mostly conducted by irregular soldiers (*Hamidiye* Kurds), often with the support of local government and probably instigated by Sultan Abdul Hamid II. They caused between 200,000 and 300,000 Armenian casualties, not to mention abductions, rapes, forced conversions and marriages.[2]

Rawnsley's relentless fundraising efforts were just one aspect of the entangled British-American response to the Hamidian massacres with which this chapter deals.[3] In particular, the chapter focuses on the two main collecting organisations that operated at the national level with governmental acknowledgement on both sides of the Atlantic: the ARF and its American counterpart, the National Armenian Relief Committee (NARC). Currently absent from the historiography, this joint perspective allows for the investigation of the two organisations' strategies in light of developing norms of humanitarian accountability, shedding new light on foreign interference in the Ottoman Empire and on ongoing debates over humanitarianism at a time when clearly established international relief patterns were still relatively absent from international law.[4] Inspired by the work on late-Victorian humanitarian accountability norms engaging with the concept of 'gift reciprocity and transactional charity' in the work of Marcel Mauss, this chapter asks what moral contract these norms imposed on the ARF and the NARC vis-à-vis donors, governments and victims.[5]

This chapter argues that the discreet, though strong, bond between the ARF and the NARC opened new perspectives for Anglo-American collaboration in the field of aid, which *in fine* marked a turning point in the history of humanitarianism. When Anglo-American diplomatic cooperation in response to the massacres was ruled out in early 1896, these organisations sought to devise new solutions for Armenians on the margins of interstate diplomacy. They did so by working hand in hand with the representatives of their respective countries on the ground in the Ottoman Empire. Through this process, the boundaries between the political or diplomatic and the humanitarian were blurred and redefined, and the principle that relief alone was not the solution to the Armenian Question came to be embedded in Armenophile circles.

First, this chapter explores the ARF's endeavours to establish itself as an accountable private aid agency, officially acknowledged by the Foreign Office and representing the whole British world. It then turns to the NARC and the shifting public expectations of its role and accountability in the American sphere. In both cases, the chapter demonstrates, attempts to maintain transparency and accountability were challenged by the complexity of the networks and processes involved in delivering aid. The final section discusses how relief was conceptualised and implemented in the Ottoman Empire. It examines how British and American organisations and individuals together played a role in shaping it, how local Armenian actors were involved, and how developments on the ground helped shift conceptions of the purpose and limits of international responses to Armenian suffering.

Greater Britain aids Armenians through the ARF

From its onset, sustained relief and activism in Britain and the USA had much to do with the press coverage of the three waves of massacres striking Ottoman Armenia, the vilayets of Trabzon and Zeytun, as well as Constantinople. Before disclosures of massacre rumours in the *Standard* and the *Daily News* in November 1894, few beyond evangelical circles in Britain, philologists, public statesmen and intellectuals involved with the Anglo-Armenian Association – the 1879 brainchild of English jurist, Liberal and fervent Armenophile James Bryce – were familiar with Ottoman Armenians' plight. The 1856 Paris and 1878 Berlin Treaties had made Britain, like other European signatories, a guarantor of promised Ottoman reforms for equality among all subjects, but it took the 1894 Sasun massacre to mobilise public opinion on a large scale.[6] Constructed as evidence of the massacre, 'The Truth about Armenia' series, which appeared in the highest-circulation newspaper the *Daily Telegraph* between February and May 1895, inspired an early agitation movement in both Britain and the US.[7]

The ARF emerged from this context, when just over £14 were spontaneously donated to relieve Armenian refugees at the end of a mass political meeting denouncing the massacres.[8] The latter had been organised by Hugh Lupus Grosvenor, Duke of Westminster, in May 1895 to translate the specific responsibility of the whole nation (beyond political, religious, gender, class and nationality divides) towards Ottoman Armenians. The Grosvenor House Committee, formed out of the meeting, regarded this unexpected contribution as a test case for establishing a national centralising fundraising organisation that would cooperate with the Foreign Office to distribute funds on the ground. The ARF was officially launched in the *Daily News* issue of 17 June, 1895. As it wound up in late 1898, Westminster announced that the organisation, which he had founded, had altogether collected £100,000.[9]

The ARF was the largest, but not the sole organisation fundraising on behalf of Armenians, and British Armenian relief in total probably neared £150,000 (leaving aside despatched goods).[10] Thus British relief for Armenians was the largest humanitarian campaign in aid of a single ethnic group outside of the Empire.[11] It outsized the 1876 agitation denouncing the 'Bulgarian atrocities' by far.[12] By comparison, available estimates of US relief oscillate between $300,000 and $837,353.[13]

The ARF's success built upon lessons from previous humanitarian campaigns for the Ottoman Empire, especially the 1876 Bulgarian relief campaign in which ARF executive committee members had been involved either as fundraisers or donors (sometimes both). Memories of the Stafford House Committee's difficulties during the 1877–78 Turkish War relief operations meant that the ARF was at pains to present itself as fully accountable to its donors.[14] In order to avoid appearing as a one-man charity, the Duke of Westminster, a respected philanthropist, selected the George John Douglas Campbell, 8th Duke of Argyll as chairman, rather than himself. The steering committee was to be politically neutral: although heavily drawing on the ranks of distinguished Liberal Armenophile politicians (James Bryce, Arthur Hayter, Francis Stevenson, Charles E. Schwann or Francis A. Channing), it included two prominent Conservative politicians. The steering committee was also religiously diverse, including Wesleyan theologian J. Agar Beet, Congregationalists James Guinness Rogers and Robert Forman Horton, Reverend John Clifford (then acting as president of the Baptist Union) and Sukin Baronian, archpriest of the Armenian Apostolic Church of Manchester and representative of the Armenian community in Britain. Anglicans were also involved, notably Gladstone's son, the rector of Hawarden, and High Anglican Malcolm MacColl.[15]

To maximise efficiency, Westminster was against fragmenting relief funds, which had been detrimental to the 1876 Bulgarian relief effort.[16] He thus designed the ARF, which benefited from Foreign Office support at its onset, as an umbrella structure and invited other aid structures to collaborate rather than compete.[17] It proved a successful strategy, at least until early 1896. The Anglo-Armenian Association's Armenian Relief Fund, established in April 1895, systematically transferred all money collected at conferences that their members organised, while the Women's ARF, formed in March 1895, did so episodically and otherwise sent the remainder directly to local actors, either Philip Currie, British ambassador at Constantinople since 1893, relief agents or British consular staff in devastated provinces.[18]

The distance separating British donors and recipients in the Ottoman Empire placed an extra responsibility on the ARF as reliable third parties had to be entrusted for aid distribution. The ARF had to give donors and other relief funds sufficient accountability guarantees to ward off embezzlement suspicions. All subscriptions were thus acknowledged in the column of the *Daily News*, on a daily basis until late

July 1895 and then mostly weekly. John R. Robinson, its editor, participated in the ARF steering committee and the *Daily News*, just like the Duke of Westminster, was enabled to receive funds on its behalf. Collected sums were handled by Edward Atkin, whose legal and financial professional background proved assets in his role as ARF treasurer. Announcements about how funds were used for Armenians also appeared in a series of letters to *The Times*.[19]

The ARF's success was immediate, with subscriptions worth £1,001 collected within a week of its launch.[20] After a lull in summer 1895, the broadening of the steering committee allowed the ARF to mobilise wider political, religious and civic networks, which raised large sums throughout the country immediately upon the release of the gruesome official investigation report in late August and ahead of the clamour of 'renewed Armenian horrors' in the British press on 29 October, 1895. With its Armenian community and local ARF Armenophiles, Manchester was a case in point: it transferred six subscriptions of £1,000 each between 5 October, 1895 and 15 February, 1896.

The press also published photographs, such as those commissioned in *The Graphic* of the Erzerum massacre in December, 1895. Around the same time, local branches of the ARF sprouted all over Britain and expressed strong local/regional identities. A Scottish Armenian Relief Fund was established in October 1895; an Irish Armenian Relief Fund brought together Catholics and Protestants; and in March 1896, the Armenian Relief Fund (Wales) was launched. In January 1896, the ARF also approached the mayor of London with the view of opening a Mansion House Fund to aid the ARF collect money there.[21]

From its establishment, the ARF sought to maximise publicity as part of its fundraising agenda and successfully cultivated an international strategy to represent Greater Britain (especially Canada, Australia, Cape Colony, Java and India). Subscriptions to the ARF were sent from Calcutta, where there was a historic Armenian community, as early as 27 June, 1895, and an ARF branch emerged there in January 1896.[22] ARF relays in the Empire had much to do with a burgeoning imperial press system and news agencies like Reuters (Australia) and the US Associated Press (Canada), which diffused ARF news.[23] In both Dominions, the Evangelical Alliance further facilitated the organisation of local committees and money transfers to Britain – although not always to the ARF.[24]

Yet, by early 1896, its mass diffusion strategy was being questioned for lack of transparency by both other Armenophile organisations and opponents to the Armenian agitation.[25] Suspicions towards the ARF resulted in alternative smaller-scale, local and/or network-based initiatives, such as the Friends' Armenian Relief Committee (FARC). Launched in January 1896, the FARC despatched its own relief agents, biblical scholar James Rendel Harris and his wife, to distribute FARC funds in Armenia (March–November 1896). Structures for distributing aid became more complex. In the field, the British Ambassador, as the President of the International Committee at Constantinople, sent money received (from the ARF and others), to the 'British' Committee, chaired by the President of the British Chamber of Commerce.[26] This was distributed to the devastated areas through local actors (including the Harrises) and the fourteen local Union Relief Committees. The ARF's attempt to manage fundraising and distribution was therefore ultimately subsumed by Currie's wider programme of foreign aid management at Constantinople.[27]

As a third wave of massacres struck, just after Armenian revolutionaries seized the Imperial Ottoman Bank in Constantinople in August 1896, suspicions of accounting mistakes further destabilised the ARF in Britain.[28] Concurrently, Canon MacColl, the linchpin of Westminster's relief scheme and a friend of Liberal icon Gladstone, became the butt of mounting distrust among Liberal circles. He was accused of being instrumental in the Liberal Party's defeat at the 1895 General Election and of pursuing a sustained anti-Rosebery campaign through another Westminster-headed structure on Armenian affairs, the Grosvenor House Committee, with the help of the *Daily Chronicle*.[29] Influential Liberal editors had unanimously resented MacColl's endeavours at containing a pro-Armenian mobilisation since the formation of Robert Arthur Talbot Gascoyne-Cecil, 3rd Marquess of Salisbury's Conservative–Unionist government in July 1895. They rejected his argument that it would weaken British diplomacy in Constantinople and imperial relief operations.

These tensions within the Liberal Party coupled with an official statement of powerlessness on the part of the British Prime Minister (and Foreign Secretary) in the context of halted Ottoman reforms and of European diplomatic stalemate over the Armenian Question made the continued provision of aid appear the only option for Liberal networks. The following statement from Manchester progressive Liberal MP Charles E. Swann typified the sense of resignation: 'there is nothing to do at present except to send all the funds to the Grosvenor House Committee [ARF] to be distributed to suffering martyrs in the amelioration of their sad lot'.[30] Fearing dejection, Westminster invited all to keep faith and keep donating. He stressed that in the name of oppressed humanity, the three main political figures of humanitarianism (Gladstone, Argyll and Westminster) now stood re-united beyond their own divisions (especially over Home Rule). Aware that needs exceeded what British relief could achieve, he pointed to America for hopes of further support.[31]

Anglo-American cooperation for Armenians at interstate level: A lure?

Since 1854, British and American missions had cooperated in Anatolia through the American Board of Commissioners for Foreign Missions (ABCFM), while the Bible Lands Missions Aid Society (the name of the British Turkish Missions Aid Society since 1893) provided moral and financial support. In pursuit of their millennial dream, ABCFM missionaries in the region placed energy in converting Armenians, who represented the largest non-Muslim community in the region and whom they regarded as 'nominal Christians' in need of regeneration through a purer form of

Christianity – Protestantism.[32] In the face of the massacres, the twelve ABCFM 'principal' stations in Ottoman Armenia as well as colleges at Harput, Marsovan, Marash and Ayntab proved to be essential relief centres from which itinerant relief agents, like the British Quaker couple the Harrises, could operate in 1896.[33] Westminster hoped to rely on this long-standing Anglo-American cooperation in the Ottoman missionary field.

Reports on the first wave of massacres in the American press spurred an outcry on the other side of the Atlantic.[34] On Thanksgiving Day, 1894, Herant Mesrob Kiretchjian, a former Armenian student at Robert College who had settled in the USA in 1888, called 'the thrice blessed people of the land of the free' to form 'a national Armenian fund' from existing local Armenian associations for immediate relief.[35] Although Armenians represented a small community in the USA, numbering about 1,500 in the 1880s, the recent development of a connection in the USA between evangelical and humanitarian causes (for example, the 1891–92 Russian famine) and the long-lasting fascination with Bible lands spurred Kiretchjian on in his endeavour.

A few months later, shortly after the birth of the ARF and Currie's revival of the International Committee at Constantinople, Gladstone's awaited return to politics provided the trigger for joint Anglo-American relief.[36] His speech at Chester on 6 August 1895 (invited by the Duke of Westminster) made history as he summoned the nation, without party distinction, to support the newly appointed Prime Minister Salisbury's forthcoming efforts to secure the implementation of Article 61 as he begged for Anglo-American sympathy on behalf of oppressed Armenians.[37] Two days later, a New York relief committee was set up around leading philanthropic figures in business and industry (Spencer Trask and Mrs Henry Willard of the Grand Washington hotel), banking (Morris K. Jesup and Jacob H. Schiff), education (Republican Professor Nicholas Murray Butler), medicine (Armenian Dr Arthur A. Avayzian and surgeon Robert Abbe's wife) and law (Everett P. Wheeler).[38] Other relief funds emerged throughout the US – sometimes with factions rivalling over chairs, strategies and aims.[39] This rendered a national coordinating structure essential.

Meanwhile, Kiretchjian had failed to obtain official endorsement from President Cleveland, Queen Victoria, US Secretary of State Walter Quintin Gresham, or even the Tsar, but had still succeeded in establishing the Armenian Relief Association (ARA) in New York on 1 September 1895. It remained separate from Trask's New York relief association, which would eventually go national under the name of National Armenian Relief Committee in December 1895, when it teamed with ABCFM missionaries to bring relief to Armenians.[40] For the ARF, confusion prevailed as to which body – the ARA or the NARC – was the legitimate voice of US philanthropy. Nonetheless, the ARA, in need of international recognition, feigned Westminster's support and by doing so suggested that he approved of the ARA's overtly political agenda 'to induce the Powers of Europe to fulfil their pledges and establish the security of life, honor, religion and property in Armenia'.[41]

Regardless of how much some NARC executive members, like its secretary and former ABCFM missionary at Van Frederick D. Greene, might have wished for a *rapprochement* with the ARF, regardless of British Secretary for Colonies Joseph Chamberlain's renewed invitation for British–US interstate collaboration over Armenia, or Westminster's call to the same in a February 1896 New York Times letter, deteriorating British–US relations over the Venezuela boundary dispute precluded such cooperation in the spheres of Armenian intervention and relief.[42] While President Cleveland reasserted that the Armenian Question was primarily a European question, which the USA would stay clear of by virtue of the Monroe Doctrine, the Venezuelan affair had spurred such Anglophobia in the American public sphere that relieving Ottoman Armenians was turned into America's 'sacred duty' in the face of Britain's failure to secure the implementation of Article 61.[43] The NARC could not therefore associate with the ARF publicly, for fear of endangering its *raison d'être*.

Vying with the media-savvy ARA, the NARC strove to impose itself as the authorized agency throughout the country for raising funds and supplies to be distributed by the American Red Cross through its founder, Clara Barton.[44] Secretary of State Richard Olney had suggested this approach, as the NARC could not become an official US aid agency. Although most branches approved, the NARC remained the focus of criticisms, including from within, as it submitted to Barton's strict terms that she should have ample financial support before leaving, that she was organising relief operations herself and that she excluded Armenians as aid workers (to increase Ottoman credence in the Red Cross mission).[45] When the Sultan denied Barton and her party entry in January 1896, the NARC was further criticised for assuming that the Red Cross would necessarily be allowed in the Ottoman Empire – a diplomatic *faux pas* decried by Ottoman minister in Washington Mavroyeni Bey, who denounced Barton's enterprise as anti-Turkish.[46] The NARC's fundraising strategy was on the verge of collapse when Barton learnt that her mission would not be officially endorsed by the International Committee of the Red Cross in Geneva. The NARC had to design a way of maintaining trust at home by securing an alternative distribution channel that would still frontstage the American effort.[47] Subscriptions were then sent directly to Currie's International Committee at Constantinople, but the NARC erased all mentions of British handling.[48]

Whereas the ARF (and to a certain extent its sister structure the NARC) failed in establishing an official Anglo-American alliance at interstate level (especially through Chamberlain and Olney), on the spot nonetheless, Anglo-American cooperation was the uncontested norm. American minister at Constantinople A. L. Terrell's leave in March 1896 heightened British ambassador Philip Currie's central role in coordinating relief.[49] He negotiated with Ottoman authorities for special passports into the interior, liaised with ABCFM missionaries about local needs to direct funds to these areas – and redirected Barton's first expedition towards Marash and Zeytoun, where European consuls convened to organise relief.[50] Stationed in Constantinople to coordinate the four American 'Red Cross' expeditions to Anatolia (March–August 1896), Barton worked jointly with Currie and the British Committee, the British Quaker Armenian Relief Committee treasurer and ABCFM institutions to provide general and medical relief. Upon their arrival at Constantinople in March 1896, the Harrises could thus rejoice at the British Committee being 'mixed in nationality. Americans and English working [...] in perfect harmony'.[51] A burning question remained, 'What [was] to Become of Armenians?'[52] This resonated through heated debates in Britain, the US and the Ottoman Empire as to what relief should accomplish on behalf of those who suffered, but also of those who gave.

Debating the ethics of relief and qualms over 'new humanitarianism'

'Never be interested in politics, concern yourself with your religious duties', ABCFM secretary Judson Smith enjoined US missionaries in the Ottoman Empire.[53] Not only could participation in political provocation ruin evangelical work, it could also endanger missionaries themselves. In the context of renewed massacres, such recommendations applied to all public statements (including outside the Ottoman sphere), as denunciations of Ottoman rule might both spur relief donations from abroad and hamper distribution. Indeed, in the absence of an international framework for humanitarian intervention validated by all 1878 Berlin Treaty signatories (namely European powers and the Ottoman Empire), relief operations for Anatolian Armenians required Ottoman official approval.[54] Yet, hindrances remained frequent, even after permission had been granted to the American Red Cross. In April 1896, Quaker Edward M. Vistar lamented that he and his Red Cross co-worker had been delayed a week at Urfa by the Ottoman governor who refused to let them proceed to Harput, as their passports had not been stamped.[55] Pursuing the itinerant relief mission alone, in the aftermath of the raid on the Imperial Ottoman Bank by Armenian revolutionaries, Helen B. Harris encountered bitter reluctance in obtaining passports for her travelling party (which sometimes included Armenians), as Ottoman officials feared that they were collecting testimonies for posterity and colluding with revolutionaries.[56]

To relief workers, collaboration with Ottoman authorities was always ambivalent. The Sultan allowed foreign relief on the *sine qua non* condition of neutrality, so did local Ottoman bureaucrats, who were present at the distribution of relief on his orders. Relief money transfers systematically underwent Ottoman supervision and both the American Red Cross Relief and the ARF had transactions go through the Imperial Ottoman Bank, which although private, foreign and investment, remained a state bank.[57] In the US, Barton was berated for complying in this way with Ottoman authorities, whose duplicity in the massacres she seemed to overlook when accepting an Ottoman insignia.[58] Yet, before drafts were allowed in the interior, relief despatch – in the form of coins wrapped up into a package entrusted with the Imperial Ottoman Post and insured in an English company to wherever relief was awaited – was particularly precarious and its success partly depended on Turkish-Ottoman willingness to help, sometimes circumventing official orders.[59]

A December 1896 revelation in the *Manchester Guardian* that about £50,000 had been wasted by the employment of unsuitable agencies further gloomed the whole relief enterprise at a time when Currie pleaded for a further £100,000 to save Armenians from famine during the winter.[60] Since the spring, Edward M. Wistar, Barton and the Harrises had all privately expressed despair about the scope of needed aid and about the future of Armenians. Yet in their published accounts, they tried to tone down such feeling so as to not hamper fundraising and increase confusion. Already in January 1896, NARC secretary F. D. Greene privately ranted against the ARA's media strategy that 'much harm ha[d] been done, by painting the subject in colors so black as to paralyze all effort to relieve it and even to make such an effort absurd'.[61] In particular, Greene had Willard William Howard's 'story of an eye-witness' in mind. 'It is hopeless to try to feed the Armenians until the Turk grows tired of persecuting and murdering them', Howard pronounced in *Horrors of Armenia* (1896), thereby disparaging temporary relief altogether at a time when it was most needed.[62] Howard's testimony was printed on behalf of the ARA and widely diffused in the American press.[63] He claimed that the sole remedy was an 'emigration plan', which he considered extending to the whole Ottoman Armenian population with a view to building a 'free Armenia' without the Ottoman Empire. This, he said, had been 'discussed with missionaries, consuls, merchants and refugees', thereby giving him – and by extension the ARA – further authority.[64] In reality, field relief operations were complicated by contradictory local and international understandings of what relief should and could achieve.

Greene was infuriated by Howard's publication, and suspected collusion with Armenian patriotic parties, especially the Hunchakian party, formed in Geneva in 1887, with which Kiretchjian's name was associated and which favoured establishing an independent homeland.[65] For the New York periodical *The Evangelist*, the miscegenation of humanitarianism with a covert political agenda characterised the 'new humanitarianism' that Greene was combatting.[66] While he had no amity for Hamidian rule, the ARA's covert revolutionary ideal was far too radical to be acceptable. Besides, Kiretchjian, who tried to infiltrate relief parties in Eastern Anatolia, where Howard was based, was under close surveillance by the American and British governments, as well as Ottoman diplomatic staff, due to his alleged revolutionary sympathies.[67] Howard then became the *bête noire* of the Prudential Committee (the ABCFM executive board in the US), which sought to expose him for misappropriation of relief funds and for contravening the ABCFM code of conduct, which prescribed that ABCFM agents and collaborators abstained from politics.[68]

More generally, Howard's scheme challenged ABCFM regular accountability procedures. The Prudential Committee advised against the use of missionary funds for the material relief of converts, indigents or victims, recommending that 'they must seek first the kingdom of God and his righteousness and trust in Him for all things'.[69] If relief was exceptionally to be provided with ordinary missionary funds, the Committee advised distributing practical help, rather than money. ABCFM missionary stations mostly followed suit; but were also pragmatic. Thus, in November–December 1895 at Marsovan, missionaries decided to provide clothing and bedding to protect victims from the rigorous forthcoming winter, as well as buy looms to resuscitate the main economic activity and thus help fifty families earn their bread, rather than depend on charity.[70]

Providing relief by restoring dignity through employment was common. It also made relief money last longer.[71] An early initiative was perfected by Miss Kimball, an ABCFM medical missionary at Van. Through the Women's Armenian Relief Fund, the fundraising interface of her Industrial Bureau at Van, she raised money and collected thread in Britain to sustain weaving locally. She also benefited from the support of the *Christian Herald's* editor, Louis Klopsch, to open bakeries in the Van area under the helm of W. W. Howard, who had been appointed commissioner of the American evangelical weekly's relief fund.[72] By December 1895, Kimball was feeding 1,500 mouths and maintained activity thanks to remittances from the *Christian Herald*, the Women's ARF, but also the ARF, the Red Cross and the Harrises' mission.[73]

It was from precisely this Eastern Anatolian base that Howard had proposed emigration to Persia and Russia as a permanent and efficient remedy for Armenian suffering, thereby creating tensions between relief parties in the field and back home in the USA. To legitimise their views, Howard and the ARA insisted that Armenia spread over Persia and Russia, that many Armenians lived there and that the historical highest spiritual Armenian authority, the Catholicos of all Armenians, was based in Etchmiadzin, then located in Russia.[74] Such an argument rested on the idea that the Armenian Patriarch of Constantinople, who was the recognised leader of the Ottoman *Ermeni* millet, was bound by his loyalty to the Sultan and could not really offer permanent rescue *in loco*.

The ARF felt particularly concerned as it had always promised donors to aid locally those who had been forced to flee due to massacres or who had been expelled.[75] Resettling Armenian refugees in neighbouring empires, as Howard had suggested, was not really considered by the ARF, for fear of betraying their original mission and breaking confidence with supporters, including influential Armenians.[76] But despite the ARF's and the Prudential Committee's upbraiding, some ABCFM missionaries and J. R. Harris continued to envisage emigration out of the Ottoman Empire as a possibility, due to continued persecution and perilous circumstances. With Currie's complicity, emigration started thanks to relief money, but the ARF and possibly the NARC were kept in ignorance; and although sharing some of their concerns about Howard, the FARC did not altogether decline working with him.[77]

With the end of the Red Cross mission in August 1896 and emigration well under way (to Britain, France, the USA, Canada, Egypt, South Africa, Russia, Persia, Cyprus, Greece and Bulgaria), the ARF and the NARC shifted gears. The ARF did not exfiltrate Armenians, but under pressure of a rather sceptical Salisbury – who asked Westminster to consider refugee resettlement as a *fait accompli*, which should not be encouraged, but which presently required aid – the latter agreed to open two ARF-affiliated funds aimed at relieving Armenian refugees in Greece (the Cretan Distress Fund) and Bulgaria (the Fund for the Relief of Armenian Refugees). The NARC supported US Temperance leader Frances Willard and her British correlate Lady Somerset in relocating Armenians in Marseilles, France, through their Woman's Signal Armenian Refugee Fund.[78] Neither the ARF nor the NARC cooperated with Howard's Rescue Fund, due to suspicions of its being a lure for Armenian revolutionaries. However, the NARC did join forces with the ARA to help welcome refugees once they had arrived on American soil, after Ellis Island immigration services caused difficulties.[79]

Whatever form relief took, ABCFM missionaries and the Harrises appraised local dynamics and relied on British consular staff, but also Ottoman Armenian community leaders.[80] Modelling their approach on that of local ABCFM missionaries, who generally entrusted part of their activities to trusted Evangelical and Protestant Armenians, the Harrises consulted Armenian community leaders (including members of the Armenian Apostolic Church) about reconstruction priorities and proposed a joint approach in the context of restricted relief funding.[81] Instances of collaboration between Armenian Evangelical pastors and Gregorian prelates were not isolated, as the Harrises witnessed when stopping at Ayntab in May 1896. Their private papers preserve accounts of the local Union Relief Committee, which was mixed in nationality and confession, and which, over the period December 1895–May 1896, liaised between the International Committee at Constantinople, the Armenian patriarch (whom Currie had invited to officially sit in the International Committee), Americans at Ayntab, local Gregorian and Protestant communities of nearby Aleppo and the Red Cross so that their collections and other individual donations were best distributed.[82] At Harput, Helen Harris rejoiced that the rebuilding of a new school for both Gregorians and Protestants, with a special grant by the Duke of Westminster, had been made possible by 'this union of the ancient and more modern Churches in joint work' – 'a most blessed thing', she wrote.[83] Amid the complexities of transnational relief networks this statement stands out as a reminder that the voices and contributions of the recipients of aid, so often lost in histories of humanitarianism, was dear to many international actors, not least Helen Harris, her husband and the wider ARF leadership.

Conclusion

Retracing the entangled paths of British and American relief for Ottoman Armenians in the late 1890s sheds light on the early stages and challenges of humanitarian accountability for both the ARF and the NARC. It also reveals ambivalent understandings of relief (during fundraising and distribution), reminding us that relief involves complex interactions between fundraising bodies, donors, governments, relief workers and recipients *in loco* in order to decide what may ethically be acceptable or achievable. Despite the ARF and the NARC originally sharing a conception of relief as temporary, geopolitics and jingoism prevented a *rapprochement* between the two. This points to the weight of public opinion in defining the agendas of humanitarian enterprises that present themselves as 'national'. British agency was consequently downplayed in ABCFM/NARC press reports, whereas the partnership between American (the Red Cross and ABCFM missionaries) and British (consular or private) relief actors in the field was in reality thriving under the British Ambassador's leadership.

Ambassador Currie's prime position as organiser of the International Relief Committee at Constantinople made him accountable to all fundraising bodies whose collected money he handled, to the Ottoman authorities and primarily to the British Foreign Office. At the same time it also gave him leeway to work with local actors (including Armenian leaders and victims) in order to decide the best way to proceed with temporary relief and then to shift the focus from relief to rescue through supporting emigration. This change of priorities emerged from the situation on the ground in Eastern Anatolia and was largely imposed on the Foreign Office and onto the ARF and the NARC. The latter organisations eventually adjusted their strategies. While still trying to hold true to their original mission, they took their cue from Currie that the Hamidian massacres represented a turning point in the Armenian Question, but also for the history of relief – temporary material relief was no longer a realistic solution to Armenian suffering. Currie called on all Protestant Armenophiles who had sought to devise a permanent solution to the Armenian Question through relief to create an international, permanent organ to promote their cause, for fear that the Armenian massacres would be superseded by other humanitarian crises and fall into oblivion.

In 1897, the NARC (renamed National Armenia and India Relief Association) remained involved in the management of Anatolian ABCFM orphanages, but widened the remit of its work to include relief for India in the context of the ongoing famine. In Britain, from December 1896, the International Association of the Friends of Armenia became a new umbrella structure, which conceived of relief as indivisible from political reforms. This was a duty in the name of humanity that, they argued, bore heavily on Britain.[84] Westminster eventually distanced himself from the new association, which he described as proselytising and as threatening the lives of Armenians in distant Ottoman Armenia. However, the Friends of Armenia (as they became known by 1897) began reflecting on integrating humanitarian principles in international law from the test case of Armenia with the help of other Armenophiles abroad. Thus, the response to the Hamidian massacres may be seen as the starting point for an attempt by Armenophiles to craft a 'humanitarian diplomacy', in the words of historian Dzovinar Kévonian, which would combine openness and multilateral international relations through state and non-state actors. As such, the relief movement for Armenians can be identified as a pivotal point in international history, posing a challenge to the common assumption that such ideals emerged only in the context of the First World War.[85]

Notes

1 Papers of J. R. Harris, Cadbury Library, Birmingham, DA/21/1/1/26, f. 171. See also 'Armenia', *The Parents' Review*, VII (1896), 681–4.
2 S. Deringil, '"The Armenian Question Is Finally Closed": Mass Conversions of Armenians in Anatolia during the Hamidian Massacres of 1895–1897', *Comparative Studies in Society and History* 51:2 (2009), 344–71; *Etudes Arméniennes Contemporaines* 10 (2018), 'The Massacres of the Hamidian Period (I): Global Narratives and Local Approaches' special issue.
3 I am particularly grateful to staff at the Friends' Library (London) and at the Cadbury Library (Birmingham) and Boris Adjemian (Nubarian Library) for facilitating research in their collections and to Lorans Tanatar Baruh (Associate Director of Research and Programs at SALT, Istanbul) for verifying information in the Imperial Ottoman Bank's Collection. Special thanks to Rebecca Gill and Bertrand Taithe for their encouragement.
4 On the American relief effort, see especially: M. Curti, *American Philanthropy Abroad* (New Brunswick, NJ: Rutgers University Press, 1963), pp. 119–26; I. Tyrrell, *Reforming the World: The Creation of America's Moral Empire* (Princeton, NJ: Princeton University Press, 1991), pp. 101–17; A. M. Wilson, 'In the Name of God, Civilization, and Humanity: The United States and the Armenian Massacres of the 1890s', *Le Mouvement Social* 2:227 (2009), 27–44. On the less well-known British effort, M. Tusan, 'Humanitarian Journalism: The Career of Lady Henry Somerset', in E. Gray (ed.), *Women in Journalism at the Fin de Siècle: Making a Name for Herself* (Basingstoke: Palgrave, 2012), pp. 91–109 and 'The Business of Relief Work: A Victorian Quaker in Constantinople and her Circle', *Victorian Studies* 51:4 (2009), 633–61. Also see D. Rodogno, *Against Massacre: Humanitarian Interventions in the Ottoman Empire: The Emergence of a European Concept and Practice* (Princeton, NJ: Princeton University Press, 2012) e-book, location 195.
5 S. Roddy, J.-M. Strange and B. Taithe, 'Humanitarian Accountability, Bureaucracy, and Self-Regulation: The View from the Archive', *Disasters* 39:2 (2015), 188–203, 190.
6 'The Truth about Armenia', *Daily Telegraph* (27 February 1895), p. 5.
7 S. Prévost, 'L'opinion publique britannique et la Question arménienne (1889–1896): quelles archives pour quel récit?', *Etudes Arméniennes Contemporaines* 8 (2016), 51–90, 78.
8 Though a relatively small amount by comparison to the scope of the relief movement, £14 in 1895 equates to £1,749.84 in 2017 in terms of purchasing power, according to the Official Data Foundation, www.in2013dollars.com/1895-GBP-in-2017?amount=14 (accessed 24 March 2019).
9 Westminster, 'The Grosvenor-House Committee & Armenian Relief Work', *The Times* (3 October 1898), p. 6.

10 A private reporter sent by Sultan Abdul Hamid to the 1898 relief conference evoked an even larger figure: £250,000. BOA, Y.A. HUS, 391/5, quoted in: *Osmanlı Belgelerinde Ermeni- İngiliz İlişkileri*, IV: 1896–1922 (Ankara: T.C. Başbakanlık Devlet Arşivleri Genel Müdürlüğü, 2005), p. 68.
11 Roddy, Strange and Taithe, 'Humanitarian Accountability', 191, record £106,221 having been collected for 1877–78 Russo-Turkish war victims. In *Calculating Compassion: Humanity and Relief in War, Britain 1870–1914* (Manchester: Manchester University Press, 2013), p. 75, p. 95, Rebecca Gill estimates that about £250,000 were collected 'for those affected by war in the Balkans' over the period 1876–78. Neither campaign targeted a single ethnic group.
12 Prévost, 'L'opinion publique britannique', 66. The article discusses earlier insights by D. W. Bebbington (1982), E. F. Biagini (2007), S. J. Brown (2008) and M. Tusan (2012).
13 Curti, *American Philanthropy Abroad*, p. 125 and *The Independent* (23 July 1896).
14 Roddy, Strange and Taithe, 'Humanitarian Accountability', 193.
15 'The Armenian Relief Fund', *Daily News* (17 June and 24 August 1895), both p. 5.
16 D. Anderson, *Miss Irby and her Friends* (London: Hutchinson, 1966), p. 128; S. Prévost, 'La question d'Orient dans la culture politique Britannique (1875–1898)', vol. 1, unpublished PhD dissertation, Tours University, 2010, p. 129; Gill, *Calculating Compassion*, p. 75.
17 The National Archives of the UK (TNA), FO 78/4693, f. 34. Note by T. H. Sanderson to Foreign Secretary Kimberley, 24 June 1896.
18 'Manchester & Salford Women's Armenian Relief Fund', *Manchester Guardian* (27 March 1897), p. 12.
19 'The Armenian Relief Fund', *The Times*, (13 June 1895), p. 6; (27 August 1895), p. 6; (21 September 1895), p. 7.
20 'The ARF', *Daily News* (25 June 1895), p. 6.
21 TNA, FO 78/4792, f. 4., ARF to FO, 7 January 1896.
22 'The ARF', *Friend of India and Statesman* (29 January 1896), p. 11.
23 'The Starving Armenians', *The Brisbane Courier* (11 May 1896), p. 3. On duplicated cable news, see S. J. Potter, *News and the British World: The Emergence of an Imperial Press System, 1876–1922* (Oxford: Clarendon Press, 2003), pp. 90–2.
24 'The Evangelical Alliance', *Daily Telegraph*, Sydney (27 March 1897), p. 11.
25 'The ARF', *Daily News* (5 November 1895), p. 3.
26 Also known as the General Relief Fund. A dormant structure that originally had been active in between 1878 and 1881 to help Turkish refugees in and in the aftermath of the 1877–78 Russo-Turkish war ('Turkish Refugee Fund', *Frome Times*, 20 March 1878), and that was also activated in the context of earthquake relief.
27 TNA, FO 78/4792, f. 16, Currie to FO, 11 January 1896, 'The Armenian Relief Committee', *Morning Post* (5 July 1895), p. 5.
28 *Manchester Guardian* (3 December 1896), p. 5.
29 'Lord Rosebery Has Broken Silence', *Scotsman* (30 December 1895), p. 6.
30 Manchester Central Library, Manchester Liberal Union Archive, M283/1/1/3, 24 March 1896.
31 'Needs of Armenians', *New York Times* (*NYT*) (8 February 1896), p. 16.
32 M. A. Doğan, 'American Board of Commissioners for Foreign Missions and "Nominal Christians": Elias Riggs (1810–1901) & American Missionary Activities in the Ottoman Empire', Unpublished PhD Thesis, University of Utah, 2013, p. 85.
33 Friends' House Library, London, TEMP MSS 13/6, p. 9.
34 Tyrrell, *Reforming the World*, pp. 103–4.
35 'Armenia's Heavy Burden', *Omaha Daily Bee* (26 November 1894), p. 1.

36 'Words of Warning', *San Francisco Call* (7 August 1895), p. 2.
37 'Mr. Gladstone and the Armenians', *The Times* (7 August 1895), p. 7.
38 'Threatened by Famine', *NYT* (8 August 1895), p. 9.
39 'Riot Over Armenian Relief Funds', *NYT* (20 August 1895), p. 8.
40 *Armenian Relief Bulletin*, No. 1, New York, October 1895, p. 1; 'An Appeal for Armenia', *The Sun* (31 December 1895).
41 'Relief for Armenia', *Indianapolis Journal* (16 November 1895), p. 2; *Armenian Relief Bulletin*, No. 1, p. 11; 'To Save Poor Armenians', *NYT* (8 October 1895), p. 13; 'Chickering Hall Too Small', *The Sun*, New York (21 November 1895).
42 Bodleian Library, Oxford, Bryce Papers, MS. Bryce 196, ff. 10–12; Chamberlain to Salisbury, Chamberlain Papers, Cadbury Library, Birmingham, 1 December 1896, JC5/67/45; 'Needs of the Armenians', *NYT* (8 February 1896), p. 16.
43 'United States Out', *Highland Recorder*, Monterey, Va. (21 December 1894), p. 1; 'Cullom Resolution Worries Cleveland', *The Journal*, New York, (29 January 1896), p. 3; 'The United States & Armenia: An Open-Letter from John C. Havemeyer', *NYT* (12 January 1896), p. 16.
44 'Cabled to Queen Victoria', *NYT* (16 January 1896), p. 5; Curti, *American Philanthropy Abroad*, p. 126.
45 'Red Cross Work in Armenia', *Pullman Herald*, Washington (4 January 1896), p. 9.
46 M. M. Jones, *The American Red Cross from Clara Barton to the New Deal* (Baltimore, MD: Johns Hopkins University, 2013), Kindle edition, location 1939; 'Crescent and Red Cross War', *NYT* (15 January 1896), p. 5; on Barton's participation at political meetings, see Barton, *America's Relief Expedition to Asia Minor under the Red Cross* (Washington DC: US Red Cross, 1896), p. 11.
47 For chauvinistic readings, see: 'Forwarded $10,000 for Relief', *Greencastle Banner and Times*, Indiana (20 March 1896), p. 3.
48 Editorial of the April 1896 issue, *The Missionary Herald*, 92, p. 134.
49 Relief was rather a consular mission. See M. Tusan, *Smyrna's Ashes: Humanitarianism, Genocide and the Birth of the Middle East* (Berkeley, CA: University of California Press, 2012), p. 76. See also TNA, FO 4793, ff. 53–6 and f. 66, E. Atkin to FO, 7 September 1896, and FO telegram to Currie on 8 September 1896.
50 Barton, *America's Relief Expedition*, p. 12.
51 L. L. Gould, *Alexander Watkins Terrell: Civil War Soldier, Texas Lawmaker, American Diplomat* (Austin, TX: University of Texas Press, 2010) p. 139; FARC, Friends' House Library, MS Box T2/1, Helen B. Harris, Circular letter no. 2, 1 April 1896.
52 Cadbury Library, Birmingham, Papers of J. R. Harris, DA/21/1/1/26, f. 21, Title of a 'Proposal'.
53 Quoted in Doğan, 'American Board of Commissioners for Foreign Missions and "Nominal Christians"', p. 178.
54 Rodogno, *Against Massacre*, Location 4773.
55 R. Russell, 'Insights into the 2nd Expedition of the American Red Cross in 1896', *Houshamadyan*, www.houshamadyan.org/oda/americas/wistar-archive-usa.html (accessed 14 July 2018).
56 Helen B. Harris's report from Harput, 21 September 1896, Papers of J. R. Harris, DA/21/1/1/26, f. 53. In August 1896, the Red Cross ceased operations and James R. Harris returned to England for professional reasons.
57 C. Barton, *The Red Cross: A History of this International Movement in the Interest of Humanity* (Washington DC, 1898), p. 333; Cash book of the Ottoman Bank Accounting Department (September–December 1896), Ottoman Bank Archives, SALT, Istanbul, MCI078, f. 203.

58 E. B. Pryor, *Clara Barton, Professional Angel* (Philadelphia, PA: University of Pennsylvania Press, 1987) p. 295.
59 Barton, *America's Relief Expedition*, p. 44; James R. Harris and Helen B. Harris, *Letters from Armenia* (London: James Nisbet & Co., 1897), p. 36.
60 E. Atkin, 'The Armenian Relief Fund', *Manchester Guardian* (5 December 1896), p. 7.
61 Cited in R. L. Daniel, *American Philanthropy in the Near East, 1820–1960* (Athens, OH: Ohio University Press, 1970), p. 118.
62 W. W. Howard, *Horrors of Armenia: The Story of an Eye-Witness* (New York: Armenian Relief Association, 1896), pp. 50–1.
63 See for instance 'The Condition of Armenians', *NYT* (23 August 1896), p. 4.
64 Howard, *Horrors of Armenia*, pp. 48–58.
65 L. Nalbandian, *The Armenian Revolutionary Movement: The Development of Armenian Political Parties in the 19th Century* (Berkeley, CA: University of California Press, 1963) p. 169. The ambition behind the 'emigration plan' shared features with Hunchakian leader Avetis Nazarbek's proposition for Armenian autonomy. See his *The Voice of the Armenian Revolutionists upon the Armenian Problem and How to Solve It* (London: Ward & Foxlow, 1895), pp. 11–12.
66 'New Humanitarianism', *The Evangelist*, New York (25 June 1896), p. 3.
67 TNA, FO 78/4793, ff. 186–9, Elliot (GB Consul at Sofia) to FO, 6 December 1896.
68 Papers of J. R. Harris, DA/21/1/1/26, f. 52, Ward to Harris, 18 September 1896.
69 Morgan and Schauffler, 'Should Missionary Funds Be Applied to the Temporal Relief of Converts?', SALT, Istanbul Amerikan Bord Heyeti (ABCFM) Archives, ABA001801463.
70 Report of Marsovan Station for 1895, Amerikan Bord Heyeti Archives, ABAASR000323.
71 Bryce Papers, MS. Bryce 197, f. 186, Trask to Bryce, 16 November 1896.
72 Curti, *American Philanthropy Abroad*, p. 121.
73 E. B. Thelberg, 'An American Heroine in the Heart of Armenia: Dr Grace Kimball and her Relief Work at Van', *The Review of Reviews*, April 1896, in A. J. Kirakossian, *The Armenian Massacres 1894–1896: US Media Testimony* (Dearborn, MI: Armenian Research Centre, University of Michigan, 2004), p. 162.
74 On the debate, see T. Peterson, 'Turkey and the Armenian Crisis', *The Catholic World*, August 1895, in Kirakossian, *The Armenian Massacres*, p. 70.
75 'The Armenian Relief Fund', *Daily News* (19 June 1895), p. 5.
76 Westminster, 'The Grosvenor-House Committee & Armenian Relief Work', *The Times* (3 October 1898), p. 6.
77 *Cf.* Mellinger to Harris, 11 June 1896, FARC Archives, Box T2/2; Trask to Bryce, 16 November 1896, Bryce Papers, MS. Bryce 197, f. 187; E. W. Brooks to J. R. Harris, 9 October 1896, Papers of J. R. Harris, DA/21/1/1/26, f. 59.
78 C. de Swarte Gifford and A. R. Slagell (eds), *Let Something Good Be Said: Speeches and Writings of Frances E. Willard* (Urbana, IL: University of Illinois Press, 2007), p. xxi.
79 'Refugees Are Welcomed', *San Francisco Call* (27 October 1896), p. 3 In late October 1896 ('Armenian Refugees', *The Indianapolis Journal*, 20 October 1896, p. 5), 167 Armenian refugees were detained on Ellis Island pending investigation. As D. Gutman shows in 'The Political Economy of Armenian Migration from the Harpoot Region to North America in the Hamidian Era, 1885–1908', in Y. T. Cora, D. Derderian and A. Sipahi (eds), *The Ottoman East in the Nineteenth Century: Societies, Identities and Politics* (London: I.B. Tauris, 2016), pp. 42–61, Armenian emigration channels to the USA already existed, especially from the Harput region. What worried Ellis Island authorities was a mass influx of Ottoman Armenian paupers. Beyond that, they realised that the Sultan's recent edict changed immigration/emigration

rules for Ottoman Armenians and that the 1896 Ottoman–American bilateral agreement on naturalisation made it compulsory for them to report Armenian revolutionaries' movements. In such conditions, the release of the 167 refugees, who had transited via Marseilles where Lady Somerset and Frances Willard helped them reach the USA, required authorisation both from the Ottoman minister at Washington (who, in exchange, negotiated that he should be given lists of landees' names) and French authorities. In the absence of a definitive study of ship manifests, the exact number of refugees arriving in the US in 1896 remains unknown. Thanks to the tool developed by Stephen P. Morse (*Ellis Island Gold database*), the number of Armenian entries at Ellis Island for 1896 can be estimated at 1,410 – some of whom had already resided in the US.

80 TNA, FO 78/4792, f. 98, Report from Harput to the Members of the Armenian Relief Committee (Constantinople).
81 Turkish Missions' Aid Society, 27th Annual Report, London, 1883, p. 11; FARC Archive, MS Box T2/1, Helen B. Harris, Circular letter no. 2, 1 April 1896.
82 Papers of J. R. Harris, DA/21/1/1/26, ff. 25–6, 'News Notes N°12', 4 June 1896; TNA, FO 78/4693, f. 21, Currie to FO, June 1895.
83 Harris and Harris, *Letters from Armenia*, p. 192.
84 See 'Armenian Leaflets', London School of Economics, Coll. Misc. 0019.
85 D. Kévonian, *Réfugiés et diplomatie humanitaire: Les acteurs européens et la scène proche-orientale pendant l'entre-deux-guerres* (Paris: Publications de la Sorbonne, 2004), p. 17. K. D. Watenpaugh, *Bread from Stones: The Middle East and the Making of Modern Humanitarianism* (Oakland, CA: University of California Press, 2015), p. 33.

2

Pragmatism and personalities: Etienne Brasil and Brazilian engagement with Armenia, 1912–22

Heitor Loureiro

On 29 May 2015, coinciding with the one hundredth anniversary of the Armenian Genocide, the Armenian press in Yerevan reported with excitement that Brazil would recognise the massacres of the Ottoman Armenians as genocide, following – after decades of delay – the actions of many other countries, including neighbouring Argentina and Uruguay.[1] Although the news was released by the Ministry of Foreign Affairs of the Republic of Armenia, replicating information from the Armenian embassy in Brasília, neither the Brazilian press nor the Brazilian Embassy in Yerevan confirmed the recognition. After some confusion, it was discovered that what the Armenian Embassy in Brazil had presented as Brazilian recognition was, in fact, the approval of a 'Vote of solidarity with the Armenian people on the passing of the centennial of the campaign to exterminate its population.'[2]

This was not the first time that Armenian representatives in Brazil tried to take advantage of the local political scenario in order to advocate for their own agenda. In the 1910s, a small group of Rio de Janeiro-based Armenian immigrants pushed the government to defend the interests of Armenians who sought the creation of an independent state in territories that included parts of the Ottoman and Russian Empires. This group was led by Etienne Brasil, an intellectual, former Catholic priest, and the first diplomatic representative of Armenia in South America. For Brasil, recognition by Brazil of the newly independent Armenian Republic and Brazilian support for Armenian territorial claims meant the recognition of Armenian deaths in the massacres perpetrated by the Ottoman government since 1915.

In order to make the claims of a small and distant country like Armenia seem relevant in Brazil in the 1910s and 1920s, Brasil and his allies deployed a combination of pragmatism and humanitarianism to convince wider society and political decision-makers that supporting the Armenian cause would be in their mutual interest. In the aftermath of the Genocide their aims were partially realised as, under the leadership of Epitácio Pessoa, the Brazilian government began use the Armenian cause as a means of strengthening Brazilian participation and leadership into global governance at the League of Nations (LON).[3]

Drawing on archival sources from Brazil, the USA and Armenia, as well as the Brazilian and international press, this chapter provides a transnational analysis of Brazilian engagement with Armenia before, during and in the aftermath of the Genocide. Armenia and the Armenians occupied the pages of leading newspapers in Brazil during the 1910s and the issue reverberated in the Brazilian foreign agenda into the post-war period. However, the Brazilian engagement with the Armenian cause is sharply different from other cases described in this volume. This chapter therefore examines how the Armenian question was inserted into the Brazilian political agenda by a small interest group, paying particular attention to the way in which this process was shaped by the agendas and ambitions of one man, Etienne Brasil. It demonstrates that while advocates of the Armenian cause in Brazil deployed a language of humanitarianism that echoed the one which had emerged in the USA and Europe, the Brazilian response was not characterised by the emergence of a large-scale relief effort of the kind described in chapters in this volume by Rebecca Jinks and Inger Marie Okkenhaug but by diplomatic measures driven as much by pragmatic concerns as by humanitarian sentiments.

Etienne Brasil

Etienne Brasil's biography is unclear and eclectic. The sources do not even agree on his real name.[4] Born between 1882–83 in an unknown town of the Ottoman Empire, Brasil studied at the French lycée Saint-Benoît in Istanbul and then migrated to France to become a Catholic priest and obtain a degree in pharmacy and a doctorate in philosophy. After reaching Rio de Janeiro, in 1907 Brasil spent one year in Salvador, Bahia.[5] There, he studied the religion of local African heritage populations. In 1909 he published *Os Malês*, an analysis of the anti-slavery uprising in the region in 1835. This text featured many of the Orientalist and anti-Islamic elements that Etienne Brasil would present in dozens of other works during the 1910s. In the preface to the Brazilian edition, for example, he suggests that the violence of the Malê revolt was characteristic of Muslims, referencing the massacres of Armenians in Adana in 1909 as 'proof' of this hypothesis.[6]

Jo Laycock claims that in Britain it was common to mention massacres committed by the Turks against Christian minorities to serve as a key to explain the 'nature' of the Ottoman Empire and to arouse sympathy for the cause of the Armenians.[7] Etienne Brasil took this logic a step further, using the Adana massacres to explain the Muslim 'ferocity' that made the 'white population of Bahia' experience a 'horrible slaughter' in the 1830s.[8] In his later writings on Armenia, Brasil employed an image of Armenian suffering which had framed Western European and North American engagements with the Armenian Question since the late nineteenth century. Armenia was represented as the last Christian bastion in the East, crucial in defending Christianity and civilisation against Muslim barbarism. In the face of the Armenian Genocide, like European and American advocates of the

Armenian cause he emphasised Armenian Christianity, the efforts that Armenians made in favour of the Allies during the First World War and the high price they paid in human lives, both on the battlefield and as a result of Ottoman massacres. These representations were central to the emergence of 'organised compassion' for Armenian suffering in the West, which Keith David Watenpaugh identifies as central to 'modern humanitarianism'. In the Brazilian context, they would not underpin the provision of relief, rather they would be used to support Brasil's advocacy for the recognition of Armenian national rights.[9]

'We Are Not Turks! Open Letter to Mr. Munir Suraya Bey' was the first article authored by Etienne Brasil about Eastern affairs and was published in *A Epoca* in November 1912.[10] In this article Brasil fiercely attacks the representative of the Ottoman Empire in Brazil, stating that the so-called consul had no authority over the peoples from the Ottoman Empire living in Brazil: 'For us [Syrians, Armenians, Greeks] the Turkish Empire is an execrable plague … which has been afflicting our beautiful country [Armenia] for centuries.'[11] The reason for this challenge was the call made by the Ottoman Consul to the citizens residing in Brazil to send funds to Istanbul to finance the army fighting in the Balkans. After this article, Rio de Janeiro's press treated Brasil as a 'well-known Orientalist', inviting him to write pieces that would transmit to the reader 'the Orient, so unknown to our public'.[12]

In February 1916, the newspaper *A Rua* published another piece by Brasil entitled, 'Armenia Is Almost Freed from Turkish Rule'. Excited about Ottoman defeats on the Caucasus front, Etienne Brasil argued that the Armenians were crucial in deciding battles in favour of the Russians, therefore 'the Turks, furious over this failure, began to persecute atrociously the Armenians residing in Turkey'. Brasil presents a heroic image of the Armenians, 'those who fell, defended themselves as lions. Women and children sold their skin dearly … in a word, Armenia is standing and is gloriously fighting.' At that time, he hoped that the Ottoman Empire would lose the war and the Armenians, organised by the revolutionary parties, would resist and inflict defeat on the Ottoman troops.[13]

In the second half of 1916, Brasil began to advocate politically so that the Armenian cause would reach the ears of decision-makers more directly. In 1917 he expanded his political-diplomatic incursions. On 1 November, a week after Brazil declared war on Germany, Etienne Brasil addressed a telegram to the Minister of Foreign Affairs, congratulating him on Brazil's attitude and placing himself at the disposal of the Chancellor: 'The name of Brazil will electrify hope in the oppressed of the Caucasus. Armenia, the well-cultured and eternal martyr, begs for a gesture that is ultimately the saviour from the largest republic in South America. Accept, Mr. Minister, the unconditional services of the small Armenian colony of Rio.'[14] Brazil's entry into the First World War had thus given Brasil the opportunity to use the influence and notoriety he had gained to have access to Itamaraty in order to glean support for the Armenian cause. This telegram marks the first of many contacts that he would make with the Brazilian government, seeking out its sympathy.

Brasil's first article of 1918 about the situation of the Armenians was published on 20 May, to refute the 'fake news spread by Turks'.[15] In this piece, Brasil denies that massacres of the Armenians were taking place in the Caucasus and claims that the region has been independent since November 1917. According to Brasil, the experienced and victorious Armenian army would be able to march to Istanbul and occupy the city within three months if they received military and logistic support from the US and France. A week later the Armenians of the former Russian imperial territories of Transcaucasia, left vulnerable by revolution and imperial collapse, found themselves with no choice but to proclaim independence. From then on, Etienne Brasil would play a pivotal role in the recognition of the new Armenian Republic by the South American nations and would garner support to assist Armenians in a humanitarian crisis.

The Armenian cause in Brazil after the First World War

As the only South American country to send troops to Europe during the war, Brazil had the right to send three delegates to the Paris Peace Conference. The prestige of Brazil at the conference led Etienne Brasil to see the possibility of inserting the Armenian cause into the multilateral sphere through the Brazilian representatives to Paris. By entering into the war claiming 'continental solidarity', Brazil aligned itself with US interests and demonstrated the willingness to participate as a protagonist in the international system.[16] The Brazilian delegation, headed by Epitácio Pessoa – who was elected President of the Republic during the conference – went to Paris with the intention of approaching the US, but also to defend the interests of his own country.[17]

The beginning of Brazil's political engagement in the LON was not without tensions. Brazil complained that the powers seemed to have come to an agreement on how the Peace Conference and the LON would work even before engaging the other nations in dialogue.[18] Epitácio Pessoa went even further by stating that the presence of the smaller countries at the conference was 'merely to give the meeting a liberal appearance'.[19] To assuage the mood of these countries, Woodrow Wilson proposed in plenary session on 28 April 1919 that Brazil, Belgium, Spain and Greece should occupy the elective seats in the Council.[20] It was in this context that the Pessoa administration showed interest in the Armenian demands, trying to instrumentalise them, taking advantage of the moment of humanitarianism in the West to raise political capital for Brazil in the international system.

Brazil's path towards a more prominent place in international affairs was smoothed by the American Congress' non-ratification of the Treaty of Versailles. This unexpected turn allowed Brazil to position itself as the representative of the American nations, seeking to act, according to historian Eugenio Garcia, as mediator between the powers and less influential nations.[21] However, over time, Brazil's 'implicit mandate' thesis – the idea of Gastão da Cunha, the first Brazilian representative in Geneva – to speak on behalf of American interests collapsed with the constant divergences between the propositions of Brazil and other American countries such as Argentina.[22]

Against these changing circumstances, Etienne Brasil began an intensive campaign of letters to prominent Brazilian personalities who might show an interest in the Armenian question. For example, in 1919 Brasil wrote to Domício da Gama from the Ministry of Foreign Affairs: he protested the Syrian requests at the LON for the control of Cilicia on the basis of a much longer Armenian presence in the region and equated Cilicia to the much contested Alsace-Lorraine.[23] This position echoed the claims of Boghos Nubar, leader of the Armenian National Delegation in Paris, and other members of the Armenian diaspora elite who hoped to unify that region with the new Armenian Republic, which had been established in the South Caucasus in May 1918 following the collapse of Russian imperial power in the region.[24] Also in February 1919, newspapers from various states gave wide coverage to a letter Etienne Brasil sent to Albert I of Belgium, to whom he called for support for the Armenian cause, 'because Belgium was the Armenia of Europe'.[25] All of these letters were the result of the proactive attitude of Brasil, rather than orders issued by the Armenian decision-making centres in Paris and the Caucasus.

The institutionalisation of Armenian–Brazilian relations

In October 1919, with other Brazilian-Armenian leaders, Brasil visited and thanked President Epitácio Pessoa for Brazil's role at the Paris Peace Conference in advocating for Armenian demands. During the meeting, the group of Armenian-Brazilians not only inscribed President Epitácio Pessoa's name 'alongside those of Gladstone, James Bryce, Wilson, Clemenceau and other defenders of Armenia' but also asked for a further commitment of his government regarding the 'final destiny of glorious and martyred Armenia'.[26] Thus encouraged by the information provided by Etienne Brasil and his construction of the idea of Brazil both as an ally of the Armenians and an emerging international power, the Armenian leaders were clearly making the effort to cultivate Brazilian support, envisaging the country as a strategic ally for their cause.

Late 1919 and early 1920 were marked by strong pressure from Armenian leaders around the world to encourage as many states as possible to recognise the Armenian Republic. It was in this context that Etienne Brasil received, on Christmas Eve 1919, his appointment as the diplomatic representative of the Armenian Republic in Brazil.[27] He lobbied Brazilian politicians to receive him and wrote to Epitácio Pessoa, reminding the President of the words of support for the Armenian cause spoken as head of the Brazilian delegation at the Peace Conference. He concluded his arguments with a final appeal: 'the recognition of the Armenian Republic will not only be welcomed by Europe, because the voice of Brazil is disinterested; it will also provoke the recognition by the other Powers; two South American Republics promised to immediately follow Brazil. This noble gesture will facilitate the defense of our claims to the table of Peace.'[28]

Renewed by the apparent successes of the Armenian campaign in Europe, Etienne Brasil wrote to Avetis Aharonian, representative of the Armenian Republic in Paris, requesting that credentials be issued to enable him to be plenipotentiary Minister of Armenia for all South America. Brasil had been negotiating with the South American ministers for a while and obtained the support of Chile for the Armenian Republic.[29] The same approach would be used with the Minister of Uruguay, Manuel Bernardes.[30] In this sense, he asked Aharonian to send documents that gave him 'powers before the governments of Chile, Uruguay, Paraguay, Argentina, Peru, Colombia, and Venezuela', as, Brasil continued, 'America forms a whole whose spiritual forehead is Brazil'.[31]

The meeting between President Epitácio Pessoa and Brasil eventually took place in late February 1920. Pessoa confirmed that he 'must publish the decree recognizing Armenia in the following days' and even asked for a map of the country.[32] Brasil, from his end, provided evidence that other European countries had previously recognised the Armenian Republic, thus the Brazilian one would be 'a mere formality, to a simple act of consideration'.[33] Despite this tone, the diplomat made a list of demands: an act by the Brazilian government officially recognising Armenia; the acceptance of his credentials as a diplomat and the issuance of the exequatur; sending a political-commercial mission to Yerevan; Brazil's support for the liberation of Cilicia and other territories and its consequent restitution to the Armenians, freeing them from 'the sultan's tyranny'.[34]

On 28 February 1920, it was the turn of the Argentine minister in Rio de Janeiro, Ruiz de los Llanos, to address the Brazilian government requesting the recognition of Armenia.[35] The Argentine diplomat was the intermediary between Etienne Brasil and Buenos Aires and the recognition of Armenia by Argentina happened in the first days of May.[36] The same tactic was used to obtain recognition from other Latin American states.[37] Eventually, in March 1920, Etienne Brasil received documents investing him with powers to speak on behalf of the Armenian Republic in South America.[38]

Following these negotiations, Brasil made a list of suggestions: Armenia should consider as a citizen anyone who claims Armenian nationality and for those born outside the Armenian Republic (like himself) the government should 'give a supposed birthplace in a town of the Republic'.[39] In addition, to help increase the population, he suggested that Armenians from abroad should adopt 'poor orphans and Armenize them'; all citizens should pay a military tax, which would include the Armenians from the diaspora; and a 'foreign guard', inspired by the Brazilian National Guard, should be organised in parallel to the national army.[40] Of all these proposals, the adoption of 'poor orphans' is the most peculiar. What Brasil proposed was the adoption of children by wealthy Armenians of the diaspora in the host countries – not the thousands of Armenian orphans who were in the local and international humanitarian aid institutions in the Levant – so that they would be considered Armenian citizens, and so the population of Armenia would be numerically increased. Brasil seemed to be less concerned with moral and humanitarian issues than with demographic, statistical population increase, which could be used by him as an argument at negotiating tables around the world.[41]

The hope for a Brazilian mandate over Armenia

May 1920 was a particularly busy month for Etienne Brasil and one of the most remarkable moments for the Armenian cause in Brazil. On 15 May 1920, the newspaper *A Noite*, the largest paper in Rio – with a circulation of over 50,000 copies – had a dramatic headline: 'The mandate of the League of Nations over Armenia was offered to Brazil.'[42] In reality the situation was unclear after the US Congress had indicated that it would veto the proposal for a US mandate for Armenia. According to *A Noite*, realising that defeat was certain, the President of the United States had suggested that the mandate should be assumed by 'one of the richest nations of South America'. Based on information said to be from Etienne Brasil and drawing on information originally published in the British newspaper, *The Times*, the article suggested that after refusals from Canada, Holland, Sweden and Norway, the mandate would be offered to Argentina and/or Brazil.[43]

Notwithstanding the prominence given by *A Noite* to the news (which was also widely reproduced by press agencies of several cities), no archival documents confirm that Wilson had made plans for a Brazilian mandate. It might thus appear that this was simply a story developed by Etienne Brasil in order to raise the profile of the Armenian issue. The reality was slightly more complex. On 10 May 1920, five days before the article, a letter was published in the London newspaper *The Times*. The letter was a response to articles published over the previous weeks that discussed the fate of the mandate over Armenia in the face of imminent US rejection of this role. Signed by Sir Robert William Perks, baronet and former member of the British Parliament, it asked, 'is it beyond the region of hope that this Christian and humane task, which the powerful Republic of North America may find herself unable to undertake, one of the wealthy and progressive Republics of South America, aided by British administrative experience, may attempt and to her lasting honour successfully achieve?'[44]

Thus, the suggestion that one of 'the rich and progressive republics of South America' would take on the mandate had been made not by Wilson but rather by an ally of the Armenian cause in Britain, who had struggled alongside such figures as former Prime Minister William Gladstone and James Bryce.[45] The letter published by *The Times* was just one statement among so many others expressing apprehension about the consolidation of the Armenian Republic and its territories. The request for a South American nation to assume the mandate, therefore, was more a hope than a reality. Nonetheless, it was a hope that Etienne Brasil would manipulate in order to promote his cause in Brazil and beyond.

The vague mention of a South American mandate allowed Etienne Brasil to take the lead and use a newspaper with which he had maintained close ties for years to make his own pronouncements on the subject, presumably assuming that the information coming from London referred to a resolution taken in the top decision-making circles of world politics. He gave *A Noite* an interview saying that the matter was treated with secrecy, but 'our great protector, President Wilson' had indicated that either Brazil or Argentina should assume responsibility.[46] Historian Richard Hovannisian believes that Brasil himself was the author of the idea concerning a Brazilian or Argentinian mandate over Armenia.[47] However, the inspiration may indeed have had an American source. In one of the letters sent by Brasil to Aharonian the day after the publication of the article, he stated that, in a meeting with the US ambassador in Rio de Janeiro Edwin V. Morgan, the American diplomat proposed a 'magnificent solution: a collective mandate of two or three American powers'.[48] However, it is impossible to conclude if Morgan actually mentioned this solution and if so, to what extent it was a diplomat's personal opinion or instructions from the capital.

It is not known precisely how the article in *A Noite* and the interview with Etienne Brasil reverberated in the Brazilian government, but on 22 May 1920 Brasil met President Epitácio Pessoa. Brasil then reported to Aharonian in Paris that the Brazilian President had authorised him to write stating that Brazil would be sympathetic to the idea of a 'mandate or protectorate'. Quoting Pessoa, Brasil wrote: 'I sympathize with the idea of a protectorate or a joint mandate over your country. Brazil may enter into an agreement with the United States on the partnership. I will put myself in dialogue with the ambassador of the United States and I will examine this question carefully ….'[49]

This fired the enthusiasm of Etienne Brasil so much that he drafted possible scenarios for the joint mandate over Armenia and sent them to Aharonian. For Brasil, there were three possibilities for the mandate: a mandate taken by Brazil or Argentina; Brazil or Argentina, with the help of the US; Brazil, Argentina and the US collectively. Officials would be required to supply Armenia with weapons, ammunition and provisions; caring for institutions and administration; having the responsibility of bringing together the 'poor Armenians from dispersion and the Turkish cities in the territory of the Armenian Republic' over a term of five to ten years.[50] Fully convinced of the effectiveness and feasibility of his plans, Brasil requested Aharonian to formally request the protection of Brazil and Argentina in the terms he devised. Despite his proactiveness, enthusiasm and optimism, there is no evidence that Armenian decision-makers considered the plan made by Brasil. At the end of May 1920, Brasil complained that eight of his letters had gone unanswered.[51]

Sèvres's repercussions

On 10 August 1920, the Treaty of Sèvres defined the new frontiers of the defeated Ottoman Empire. While the Turks protested the retribution against the Ottoman Empire, the Armenians celebrated the award of the territories that they demanded. Two days after Sèvres, Etienne Brasil sent a document to Rodrigo Octávio, the Brazilian representative at the LON, informing him of the new territorial limits of the Armenian Republic. He stated that Armenia 'is not and will never be Soviet; the Russians, in turn, have respected our borders to this day'.[52] This statement makes more sense if one takes into account how much Etienne Brasil would personally have to lose in terms of his own power and influence as the Armenian diplomat in South America if the Bolshevik Russians took control over Armenia.

On 20 September 1920, after much speculation and little action on who would assume the mandate over Armenia, the Council of the LON consulted the Supreme Council of Allied Powers on the possibility of the Armenian issue to be brought to the Assembly of the League scheduled for the following November. Woodrow Wilson stated that he could offer his influence with other presidents to garner moral and diplomatic help from the Powers and he would personally provide a mediator for dialogues between the Armenians and the Kemalists.[53] Spain was the first nation to welcome the call, stating that it would voluntarily support any moral and diplomatic action aimed at achieving peace between Armenians and Turks. Later, Azevedo Marques, Minister of External Relations of Brazil, wrote that Brazil could act individually or collectively, along with other powers in Armenia. In doing so he was asserting Brazil's place among the world powers.[54]

Meanwhile, in Brazil, in a message to the Congress, Epitácio Pessoa reported that 'Brazil, at the invitation of the Executive Council of the LON, accepted the task, together with the United States of America and Spain, to serve as a mediator in the struggle between the Armenians and the Turkish nationalists.'[55] Despite the Brazilian President's personal admiration for his American counterpart and his foreign policy of rapprochement with the United States, Brazil's engagement in resolving the Armenian issue was not decided with only American relations in mind. In a postwar climate characterised by the emergence of 'modern humanitarianism' Etienne Brasil's appeals on the grounds of 'high humanitarian spirit' or 'humanitarian action' had particular purchase with a Brazilian government seeking a place on the world stage. However, this was not only a humanitarian moment, it was also 'the Wilsonian moment', when minorities, colonised peoples and less powerful countries placed their demands for self-determination on the international agenda, which also made the Armenians 'matter' to the Brazilian government in the international relations.[56]

Although there had been reasonable media coverage of what was happening in Armenia, as well as a number of immigrants who were beginning to organise and gain visibility within Brazil, there was no popular movement in support of the victims of the Armenian Genocide, as there were in the other cases documented in this volume. The interest in the Armenian issue was primarily played out in elite and governmental circles. It was pragmatic and primarily motivated by two objectives: to strengthen diplomatic ties with the United States, and to guarantee a permanent seat in the Council of the LON. For Epitácio Pessoa, demonstrating Brazil's growing prestige on the international scene in this way was useful for his attempt to consolidate himself as a *national* leader.

In addition to the question of the mandate, the recognition of the Republic of Armenia provided another way for the Pessoa government to engage with the Armenian cause on the international stage. In October 1920, Etienne Brasil was invited to an interview at the Ministry of External Relations on the 'Recognition of Armenia'.[57] Brazilian recognition was an important political victory for the Armenians in the context of international relations. It was also a personal victory to Etienne Brasil. He was interested in reinforcing the image of Brazil as a 'leader of the South American nations'. According to him, 'all the small republics here will quickly follow' the Brazilian decision to recognise Armenia, because 'the great difficulty was here and we won'.[58] Although Brasil officially reported to Paris that the Brazilian recognition had happened on 9 October 1920, the official publication by the executive would only happen in November, receiving wide coverage in Rio de Janeiro's press.[59]

Recognition coincided precisely with a new phase of Brazilian foreign policy which advocated, on the one hand, relations with the United States and other 'major' powers, but also with emerging and newly independent countries. It also coincided with a key moment for the Republic of Armenia. After the Treaty of Sèvres was rejected by Mustafa Kemal and the national government in Ankara, Kemalist troops marched east. The Armenian Republic was threatened on the one hand by this Turkish advance, and on the other by the Bolsheviks. Aware of these threats, Etienne Brasil, in a telegram to the Minister of External Relations, thanked Brazil for the recognition and said that 'the noble gesture of the Brazilian Government came to comfort us on a painful occasion'.[60] In addition, he requested that Pessoa intervened with the other powers to provide weapons, ammunition and credit to the Republic, as well as to find a 'just solution' to the Cilicia issue in favour of the Armenians.[61] Later that month, Brasil sent a telegram to Aharonian trying to obtain information about rumours of the sovietisation of Armenia. In the last sentence of the telegram, Brasil reported that he would again request an audience with Pessoa to try to persuade the President to intervene.

The decree signed by Pessoa recognising the Republic of Armenia on 3 November 1920 turned out to be of little significance. A month later, on 2 December, representatives of the Armenian government and Soviet Russia would sign an agreement that annexed Armenia to Bolshevik territories. On 20 November 1920, the LON negotiated with Woodrow Wilson and the representatives of Brazil and Spain to stop the escalation of violence between the Turkish troops commanded by Mustafa Kemal and the Armenian army. On 3 December the Assembly of the LON granted 'moral support from the LON and the civilized world' to the US,

Brazil and Spain for negotiating with the 'Turkish nationalists' a peaceful solution for the conflict with Armenia.[62] However, the signing of the Armenian–Bolshevik pact rendered this useless.[63]

Etienne Brasil still held out the hope that the Russian occupation would be a strategy to end 'the invasion of the infamous Turks and win the friendship of the Russians' while the USA and the LON made possible the much-awaited and promised aid to Armenia.[64] 'A long time ago', he wrote to Aharonian, 'we have been playthings of the Powers of Europe ... This time, if necessary, we will unite even with the devil so that we can save our Armenia.'[65] Amid all these uncertainties, Epitácio Pessoa once again met with Brasil, who suggested that 'two major Brazilian cities adopt two Armenian towns to protect them'.[66] He ended his activities in 1920 by distributing a press release denying 'rumours coming from Constantinople' about the sovietisation of Armenia: 'In no case will we renounce the Treaty of Sèvres and the friendship of the Allies. Lately, both the issue of Cilicia and the liberating aid of the Armenian Republic have progressed, and there is hope that we will soon be able to liberate the country both from the assaults of Mustafa Kemal and from Soviet pressure.'[67]

Meanwhile, Brasil was desperately seeking support from the Brazilian government to salvage both the Armenian Republic and his own position. On 25 January 1921, he ignored protocol and sent simultaneous messages to Foreign Minister Azevedo Marques, the Foreign Affairs Director at the Presidency, Araújo Jorge, and the President of the Republic. To the first, Etienne Brasil requested that Brazil intervene with the 'great powers' to enforce the Armenian borders as outlined by Wilson and consolidated by the Treaty of Sèvres, as well as the creation of a mandate over Cilicia.[68] To Epitácio Pessoa, he defended his credentials as representative of the 'legitimate government of Armenia' and prayed 'for the high humanitarian spirit and great sympathy that you manifested for my unfortunate country; and of my efforts and sacrifices you yourselves have witnessed.'[69]

Soon after, Etienne Brasil's credibility fell and his articles in the press became scarce. Some sectors of the press became especially critical of the course of the Armenian cause in Brazil and the involvement of the government with a question far from the traditional sphere of influence of the country.[70] In the meantime, in Armenia, in early 1921, the Dashnak party (Dashnaktsutiun, Armenian Revolutionary Federation) was able to temporarily regain power through an uprising led by Simon Vratsian, the last Prime Minister of the Armenian Republic. This gave new hope to Aharonian and other leaders in the diaspora. In the euphoria of the resumption of power in Armenia, Avetis Aharonian finally sent the Brazilian government an official communiqué naming Etienne Brasil 'official agent of the Armenian Republic to the Brazilian government'.[71] The Brazilian embassy in Paris confirmed Brasil's appointment on 18 April 1921.[72] Once again, action came too late. By then, the Red Army had already regained control of Armenia, again deposing the Dashnaks and definitively establishing the regime that would last until 1991.

The unexpected events in Armenia had repercussions on Brasil's professional and personal life as well. He did not speak again about the country's situation either through diplomatic channels or through the press. His hopes of becoming a diplomat for an independent Armenian state being over, he changed career plans, graduated with a degree in law and began to practice in Rio de Janeiro, a job he held until his death in 1955. Once his new career began, Brasil no longer dealt with the Armenian cause. In the 1920s and 1930s, with the arrival of many more Armenian immigrants to Brazil, humanitarian engagements with Armenia and Armenians were centralised in new community institutions created in São Paulo, where they remain until the present day, even after the independence of Armenia from the USSR in 1991 and the creation of official diplomatic representations in Brazil.[73]

Conclusion

It is interesting to analyse the susceptibility of the Brazilian state to the demands of Etienne Brasil and the resonance that the Armenian cause had in the Brazilian society of the 1910s and 1920s. The case of Etienne Brasil demonstrates the importance of paying attention to the role of individuals in the diasporic and transnational connections that shaped international engagements with the Armenian cause before and after the Genocide. The access that Brasil enjoyed in the press of Rio de Janeiro was facilitated by his former belonging to the Catholic Church as a clergyman and his European education, which gave him authority. He acted, therefore, as a cultural mediator of the Orient in the Brazilian *Belle Époque*. Little by little he managed to convince his non-Armenian interlocutors of the relevance of the cause and the need to support the claims of Armenians by establishing channels of communication with potential supporters ranging from newspaper owners in Rio de Janeiro to officials of the Brazilian state to foreign diplomats. At the same time, Etienne Brasil persuaded Armenian intellectuals and politicians of his usefulness in defending Armenian interests in Brazil and he became the official representative of the Armenian Republic in South America. He thus expanded his influence in Rio de Janeiro, endorsed by wealthy Armenians in the city and the Armenian leaderships in Europe to work for the homeland he called his own, seeking a rapprochement with Epitácio Pessoa, his cabinet and other influential politicians.

As for the Brazilian government, criticism of the Pessoa administration was accentuated in late 1920, just as the Armenian demands for support and recognition increased. It is not surprising that it was during this period that Brazil recognised the independence of the Armenian Republic and accepted the call of the LON and the US for a joint effort to maintain Armenian territorial integrity. At the moment when Pessoa was surrounded by critics and opponents, he took a step towards Armenian claims, increasing his prestige among Armenians in Brazil and adopting the discourse of humanitarian responsibility towards the Armenians that circulated in the international diplomatic circles of the post-war years in order to improve his status at home and abroad. In the end, Brazilian acceptance of the joint effort on behalf of the Armenians did not materialise, but the country continued to be an important player in the international system, albeit far from the centre of power, but equally far from the space that other Latin nations occupied. This can be measured by the maintenance of Brazil's temporary seat in the Council of the LON until 1926.

In the 1920s, as new domestic issues emerged closer to home in the states of Bahia and Amazonas, the limits of the Brazilian language of humanitarianism were exposed and attitudes to displaced Christians from the former Ottoman world became less sympathetic. In the 1930s, the Brazilian government failed to support a plan of receiving a couple of thousand Iraqi Assyrian refugees – a joint plan made by Brazilian officers, the LON and the Nansen International Office for refugees – after massive opposition from a group of very influential anti-immigration Brazilian intellectuals who pressed the then President Getúlio Vargas to veto the plan. At that point, Vargas needed political support in his attempts to change the constitution and he could not displease his allies by pushing for a humanitarian plan to help Assyrians who were seen by the nativist intellectuals as 'non adaptive' and 'semibarbarians'.[74]

Decision-makers, it seemed, no longer found it useful to spend time and energy on distant issues that were less and less interesting for Brazilians. Armenians, like the Assyrian refugees described above, were no longer seen as a Christian people in danger, diminishing their capacity to generate empathy within Brazilian society. Instead attention was refocused on them as undesirable immigrants; they were labelled Turks, Asians, stateless, opium producers, viewed as undesirable and lazy. This radical change of image deserves to be analysed more closely in future research. Encouraging their immigration or incorporating their demands would mean supporting the entry of a type of immigrant that did not meet the new national project, deepened in the 1930s by the Getúlio Vargas administration. In another pragmatic response to changing circumstances, Brazil turned its back on the Armenian cause.

Notes

1 My thanks to Nareg Seferian for his helpful review, comments and friendship.
2 (*Moção de Solidariedade ao povo armênio pelo transcurso do Centenário da Campanha de extermínio de sua população*), H. Loureiro, 'Beyond the Brazilian Vote: Three Decades of Activism and Counting', *The Armenian Weekly* (12 June 2015), https://armenianweekly.com/2015/06/12/beyond-brazilian-vote/ (accessed 15 April 2018).
3 F. de Campos Mello, 'O multilateralismo na Política Externa Brasileira', *Carta Internacional (Associação Brasileira de Relações Internacionais)*, 7:2 (2012), 163–73, 164.
4 For Vartan Matiossian, based on information provided by Richard Hovannisian, the baptismal name of Etienne Brasil would be Iknadios Etian, which would have been converted into the French-speaking version of Ignace Etienne after his ordination. R. G. Hovannisian, *The Republic of Armenia: From London to Sèvres, February–August 1920* (Berkeley, CA: University of California Press, 1996, vol. III), p. 430. However, the enrolment book of the French lycée

Saint-Benoît in Istanbul where he studied records a student named 'Et. Iknadossian'. E. Brasil, *La France au Brésil* (Rio de Janeiro: Besnard Frères, 1920), p. ix and *Enrollment Book* (Istanbul: Lycée Saint-Benoît), p. 176. I would like to thank historian Cafer Sarıkaya for finding these records at the Lycée in 2015.
5 Arquivo Nacional, Rio de Janeiro, NE 3.925, year 1925, code 24391, not. 713, p. 4/30.
6 E. Brasil, 'Os Malês', *Revista do Instituto Histórico e Geográfico Brasileiro*, 72:120 (1909), 70.
7 J. Laycock, *Imagining Armenia: Orientalism, Ambiguity and Intervention, 1879–1925* (Manchester: Manchester University Press, 2009), p. 109.
8 Brasil, 'Os Malês', 70.
9 K. D. Watenpaugh, *Bread from Stones: The Middle East and the Making of Modern Humanitarianism* (Oakland, CA: University of California Press, 2015), p. 32.
10 *A Epoca* (30 November 1912), p. 3.
11 *Ibid.*, p. 3.
12 *A Rua* (3 December 1914), p. 2.
13 *A Rua* (26 February 1916), p. 1.
14 *O Imparcial* (1 November 1917), p. 5.
15 *O Imparcial* (20 May 1918), p. 3.
16 E. Vargas Garcia, *O Brasil e a Liga das Nações (1919–1926): Vencer ou Não Perder* (Porto Alegre/Brasília: UFRGS/FUNAG, 2000), pp. 27–8.
17 B. Baracuhy, 'A crise da Liga das Nações de 1926: Realismo neoclássico, multilateralismo e a natureza da política externa brasileira', *Contexto Internacional*, 28:2 (2006), 355–97, 366; E. V. Garcia, *Entre América e Europa a política externa brasileira na década de 1920* (Brasília: Editora UnB/Fundação Alexandre de Gusmão, 2006), pp. 57–9.
18 J.-J. Becker, *O Tratado de Versalhes* (São Paulo: Unesp, 2011), p. 153.
19 S. Hilton, 'Brazil and the Post-Versailles World: Elite Images and Foreign Policy Strategy, 1919–1929', *Journal of Latin American Studies*, 12:2 (Nov. 1980), 341–63, 342.
20 J. C. de Macedo Soares, *O Brasil e a Sociedade das Nações* (Paris: A. Pedone, Editor, 1927), p. 69.
21 Garcia, *O Brasil e a Liga das Nações*, p. 57.
22 *Ibid.*, p. 393.
23 Arquivo Histórico do Itamaraty, Rio de Janeiro (hereafter AHI), 281/2/4, Legação Armênia no Brasil, 'Centre Arménien du Brésil à son excellence monsieur Domício da Gama, Ministre de affaires étrangères du Brésil', 19 February 1919.
24 See V. Sahakyan, 'Between Host-Countries and Homeland: Institutions, Politics and Identities in the Post-Genocide Armenian Diaspora (1920s to 1980s)' (PhD dissertation, University of Michigan, 2015), pp. 54–64.
25 *A Epoca* (8 February 1919), p. 8.
26 *Correio da Manhã* (12 October 1919), p. 2.
27 AHI, 281/2/4, letter from Etienne Brasil to Azevedo Marques, Rio de Janeiro, 5 January 1920.
28 *Ibid.*, 9 January 1920.
29 Armenian Revolutionary Federation Archives, Watertown (hereafter ARFA), letter from Etienne Brasil to Avetis Aharonian, Rio de Janeiro, 4 January 1920.
30 *Ibid.*
31 *Ibid.*
32 ARFA, letter from Etienne Brasil to Avetis Aharonian, Rio de Janeiro, 27 February 1920.
33 AHI, 281/2/4, letter from Etienne Brasil to Epitácio Pessoa, Rio de Janeiro, 26 February 1920.
34 (*Tirania sultânica*).
35 *O Paiz* (28 February 1920), p. 4.

36 AHI, 241/2/13, letter from Etienne Brasil to Rodrigo Octávio, Rio de Janeiro, 3 May 1920.
37 ARFA, letters from Etienne Brasil to Avetis Aharonian, Rio de Janeiro, 11 April 1920; 21 April 1920.
38 ARFA, letter from Etienne Brasil to Avetis Aharonian, Rio de Janeiro, 25 March 1920.
39 (*Dar um nascimento suposto nas cidades da República*).
40 ARFA, letter from Etienne Brasil to Avetis Aharonian, Rio de Janeiro, 25 March 1920.
41 On Armenian orphans in the former Ottoman Empire see for example, L. Ekmekçioğlu, *Recovering Armenia: The Limits of Belonging in Post-Genocide Turkey* (Stanford, CA: Stanford University Press, 2016), pp. 22–3.
42 O. Compagnon, *O Adeus à Europa: A América Latina e a Grande Guerra* (Rio de Janeiro: Rocco, 2014), p. 70; *A Noite* (15 May 1920), p. 1.
43 *The Times* (22 April 1920), p. 15.
44 *The Times* (10 April 1920), p. 8.
45 There had been a movement in Britain of politicians in support of Armenian claims since the 1890s. See Laycock, *Imagining Armenia*.
46 *A Noite* (15 May 1920), p. 1.
47 Hovannisian, *The Republic of Armenia*, p. 432.
48 ARFA, letter from Etienne Brasil to Avetis Aharonian, Rio de Janeiro, 16 May 1920.
49 ARFA, letter from Etienne Brasil to Avetis Aharonian, Rio de Janeiro, 18 May 1920.
50 ARFA, letter from Etienne Brasil to Avetis Aharonian, Rio de Janeiro, 29 May 1920.
51 *Ibid.*
52 AHI, 281/2/4, letter from Etienne Brasil to Rodrigo Octávio, Rio de Janeiro, 12 August 1920.
53 National Armenian Archives, Yerevan (hereafter NAA), f. 430 op. 1 d. 1225, 'Réponse du Président des Etats-Unis', 1 December 1920.
54 *New York Times* (2 December 1920), pp. 1–2; see also NAA, f. 430 op. 1 d. 1225, 'Réponse du ministre des affaires étrangères du Brésil', Rio de Janeiro, 30 November 1920, p. 11.
55 Epitácio Pessoa, *Mensagens ao Congresso* (Rio de Janeiro: Instituto Nacional do Livro, 1956, vol. XVII), p. 255.
56 See E. Manela, *The Wilsonian Moment: Self-Determination and the International Origins of Anticolonial Nationalism* (Oxford: Oxford University Press, 2007).
57 AHI, 281/2/4, letter from Araujo Jorge to Etienne Brasil, Rio de Janeiro, 4 October 1920.
58 ARFA, letter from Etienne Brasil to Avetis Aharonian, Rio de Janeiro, 6 October 1920.
59 ARFA, telegram from Etienne Brasil to Avetis Aharonian, Rio de Janeiro, 9 October 1920, *Diário Oficial da União* (3 November 1920). The act no. 14,456, which 'recognizes the independence of the Republic of Armenia and its Government', was published in the Official Gazette of the Federal Executive on 3 November 1920.
60 AHI, 281/2/4, telegram from Etienne Brasil to Azevedo Marques, Rio de Janeiro, 5 November 1920.
61 ARFA, letter from Etienne Brasil to Avetis Aharonian, Rio de Janeiro, 9 November 1920.
62 *The Times* (3 December 1920), p. 11.
63 E. Gzoyan, *Hayastani Arajin Hanrapetutynĕ yev Azgeri Ligan* (Yerevan: Academy of Scientes of Republic of Armenia, 2013), pp. 157–8.
64 ARFA, letter from Etienne Brasil to Avetis Aharonian, Rio de Janeiro, 28 November 1920.
65 *Ibid.*
66 *Ibid.*
67 *A Razão* (27 December 1920), p. 8.
68 AHI, 281/2/4, letter from Etienne Brasil to Azevedo Marques, Rio de Janeiro, 25 January 1921.

69 AHI, 281/2/4, letter from Etienne Brasil to Epitácio Pessoa, Rio de Janeiro, 25 January 1921.
70 *Jornal do Brasil* (16 February 1921), p. 5.
71 ARFA, letter from Gastão da Cunha to Avetis Aharonian, Paris, 31 March 1921.
72 ARFA, letter from the Embassy of Brazil in France to Avetis Aharonian, Paris, 18 April 1921.
73 See P. Bogossian Porto, 'Construções e Reconstruções da Identidade Armênia no Brasil' (MA thesis, ICHF, UFF, 2011); H. Loureiro, 'O Comunismo dos Imigrantes Armênios de São Paulo' (MA thesis, PUC-SP, 2012).
74 J. Lesser, *A Negociação da Identidade Nacional: Imigrantes, Minorias e a Luta pela Etnicidade no Brasil* (São Paulo: Unesp, 2001), pp. 117–29.

3

'An appeal from afar':
The challenges of compassion and the Australian humanitarian campaigns for Armenian relief, 1900–30

Joy Damousi

'Aid for Armenia' became a familiar catch cry in Australia during the late nineteenth and early twentieth centuries. In 1896, the Sydney paper, the *Methodist*, carried lengthy reports from the British Methodist press detailing the atrocities conducted against the Armenian population.[1] The major Australian newspapers did the same, publishing stories from abroad, which were syndicated to rural and country newspapers. In 1909, largely attended public meetings were held in capital cities to express sympathy with the 'sufferers in Armenia from Turkish oppression'.[2] In 1923, Australian children in the 1,000 schools in South Australia contributed pennies in the aid of 'starving women and children of Armenia'. The aim of the campaign was to educate them in the virtues of charity and to enlist sympathy for the plight of Armenian children.[3] A year later in Melbourne in 1924, the American inspired Golden Rule Sunday was launched throughout Australia, which was a very different type of campaigning, asking the public to eat similar meals to those supplied to refugees by relief organisations.[4]

While these campaigns reveal considerable success in fundraising, this chapter explores how a study of Armenian relief efforts in one national context – Australia – points to the ongoing need to generate compassion and empathy through new fundraising methods and narratives. Pleas for compassion from fundraisers for the Armenian survivors may have been answered to a degree but this was by no means consistent nor did it arise spontaneously without generating a considerable effort towards this end. I argue that mobilising compassion for strangers in distant and remote lands – as Armenia was seen by Australians – was a highly contested, volatile and challenging endeavour throughout the first decades of the twentieth century. Compassion for Armenian aid could not be assumed as a given, a theme which scholars have addressed in recent historiography.[5]

This is revealed in a number of contexts. First, through the challenges confronting humanitarian workers of sustaining an interest in the Armenian crisis by Australians across three decades. Many campaigners often identified the exhaustion of giving to charity as an obstacle to sustained fundraising.[6] Second, in response to this, new methods of fundraising developed, which were premised on *experiencing* the refugee ordeal as much as possible and so promoting empathy through enduring and witnessing suffering that was as *authentic* as possible. Third, genuine efforts were made to change the Australian immigration policy towards Armenians through arguments of economics but also compassion – which were steadfastly resisted by government. Fourth, one of the striking narratives throughout the 1920s was the emergence of a form of exotic humanitarianism through eyewitness travel accounts conveyed in colourful language by humanitarian workers. There is a long tradition of this framing, evidenced through the writings of nineteenth-century missionaries and travel literature.[7] The emotive talks humanitarians delivered were designed to raise funds but the exotic nature of the 'dark', 'uncivilised' nation of Armenia resonated with narratives of orientalism and promoted a supposed authenticity in witnessing atrocity and genocide. These narratives were situated alongside contrasting understandings of modernity. Finally, the arguments *against* aid to Armenia are central when examining campaigns based on appeals to compassion. Those on the left and the right advanced claims which countered those of Christian liberal humanists – perspectives that have been overlooked in much of the historiography on aid to Armenia. Were those who opposed aid devoid of compassion and empathy? Critics from both the left and the right argued they were expressing both – the former towards the condition of the working classes, the latter towards the impoverished in Australia. Their opposition was based on one reoccurring theme: local before global charity.

The scholarly literature on humanitarian campaigns for the Armenian cause is extensive, covering many aspects such as imperial politics, the place of human rights, the role of Protestant religions, the impact on women and children, the views and practices of humanitarian workers and the place of relief for Armenia in the broad history of humanitarianism.[8] In the Australian context, the activities of several key activists have been the subject of a number of studies exploring the contribution by Australians, especially in terms of foodstuffs and donations sent to Armenia. Funds in Australia raised to assist the establishment of an Australasian orphanage in Antilias in 1923 was seen as a major achievement by Australian humanitarians.[9] Notwithstanding these achievements, identifying some of the challenges to such campaigns, especially around the contested concept of compassion, provides a distinctive perspective on how empathy towards the suffering of others was not always forthcoming in the Australian context given its distance and remoteness, but rather, constant campaigning was required, as was a periodic renewal of the humanitarian message. The significance of physical distance from atrocities was expressed in the opposition to aid to Armenia. Critics argued that humanitarianism should start and end domestically with priority given to worthy recipients of charity within Australia, not abroad.

The exhaustion of giving

Mary Serle was a member of the Methodist Christian Missionary Association in Hobart, Tasmania, the Christian Endeavor Union and a staunch campaigner for Armenian aid. In November 1910 under the title, 'The Cry of Armenia', Serle congratulated the *Sydney Morning Herald* on its sympathetic and sustained coverage of the Armenian atrocities, which was not altogether shared by others in the Australian community. An active supporter of raising relief for Armenia since the 1890s, the outbreak of atrocities in 1909 inspired her to conduct an Australian campaign of support. A revolutionary challenge to the rule of the Ottoman Empire in 1908 through the Young Turk revolution precipitated a counter revolution in 1909, which resulted in the massacre of thousands of Armenians by Turkish forces.[10] Serle condemned the 'apathetic attitude' of European powers. Closer to home, she believed the fact that the 'unspeakable horror' of atrocities experienced by the Armenians had 'made so little stir' was 'a significant sign of the times'. In the first decade of the twentieth century there was a 'modern craze for new things', she observed. The Armenian story was considered 'ancient history', but the suffering by the Armenian population continued. She was frustrated at how easily atrocities were forgotten and stressed the need to constantly remind the world of the ominous threat of violence. While domestic peace was celebrated, conditions that created atrocity continued, and were setting the stage for war on a larger scale, she ominously predicted. In the meantime, a few had sent contributions to assist Armenian orphans and widows who had lost breadwinners and their homes. She appealed to readers who might be moved 'to compassion' to further assist with funds.[11]

Such coverage in the press aimed to elicit funds, but these were not always forthcoming. 'If your readers', wrote Serle to the leading Hobart paper, the *Mercury*, with anger not typical in the message of humanitarians, 'are tired of hearing about famine sorrows' in Armenia, 'we are not nearly tired of receiving and forwarding relief funds'. 'So far', she reported, 'they have not been bulky enough to be burdensome ...'.[12] The exhaustion of 'giving' was identified as an obstacle in some of the discussions about the atrocities in Armenia. Serle reported how in England missionaries had observed that people were 'tired' of hearing about Armenia, so had requested they buy merchandise produced by Armenian survivors. Across the world – in Australia, and in England, 'even old friends of the widows and orphans have been tired of giving so we ask them to buy the needlework'.[13] Serle continuously promoted the cause, identifying indifference or lack of concern as a problem that needed to be addressed.

Earlier in May 1909, Serle reported more atrocities but had 'refrained' from making more appeals because she feared that the message would become too familiar, which would lead to paralysis – 'getting so used to hearing of such horrors unmoved by the impulse to do anything, that it seems almost useless to talk about them'.[14] Serle identified apathy and indifference as an issue: 'Is it not true that these very cables have been read aloud at many a well-spread table, or bright fireside, and scarcely caused a moment's check to the flow of trivial talk, or chatter of forks busy with the smoking viando so lavishly provided? Alas in some cases, winning no single word of interest or sympathy! Is it callousness?'[15] A poor child at the door begging would inspire charity in this context, she argued. 'But the wholesale slaughter of innocents in Armenia is another matter – just an unpleasant subject for a social meal, to be frozen up at once, and as soon forgotten. The experience of many of your readers will prove this is no exaggerated supposition.'[16]

Women such as Serle were not only active fundraisers, but also commentators on world affairs. Raising funds for the Armenian cause afforded Serle a platform from which to more broadly discuss international relations. Her access to information from international agencies such as philanthropic organisations provided her with material that not only promoted her cause, but which also allowed her to voice opinions. In May 1909, Serle discussed the opening of the Turkish Parliament but warned that this would not benefit the Armenian population as in the past, positive pronouncements had been undermined by atrocity and violence. Indeed, she warned, there is much reason to fear that it was 'only a ruse', a prelude to new horror.[17]

In September 1909, she wrote that it was maybe thought that 'enough' had been published regarding the Armenian massacre. But the fact that only £30 would have been subscribed in Tasmania shows 'how very few people have realized the awful suffering of our fellow-Christians. It has also not had the impact it appears. It also seems that those Christians are not following Christ's message in assisting fellow Christians.' Serle confessed that it is 'difficult to measure suffering we have never experienced', but appealed to hearts of 'compassion in this sunny island of peace and plenty'.[18] In a letter to the press, Serle continued in this vein, appealing to the humanitarianism and good will of Tasmanians, but she also berated them. In July 1908 she wrote that the Armenian struggle was long and tortured. 'Notwithstanding the publicity you have kindly given to the terrible facts of the distress in India and Armenia', she wrote to the *Mercury*, 'I am grieved to say that the assertion that it was over appears to have been all too comfortably accepted by thousands who have not contributed a penny to relieve the sufferers'.[19] Sufficient funds had not been raised through the newspapers so dropping off amounts of money outside shops seemed a new approach to raising finance. Serle appealed to the 'young ladies in Hobart' to collect small subscriptions by a house-to-house canvass, or with boxes.[20]

By 1910, funds had successfully been raised by Christian papers – the Melbourne *Southern Cross*, the *Australian Churchman* and the *Australian Christian World*. A total of £372 14s 10d was raised with £144 donated from Tasmania.[21] The response to raising these sums was overwhelmingly positive from the Friends of Armenia Society in London. As part of the British Empire, the Australian relief efforts were closely tied to British imperial networks, connections and transnational intersections. The Friends of the Armenian Society was one such group.[22] Serle quoted from a letter of appreciation from the Society, reassuring readers that 'this money has been spent in the wisest way for present and permanent benefit'. Thanks were expressed to 'the dear friends in Australia who are so kind and good'.[23]

But Serle did not hide her continuing frustration of what she felt was a general indifference and lack of interest. In 1910, she believed it was inexplicable that with modern technologies, and the 'boasted progress of nineteenth and twentieth century civilization, in the midst of surrounding Christian nations so-called', most people in Christian lands 'seem to know so little about the Armenian massacres, their cause and effect'. In Australia, it created 'absolutely no sensation' and the Churches were 'not ringing with the news and throbbing with Christian-like sympathy as might have been expected'.[24]

With the outbreak of the Armenian Genocide of 1915 and in the context of global violence of the First World War, relief funds were even harder to raise. During the war, the Genocide was reported in terms of the barbarism of Turkey, an enemy of Australia in conflict.[25] Serle made it clear she had refrained from pursuing an appeal, but the cause remained even more acute with the outbreak of war. Keeping the issue of aid to Armenia afloat during war was difficult as it provided a new context of atrocity. Her challenge was how she would continue to raise funds.[26] Rather than launch a new appeal, she targeted the 'long list of old subscribers to the relief funds' while donations were still gladly received.[27] The war overshadowed all attempts to draw attention to other humanitarian causes, but she continued to relentlessly attempt to raise funds.[28] In the aftermath of the Genocide the issue of the 'slavery' of women and girls provided Seale with a new framework with which to promote the Armenian cause and humanitarian aid. She wrote that efforts were made to arouse the twenty-five nations of the League of Nations to honour the pledges in the Lausanne Treaty, which under Article 38 provided for 'the full and complete protection of life and liberty for all inhabitants of Turkey without distinction of birth, nationality, language, race or religion'. Yet the slavery of Armenian girls continued, and more sums were desperately needed to address these abuses and violations.[29]

Sharing the experience

During the mid-1920s another strategy – Golden Rule Sunday – became a popular form of support for Armenian refugees in Australia. It shifted the focus of fundraising to the theme of sharing the experience of Armenian refugees and reflected trends in fundraising that had been emerging during the war. Originating from the USA, it involved eating a similar diet to that of Armenians. In the *International Golden Rule Sunday* handbook, Charles Vickrey, the general secretary of Near East Relief (NER), a prominent and powerful American humanitarian organisation, outlined the philosophy behind the concept. The NER was established in 1915 responding to humanitarian crises during the war, which included the Armenian Genocide. Initially, its efforts largely focused on raising funds to buy and distribute food by missionaries and staff at the American University in Beirut. As historian Keith Watenpaugh has observed, the NER shifted, throughout the inter-war years, from an organisation that distributed relief to one that promoted an American style humanitarianism which advocated modernity and progress, which it believed the Armenians were incapable of embracing without such external intervention.[30]

Golden Rule Sunday aspired to bring nations together in a dramatic show of strength for humanitarian support for Armenians. Vickrey described it as – 'a new day in the calendar of civilized peoples' with the aim to 'unify humanity through application of the principle of charity'.[31] The concept, however, became controversial, as Watenpaugh notes, and a source of tension within NER, as he attempted to build Golden Rule into a large-scale enterprise; his critics believed it to be 'ineffective and expensive'.[32]

In Australia, it gained considerable support. In 1924, Golden Rule Sunday was observed in Victoria on the 9 November – Armistice Sunday – 'a fitting memorial to the coming of peace', the *Portland Guardian* reported.[33] The Save the Children Fund and the Armenian Relief Fund – both Australian organisations with intimate British connections – were the two organisations responsible for promoting it.[34] It was not intended to be a 'fast' nor a 'starvation meal' but was food that 50,000 children were living on every day. It aimed to give children and adults a 'keener appreciation' of the value of citizenship, and 'the privileges and advantages they enjoyed'. The other lesson was its educative power, so violent conflict was avoided in the next generation. It also required that there be no meetings, or collections – just upholding the principles of Golden Rule.[35] The cost saved in the difference between the regular meal and that consumed as part of Golden Rule Sunday would be donated to the fund.[36]

Another form of campaigning that aimed to expose the world to the *experience* of Armenian refugees was the screening of *The Auction of Souls*, which included an Armenian young woman herself, Aurora Mardiganian, who took the lead part in the film representing her own life. While the Golden Rule movement encouraged identification with Armenian refugees in general, a focus on one Armenian woman who endured sexual violence and torture served as an emblem of Armenian suffering.[37] The film was shown in Sydney, at the Town Hall, in January 1920 for a fortnight to crowded attendances. It was shown in Melbourne at the Princess Theatre and was screened under the auspices of the committee of the Sydney Armenian Relief Fund.[38] The 'much-talked-of' film attracted a high profile and was shown around the country in all capital cities to much popular interest. In Sydney, it was reported that 'many hundreds had been turned away'.[39] In Perth, the 'picture was shown twice during the day, and the crowds anxious to see it were so great that the whole of the seating accommodation of the theatre was taxed to its utmost'. The film reportedly made a 'great impression' – as it was intended – on all those who saw it and many of the women were 'greatly affected'.[40] These appeals to a shared experience did not always attract the desired response, however, and at times had the opposite effect.

Rather than garner support and compassion it created a response of horror and repulsion.[41]

The *International Socialist*, the paper of radical socialists in Sydney, was not so convinced by the purpose of screening movies. Echoing some of the historical critiques of the film, it was critical of the 'melodramatic language for women to come and behold the trials and tribulations of their unfortunate sisters in Armenia. Everything is done to play on the morbid desire for horrors on the part of the public … to make large profits from the screening of the film.'[42] The *International Socialist* also highlighted the parlous state of Australian conditions, where under capitalism, men, women and children were bought and sold through a 'pitiless' system that exploited them. Until the private means of production were overturned, the proletarians would be slaves, and the 'auction of souls would go briskly on'.[43]

As the commentary in the *International Socialist* suggests, there was no consensus of support in Australia for Armenian relief. Similarly dissenting views had been expressed in earlier letters written to the press. In 1909, 'A Loyal Briton' argued against supporting raising funds for the Armenian cause. The writer attacked Serle's interest in all other countries but Australia:

> Why cannot we, as a nation, mind our own business? One day we are bothering about the Congo, another about Armenian Christians … As to the Armenian Christians … Turkey has a Parliament: let the members for the district explain the local troubles, and if necessary, let the executioners kill a few Kurds … What of Australia's poor and destitute? Who will support them if Australians don't? Are there no poor within our own gates, no sweated workers, no sick, to be cared for? When we have done our duty to the people under the Union Jack, then let us overflow. Perhaps by that time, the near East will not need our interference.[44]

This line of argument – that charity was needed at home before donating elsewhere – was a consistent theme in the early twentieth century in opposition to international humanitarian efforts. The far distance from Australia to the atrocities and suffering inflicted on Armenians was emphasised by critics of humanitarian support, leading to the view that compassion should begin locally and remain confined to domestic causes.

Smith's Weekly, a conservative paper, also put forward the claim that local causes should take priority over international campaigns. In 1924 it ran the headline: 'Australians Starve While Armenians Eat: Scandal of Overseas Philanthropy'. It was argued that in South Australia there was much charity, but it was charity that 'begins a long way from home'. It accused Australian humanitarians of showing a 'frenzied attachment' to Save the Children and to the Armenian Relief Fund, donating £5,000 to Greek and Armenian refugees. Yet locally unemployed and starving families in Australia were destitute. *Smith's Weekly* accused the fundraising bodies of negligence and ignorance. While they showed photos of farmers ploughing the lands, 'none but an expert anthropologist could distinguish as being either Greeks, Turks, Bulgars or

Armenians'. They applauded the government's decision not to allow them to emigrate to Australia. Humanitarians had collected £20,000 while 'shutting their eyes to misery at their own doors'.[45] It continued this campaign in Adelaide, noting that 'Three guineas for starving Armenians earns public acknowledgement in the press. Three shillings for starving Australians does not merit publication.'[46] *Labor News*, the organ of the New South Wales branch of the Australian Labor Party, was equally scathing of the 'pious utterances' of Americans in Armenia and critical of the alleged concern for 'saving the poor Christian people', which came with other agendas. The atrocities of the British were highlighted, wrongly excused by humanitarians as 'in retaliation, of course'.[47]

Immigration

While one way of resisting indifference and overt criticism was to disseminate more information that would generate compassion and funds, another method of campaigning was to lobby the government on the issue of the immigration of Armenians to Australia. The irrepressible Loyal L. Wirt, the International Commissioner for NER, appealed to the Prime Minister W. M. Hughes in 1922, following Wirt's promotional campaign visit to Australia in that year.

Wirt was effective in promoting the Armenian cause in Australia and transnationally in the early 1920s when he toured extensively throughout Australia and New Zealand. His visit was termed, 'Mission of Mercy'.[48] Described as a 'dapper, square-shouldered, vigorous, American', Wirt had been a Congregational Minister in Brisbane between 1904 and 1907, having also visited Tasmania in 1902 and became minister in Newcastle in that year.[49] Prior to this he was Superintendent of Education for the US (1897–1900) and then in 1900 he travelled to Manilla, China, Japan and the Philippines with the hope of establishing missionaries through the American Home Missionary Society.[50] By the time he had returned to the US in 1922, there were affiliated societies of the NER in Sydney, Melbourne, Ballarat, Adelaide, Perth, Kalgoorlie, Hobart and Launceston. In the Asian region he also set up branches in New Zealand, Japan, China, Philippine Islands, Korea and Hawaii.

The transnational nature of the cause drove Wirth around the globe with zest and enthusiasm. Wirt particularly appealed to Australians, arguing that they could make a significant and enduring contribution to the cause of Armenia. 'In helping in the Armenian cause, you in Australia are making a very great contribution to that end', a contribution that linked Australia to an entente of good will and kindly understanding comprising of Great Britain, United States, Canada, South Africa and New Zealand. He was delighted to see that Armenian relief committees were beginning their 'noble' efforts.[51] By September 1922 he 'expressed delight' at the success of his mission, having established ten committees and raised £25,000 in food and money.[52]

Wirt wrote to Prime Minister Billy Hughes, enthused with an idea to arrange for boys to find homes in rural Australia. 'As I understand it', he noted:

> the object of this effort is to assist boys from the British Isles, between the ages of fourteen and twenty, to find homes in the rural districts of Australasia, that they may be trained during their formative years in local methods of farming, to the end that later they may become successful cultivators of the soil, permanent members of the farmer class, and contented residents upon the land.[53]

Wirt was alert to the necessity of promoting this case of the boys in terms of the government immigration policy of White Australia, which excluded non-British immigrants to Australia. In 1901, the Immigration Restriction Act – more commonly known as the White Australia Policy – was introduced, which restricted the entry of non-European immigration to Australia. It enshrined the ideal of securing a 'white' nation.[54] Within this definition, Armenians were not 'deemed' white. In 1924, when the League of Nations requested that Australia accept Armenian refugees, the refusal to do so was on the basis that it would contravene Australia's White Australia Policy.[55] Stella Allen, Australia's substitute delegate to the fifth assembly at the League of Nations in Geneva in 1924 made Australia's position clear. She said that while it was the case that 'Australia's huge continent afforded boundless opportunities for the overflow of population', Australia would not open its doors to Armenian refugees, 'with whom Australia deeply sympathised'. This was because Australia was committed to 'relieving overcrowded Britain' – that is – to playing its role within the British Empire and serve its needs.[56]

Wirt argued that Armenians were derived from the same race and blood of Australians. These boys were from farming families, were intelligent and industrious. But above all, they would assimilate as they were also of the white race, Caucasian and European by blood: 'Bone of our bone, flesh of our flesh. In religion they are Gregorians – the oldest Christian organization. For the most part they are as white and as intelligent, and as easy of assimilation into the community as English boys.'[57] He envisaged that Armenians could be indentured labour or otherwise placed with farmers in Australia, to acquire knowledge or farming and stock raising. This emphasis on farming mirrored schemes of resettlement in Greece and the Middle East.[58] At the age of twenty-one it was anticipated that the boys would settle as citizens and would be an asset to Australia. Wirt also suggested that Hughes may wish to send a representative to Syria to assist in the selection of the boys from the 12,000 orphans they had housed in their orphanages. If the boys did not for any reason measure up, they could be returned, 'without prejudice'.[59] The response was emphatic from the government: 'it is considered undesirable to offer any attraction for the settlement in Australia of Armenians or other people of the Near East'.[60]

Another leading Armenian campaigner, the Congregational Minister Reverend James Cresswell wrote to the government supporting Wirt's proposal and seeking assistance.[61] Cresswell noted the desirability of securing girls for domestic service,

'An appeal from afar' 59

arguing that many of those in the Armenian orphanages had already achieved a 'certain amount of training'. In 1922, he offered to make 'personal investigations into the qualifications of these girls'. But he was informed that the government 'was unable to see its way clear to grant assistance in connection with the introduction of Armenian children'.[62]

In 1923, Marshall Fox, the British Quaker and relief worker in Egypt, also wrote with a detailed proposal on behalf of the Friends' Foreign Mission Association from Brummana, Syria. Armenians, he reassured Prime Minister Stanley Bruce, are Aryan 'like ourselves', and capable 'of doing anything the Britisher can do'.[63] Fox believed that Armenian refugees could go to a 'free life in Australia', claiming a vast, empty nation could accommodate them. With no awareness of the vast history of the Indigenous inhabitants of the land whose previous occupation stretched thousands of years, in 1930 he wrote that 'one possibility was shipping out refugees to give the young a chance of developing as far away as possible from the Turks and from the race hatred of the past [...] There are, as you know, vast tracts of land in Australia quite unoccupied – they want a white Australia – and the difficulties, if great, need not be considered insuperable.'[64] The myth of 'empty' lands for resettlement was commonly enlisted in discussions of the relocation of refugees.[65] When his own scheme did not gain support, Fox was critical of Armenians themselves, accusing the leadership of being concerned with keeping the nation intact rather than acting on behalf of individuals.[66]

Exotic humanitarianism

In the 1920s, the celebrity humanitarian speaker became keenly sought after for public presentations on the exotic Near East. Edith Glanville was an active humanitarian in support of the Armenian campaign who travelled extensively and commanded attention for her lectures both nationally and internationally. Her son, Leigh, had been killed in the First World War in 1915, at the Gallipoli landing. During the inter-war years, she went to Syria, Lebanon, Egypt and Palestine. She assisted in establishing orphanages for Armenian children in Lebanon and Syria. Glanville also served as the Liaison Officer at the League of Nations, between the League and Near East Relief, and she conducted regular lecture tours in Australia, England, USA and Canada to promote the work of the NER and report on the efforts of the Australian orphanage, which she visited regularly. Glanville became Director of the Australian Orphanage at Antilias for several months.[67]

Glanville also had connections with Karen Jeppe, a Danish relief worker appointed by the League of Nations to reclaim the thousands of Armenian women and children in and around Aleppo who had been abducted and forced to abandon their identity during the Genocide.[68] Jeppe appointed Glanville as her representative in Australia through the Sydney-based Australian Friends of Armenia.[69] By 1927, Glanville had become an Australian Ambassador for the

Armenian cause, and not merely an aid worker. It was reported that she had attended the conference of the British Commonwealth League in England. After that she travelled to Macedonia, Turkey, Syria and Palestine where she witnessed the work of American Near East Relief. Glanville attended the first convention of the League of Nations and then toured America and gave lectures on behalf of NER.[70]

Glanville became a much-celebrated speaker on the Australian lecture circuit. Her talks were not just about the Armenian cause and fundraising, but she offered an extended commentary on 'old' (primitive) and 'new' (modern) societies. In 1934, *The Sun* described her as possessing an 'interesting raconteur with a repertoire of epic tales'.[71] Her trips, too, became the source of considerable interest, depicted with a great sense of adventure. In 1926, the *Australasian* characterised her tour of Syria as an adventure:

> A thrilling tour of Syria has just been completed by Mrs Glanville ... in order to get first-hand knowledge of the work of the Armenian Relief Fund, of which she is former Australian secretary. She was warned not to go, and she was the only woman on the train entering the war zone beyond Aleppo, where under an armed guard she saw the menace of some of Syria's destitute people, numbering 80,000 ... In the refugees' camp at Beyrout [sic] children crowded in houses made of packing cases were dying like flies.[72]

The most pleasant aspect of her visit, it was reported, was the 'Australian orphanage ... over which the Australian flag was flying. There 1,000 Armenian boys are learning trades. A band greeted her with the National Anthem.'[73] The theme of adventure continued in the press when in November 1928, the *Age* announced Edith Glanville's Near East 'Adventures Among the Tribesmen'.[74] Australia's place on the world stage was amplified in Glanville's reports as a contributor to international relief efforts.

Other popular speakers on Armenian aid were the couple Ernest and Mary Bryce who were similarly inveterate international travellers. They drew parallels between Australia's Indigenous populations and that of Armenian refugees, arguing that the genocide of populations was an urgent matter. Ernest Bryce actively campaigned for investigations into the treatment of Aborigines. In July 1927, he spoke in London at the annual meeting of the Aborigines' Protection Society, commending proposals to establish a Royal Commission into the treatment of Aborigines.[75] Mary Bryce was active in the National Council of Women's League in New South Wales. Both were involved in the Armenian Relief Fund from 1922 until the 1930s. They travelled to the Middle East a number of times during the 1920s, visiting refugee camps. Mary Bryce assisted in the work of Karen Jeppe in Syria. In January 1924, she returned from a tour of the Near East, lasting five months, where she visited the various relief centres and orphanages, and brought back a collection of photographs illustrating the work among the refugees.

Mary Bryce became a leading Sydney figure and her lectures and talks were widely reported in the press. When she was elected to the executive of the National Council of Women in 1928, the Sydney *Sun* ran a feature on her. It was reported she distributed 40 tonnes of clothing collected in Australia in Aleppo, 'to the destitute fugitives as they came across the border into the safety of French territory'. She also established a needlework section where 'handwork made by Armenian women and girls, many of whom had been captives in Turkish harems, is sold'. Bryce declared herself a committed internationalist, travelling extensively and visiting thirty-one of the countries represented in the League and all the mandated territories.[76]

Bryce gave many lectures organised by women's groups to alert them of the devastation of the Armenian population and succeeded in raising material support for them through women's organisations.[77] Bryce especially promoted her cause through the accomplishments of children, and highlighted the centrality of children to many causes, including world peace. She attended the League of Nations Assembly at Geneva in 1927 and argued that women should train their children in peace principles. Unlike many of their counterparts who undertook humanitarian work for Armenian relief, however, the Bryce's were secular, they were not Christian missionaries or attached to a religious organisation.[78]

The collection of material items was also a part of Bryce's campaign.[79] Mary Bryce presented items made by Armenian children as gifts. In 1923, she had communicated that upon the return of herself and her husband from the Australasian orphanage, she was bringing with her some exquisite Armenian needlework and lace made by the girls in the orphanage.[80] As well as the lectures of adventure and exotic travel, then, one of the features of fundraising campaigns in the 1920s was the sale of this kind of embroidery work by children in the Australian orphanage. Armenian embroidery featured in 1928 in the Home Furnishing section of the *Sydney Mail*. Rosalie Wilson reported how such designs could fit into the furnishings of the modern Australian home as it was chiefly a 'peasant style' of design with motifs of animals, birds and flowers.[81] Placing the 'primitive' and 'peasant' goods in the Australian home was seen in contrast to a 'civilised' affluent Australia. The orientalist flavour of these representations fitted with the modernism of the 1920s, so assistance to Armenia was not exclusively about fundraising but also supporting an orientalist marvel of the 'peasant' works and how these might blend within a modernist environment. This presentation of Armenian craft may have generated interest in the Armenian cause but to what extent did it arouse compassion or empathy? It also brings to the fore the question of what was more important about this embroidery – that it was produced by an Armenian refugee, or that it could fit in the modern home? The tenuousness of compassion and its deep fragility is sharply revealed in this discussion.

Conclusion

A study of aid for Armenia campaigns in Australia reflects the contested and challenging task of sustaining compassion in charity campaigns over several decades for the Armenian cause. Supporters such as Mary Serle kept the commitment for it alive, but had to be inventive in how to rustle up funds, either through the narrative she developed so the message would not become too familiar or through the practical strategies she and others initiated nationally and internationally. Inadvertently, this task also provided a platform for women such as Serle, Granville and Bryce to serve as commentators on the international affairs of the Genocide of the Armenian population.

After the war, the popularity of recreating the circumstances of refugees through sharing diet and filmic representations became widespread to impress on the world the conditions endured by refugees in Armenia. But not all were convinced. Critics on both the left and right voiced concerns about what they saw as the misguided messages of liberal humanitarians. These methods also had an adverse impact of generating repulsion, not compassion. Many advocates of aid after the war promoted support through their eyewitness accounts. In these public lectures, a narrative of exotic humanitarianism emerged, which fitted into the modernist project of the 1920s, resonating as a form of orientalism. Even so, the plight of the Armenian population was not seen exclusively as an abstract concept in a faraway place. While efforts to allow Armenian refugees to enter Australia failed, this campaign pointed to attempts to challenge the overtly racist White Australia government policy through arguments of compassion for refugees – which were yet to be realised.

Notes

1 *Methodist* (19 February 1921), p. 1. See Stéphanie Prévost's chapter in this volume.
2 *Daily Post* (Hobart) (19 August 1909), p. 7.
3 *News* (Adelaide) (31 October 1923), p. 5.
4 *Argus* (3 October 1924), p. 6.
5 The history of compassion and its complexities is outlined in R. A. Wilson and R. D. Brown, 'Introduction', in R. A. Wilson and R. D. Brown (eds), *Humanitarianism and Suffering: The Mobilisation of Empathy* (Cambridge: Cambridge University Press, 2008) pp. 1–28; R. Gill, *Humanity and Relief in War, Britain 1870–1914* (Manchester: Manchester University Press, 2013); K. D. Watenpaugh, *Bread From Stones: The Middle East and the Making of Modern Humanitarianism* (Oakland, CA: University of California Press, 2015), p. 33; H. Fehrenbach and D. Rodogno (eds), *Humanitarian Photography: A History* (Cambridge: Cambridge University Press, 2015).
6 The theme of the exhaustion of giving in history is examined in B. Taithe, 'Horror, Abjection and Compassion: From Dunant to Compassion Fatigue', *New Formations* 62 (2007), 136.
7 J. Laycock, *Imagining Armenia: Orientalism, Ambiguity and Intervention, 1879–1925* (Manchester: Manchester University Press, 2009).

8 For recent studies see F. A. Keshgegian, '"Starving Armenians": The Politics and Ideology of Humanitarian Aid in the First Decades of the Twentieth Century', in Wilson and Brown (eds), *Humanitarianism and Suffering*, pp. 140–55; M. Tusan, *Smyrna's Ashes: Humanitarianism, Genocide, and the Birth of the Middle East* (Berkeley, CA: University of California Press, 2012); M. Tusan, *The British Empire and the Armenian Genocide: Humanitarianism and Imperial Politics from Gladstone to Churchill* (London: I.B. Tauris, 2017); M. Tusan, '"Crimes against Humanity": Human Rights, the British Empire, and the Origins of the Response to the Armenian Genocide', *American Historical Review* 119:1 (2014), 47–52; M. Tusan, 'Genocide, Famine and Refugees on Film: Humanitarianism and the First World War', *Past and Present* 237 (2017), 197–235; K. D. Watenpaugh, 'The League of Nations' Rescue of Armenian Genocide Survivors and the Making of Modern Humanitarianism, 1920–1927', *American Historical Review* 115:5 (2010), 1315–39; R. Jinks, '"Marks Hard to Erase": The Troubled Reclamation of "Absorbed" Armenian Women, 1919–1927', *American Historical Review* 123:1 (2018), 86–123.
9 J. Damousi, 'Humanitarianism in the Inter-War Years: How Australians responded to the Child Refugees of the Armenian Genocide and the Greek–Turkish Exchange', *History Australia* 12:1 (2015), 95–115; V. Babkenian, 'Australian Women and the Armenian Relief Movement', *Journal of the Royal Australian Historical Society* 101:2 (2015), 111–33; V. Babkenian, 'An SOS from Beyond Gallipoli: Victoria and the Armenian Relief Movement', *Victorian Historical Journal* 81:2 (2010), 250–76; V. Babkenian, 'A Humanitarian Journey: The Reverend James Edwin Cresswell and the Armenian Relief Fund', *Journal of the South Australian Historical Society* 37 (2009), 61–75.
10 Tusan, *The British Empire and the Armenian Genocide*, p. 91. See also B. Der Matossian, *Shattered Dreams of Revolution: From Liberty to Violence in the Late Ottoman Empire* (Stanford, CA: Stanford University Press, 2014).
11 *Sydney Morning Herald* (1 November 1910), p. 4.
12 *Mercury* (21 September 1908), p. 6.
13 *Mercury* (12 December 1913), p. 8.
14 *Mercury* (1 May 1909), p. 11.
15 Ibid.
16 Ibid.
17 *Mercury* (13 May 1909), p. 7.
18 *Mercury* (15 September 1909), p. 2.
19 *Mercury* (27 July 1908), p. 3.
20 Ibid.
21 *Mercury* (20 December 1910), p. 3.
22 Tusan, *The British Empire and the Armenian Genocide*; *Smyrna's Ashes*.
23 *Mercury* (20 December 1910), p. 3.
24 *Mercury* (1 October 2010), p. 3.
25 *Australasian* (15 May 1915), p. 32; *Examiner* (Launceston) (8 December 1917), p. 3; *Daily Telegraph* (Launceston) (12 March 1920), p. 4.
26 *Argus* (December 1915), p. 5.
27 Ibid.
28 *Spectator and Methodist Chronicle* (28 July 1916), p. 967; (20 June 1917), p. 665; (20 September 1916), p. 1916.
29 *Mercury* (7 December 1927), p. 8.
30 Watenpaugh, *Bread from Stones*, pp. 91–6.

31 C. V. Vickrey, *International Golden Rule Sunday: A Handbook* (New York: George H. Doran, 1926), p. 11.
32 Watenpaugh, *Bread from Stones*, p. 186.
33 *Portland Guardian* (23 October 1924), p. 2.
34 E. Baughan, '"Every Citizen of Empire Implored to Save the Children!": Empire, Internationalism and the Save the Children Fund in Inter-war Britain', *Historical Research* 86:231 (2013), 116–37.
35 *Portland Guardian* (23 October 1924), p. 2.
36 *Argus* (3 October 1924), p. 6.
37 See discussion in the introduction of this volume. See also P. Balakian, 'Photography, Visual Culture and the Armenian Genocide', in Fehrenbach and Rodogno (eds), *Humanitarian Photography*, pp. 89–114.
38 *Herald* (14 February 1920), p. 13.
39 *Sydney Morning Herald* (12 January 1920), p. 5.
40 *Daily News* (Perth) (24 May 1920), p. 5.
41 V. Babkenian and P. Stanley, *Armenia, Australia & the Great War* (Sydney: New South Press, 2016), p. 109.
42 *International Socialist* (24 January 1920), p. 3.
43 *Ibid.*
44 *Mercury* (5 July 1909), p. 2.
45 *Smith's Weekly* (27 September 1924), p. 11.
46 *Smith's Weekly* (25 October 1924), p. 11.
47 *Labor News* (10 November 1923), p. 3.
48 *Queensland Times* (22 May 1922), p. 5.
49 *Telegraph* (Brisbane) (4 May 1904), p. 3; (6 May 1922), p. 9; *Brisbane Courier* (17 October 1907), p. 4; *Examiner* (24 July 1902), p. 3; *Sun* (Newcastle) (17 May 1922), p. 6; *Sydney Morning Herald* (15 May 1922), p. 10.
50 *Examiner* (Launceston) (24 July 1902), p. 3.
51 *Daily Telegraph* (Sydney) (16 August 1922), p. 8.
52 *Register* (Adelaide) (16 September 1922), p. 8.
53 Armenians, Series number A457, Control symbol X401/2, NAA, L. L. Wirth to PM Hughes, 24 October 1922, Immigration Restriction. His interest in children predated this period. In 1907 he established the Social Service Institute to provide recreation for young people in Brisbane.
54 M. Lake and H. Reynolds, *Drawing the Global Colour Line: White Men's Countries and the International Challenge of Racial Equality* (Cambridge: Cambridge University Press, 2008), p. 137. See similar exclusions in Canada, D. Ohanian, 'Sympathy and Exclusion: The Migration of Child and Women Survivors of the Armenian Genocide from the Eastern Mediterranean to Canada, 1923–1930', *Genocide Studies International* 11:2 (2017), 197–215.
55 *Telegraph*, (Brisbane) (18 September 1924), p. 2.
56 *Daily Examiner* (Grafton) (15 September 1924), p. 5.
57 *Ibid.*
58 Watenpaugh, *Bread from Stones*, pp. 191–2.
59 *Ibid.*
60 *Ibid.*
61 Jas. E. Creswell, National Secretary, Australasian Armenian Fund, to Mr. Foster, 2 January 1923.
62 Secretary to Rev. Jas. E. Creswell, Hon. Secretary, Australian Armenian Relief Fund, 10 January 1923.

63 Armenians, Series number A457, Control symbol X401/2, NAA, Marshall Fox to PM Stanley Bruce, 25 April 1923, Immigration Restriction.
64 Quoted in P. Gatrell, 'Trajectories of Population Displacement in the Aftermaths of Two World Wars', in J. Reinisch and E. White (eds), *The Disentanglement of Populations: Migration, Expulsion and Displacement in Postwar Europe, 1944–9* (London: Palgrave Macmillan, 2011), p. 10.
65 M. Frank, 'The Myth of Vacant Places: Refugee Group Resettlement', in M. Frank and J. Reinisch (eds) *Refugees in Europe: 1919–1959: A Forty Years' Crisis?* (London: Bloomsbury, 2017), pp. 121–45.
66 *Ibid.*
67 *Sunday Times* (6 January 1929), p. 14. See also, Babkenian and Stanley, *Armenia, Australia & the Great War*, pp. 245–8.
68 P. Gatrell, *The Making of the Modern Refugee* (Oxford: Oxford University Press, 2013), p. 62.
69 *Sunday Times* (6 January 1929), p. 14.
70 *Port Adelaide News* (1 April 1927), p. 6.
71 *The Sun* (18 February 1934), p. 30.
72 *Australasian* (9 October 1926), p. 55.
73 *Ibid.*
74 *Age* (29 November 1928), p. 12.
75 *Register* (9 July 1927), p. 9.
76 *Sun* (Sydney) (5 August 1928), p. 51.
77 R. Kaplan, 'Forgotten Champions of Indigenous Rights', *Koori Mail* (13 March 2013), p. 24. See also Armenian Genocide Education Australia, 'Australia's Response', www.armeniangenocide.com.au/australiaresponse (accessed 19 March 2020).
78 See M. Tusan, 'The Business of Relief Work: A Victorian Quaker in Constantinople and Her Circle', *Victorian Studies* 51:4 (2009), 633–61.
79 *Sydney Morning Herald* (9 April 1924), p. 5.
80 *Evening News* (21 December 1923), p. 15.
81 *Sydney Mail* (26 September 1928), p. 31.

4

Humanitarian crisis at the Ottoman–Russian border: Russian imperial responses to Armenian refugees of war and genocide, 1914–15

Asya Darbinyan

In 1915 the Armenian writer Hovhannes Tumanyan arrived with his daughter Nvard in the town of Etchmiadzin, to assist with the relief of the thousands of Armenians who had arrived in the Russian imperial provinces of Transcaucasia, fleeing violence across the border in the Ottoman Empire.[1] He reflected that in 'that hell called Turkish Armenia – three armies exist. The first army is the one in combat. The second – is the army of the abandoned women and children, the sick, the famished, the naked, the refugees, which is the largest army. Third – is the army of activists and helpers, which is the smallest and the weakest.'[2] These brief reflections capture both the alarming scale of the crisis that was unfolding in the region, and the challenges facing the emerging relief effort.

The war on the Caucasus front between the Ottoman and Russian Empires began in November 1914.[3] It remains an unfamiliar part of the popular history of the First World War. Kristian Ulrichsen, for example, points out that the fighting at Gallipoli, Mesopotamia and Palestine have been the focus of many Anglophone military histories, even though 'the Ottoman military machine was largely bled dry on the Russian front'.[4] The Caucasus front was also a site of forced displacement, genocidal violence and humanitarian crisis. This chapter demonstrates how exploring its neglected history can nuance our understanding of population displacement and humanitarianism in the early years of the First World War.

While Russian and Ottoman imperial troops fought on the Caucasus front, hundreds of thousands of Ottoman Armenian subjects were targeted by Ottoman authorities as a potential 'strategic threat'. The Armenians fell victim to a systematically implemented genocide by the Ottoman state that justified their actions as military necessity.[5] Those who were not massacred outright or deported to the deserts of Mesopotamia became refugees on the Russian–Ottoman battlefront and elsewhere. The German missionary Dr Johannes Lepsius put the number of Armenian victims in the Ottoman–Russian frontier zones at 7,000 in November–December 1914.[6]

Each advance and retreat of either Russian or Ottoman troops across the imperial borderlines resulted in population movement, accompanied by violent persecutions, starvation and epidemics. Reflecting on the condition of Armenians and the Turkish atrocities at the Caucasus front, a Russian officer lamented, 'Have you seen what they [Turkish soldiers] did to the Armenian population of Ardahan and the refugees they caught during their offensive? All houses were full of corpses. They spared neither women nor children. Corpses littered along the roads. Not a single person managed to escape. They slaughtered everyone.'[7]

In this chapter, I observe the dynamics of the first mass population movements in Ottoman–Russian border regions and explore the condition of refugees streaming towards Transcaucasia between November 1914 and August 1915. During these months, refugees on the Caucasus front of the war became a major humanitarian concern for the civil and military authorities of the Russian Empire. An immense humanitarian assistance effort on behalf of Armenian refugees emerged. This chapter charts its development up to August 1915, when a single central body to coordinate and/or supervise these efforts was created.

Examining the relief effort during these first months of the war offers important insights into the history of humanitarianism. First, while there is a robust literature on international responses to the Armenian Genocide, these works focus on the Middle East and on American, British, German and Scandinavian news coverage and relief committees.[8] In contrast, both the situation in Transcaucasia and the Russian response to the crisis have prompted little scholarship.[9] This chapter contributes to the emerging literature on relations between humanitarianism and imperialism, by paying attention to the neglected case of the Russian Empire. While there is a significant Anglophone literature on Russia as a recipient of international aid, little has been said about Russia or Russians as actors in the provision of relief.[10] Previous literature on Russian responses to the Armenian Genocide has tended to emphasise Russia's imperial goals and, as in the case of Avetis Harutyunyan's work, to present Russian intervention on the part of Armenian refugees as simply a by-product of their imperial agenda.[11] More recently, Peter Holquist has suggested that Russian imperial strategy in the region must be interpreted in a more nuanced, contingent manner.[12] This chapter builds on this work by examining the range of actors and complex motivations that shaped the evolution of the humanitarian response to Armenian refugees in Transcaucasia.

Drawing upon primary sources from Armenian, Georgian and Russian archives, this chapter charts the organisation of assistance to displaced Armenians on the Caucasus front. I focus on emergency assistance provided to the Armenian refugees by Russian and Armenian organisations, as well as by local villagers and activists. The Caucasus Armenian Benevolent Society, and the Armenian Central Committee in Tiflis (Tbilisi) were among the major Armenian national organisations, providing aid to the refugees from the very first days of the population movement. Meanwhile, Russian organisations, such as the Committee of Her Highness Grand Duchess Tatiana Nikolaevna (Tatiana Committee), and the All-Russian Union of Towns (*Vserossiĭskiĭ Soiuz Gorodov*, VSG), established branches and sent delegates to various parts of imperial Russian and border regions to assist the wounded and sick soldiers at the frontlines and to resolve the refugee crises, including but not limited to the Caucasus. I show that humanitarianism on the Caucasus front of the First World War represented an intersection of complex structures and relationships between imperial and public institutions, central and local organisations. It brought together the motivations, aims and plans of multiple actors despite their contradicting perceptions and understanding of the role of the state and the public organisations in society and in relief work.

Refugees streaming into the Russian Empire

The war between the Russian and Ottoman Empires created complex movements of people, particularly civilians who escaped across the front lines into the interior of the two empires. Living in the borderlands of these two hostile empires, Armenians were in a particularly vulnerable position. The first wave of Armenian refugees crossed the border into Russian imperial territories in Transcaucasia in October 1914.[13] The Ottoman advance through Ardahan and Olti towards Kars and Sarikamish resulted in sudden retreat of Russian troops from Köprüköy (23–24 October 1914) and the Armenians of Turkish Basen (Pasin) fled to Russian Basen and elsewhere.[14]

The second wave followed in the wake of the temporary success of Turkish forces and sudden retreat of Russian forces in the Sarikamish forests in December 1914.[15] Karo Sassouni, who witnessed Russian forces abandoning their positions in Basen and those areas of Alashkert (Eleşkirt) bordering with Kars, described the retreat as 'merciless' towards the Armenians, since Russian troops 'almost ran over the Armenian refugees'.[16] The sudden refugee flow into various regions of the Caucasus from Turkey was alarming. Reported number of refugees in the region in January 1915 varied from around 43,000 to 95,000. On 15 January 1915, Samson Harutyunyants reported that the approximate number of refugees from the Ottoman Empire and bordering regions was around 80,000–95,000.[17]

From the start, keeping track of the numbers of refugees was a priority for the local authorities. A report prepared by the Erivan (Yerevan) Statistical Commission based on a one-day census conducted on 30 January 1915 provides a detailed account of the number of refugees that found asylum in the Erivan governorate, in Kars *oblast*, and in Akhalkalak *uezd*.[18] It lists 45,138 Armenian refugees (6,803 families), 6,379 Assyrian refugees (1,325 families), 8,886 Greek refugees (1,257 families), and 102 refugees of other nationalities (20 families), a total number of 60,505 (9,405 families) on 30 January 1915.[19] However, the report is only a snapshot of a rapidly changing situation. Newly arrived reserves enabled the Russians to counterattack and restore their positions in Sarikamish, and some of the displaced Armenians returned to their homes soon after.

The third large wave arrived in Transcaucasia in summer 1915. In spring 1915 Russian imperial troops advanced towards Tabriz, Urmia, then took over Alashkert,

Bashkale, Manazkert (Malazgirt), Shatakh and Van, after which the army was to move towards Mush and Bitlis.[20] The sudden success of Turkish forces in early July and the retreat of Russian troops, however, resulted in an accumulation of Turkish forces around Manazkert, Alashkert, Karakilisa, Patnos, Van, up to areas close to Kaghzvan (Kagizman).[21] The local Armenian population, terrorised, followed the troops towards the Russian border.

The condition of refugees between the advancing Turkish troops and the retreating Russian army was terrible. 'So many of them [refugees] died, that at certain areas the accumulation of corpses disrupted the communication. Countless children died, separated from their parents and abandoned.'[22] Newspapers in Transcaucasia were filled with descriptions of this immense population movement and the condition of refugees: 'Strung to the fullest stretch of anguish and terror, the procession [refugee movement] pushes forward across the lofty mountains and the deep valleys, devoured by thirst under a burning sun. There are many in that company who curse the day of their birth.'[23]

About 208,000 refugees from Turkey had reached the Caucasus by July–August 1915.[24] Two thirds of them were women, as men were slaughtered remorselessly before the flight. The refugee columns had moved towards Russian imperial territories from three general directions: Kars, Igdir and Julfa. On arrival, they were accommodated in Surmalu, Etchmiadzin, Erivan, Sharur-Daralagyaz, Nor Bayazet, Alexandropol, Borchalu, Kazakh, Elisavetpol and other *uezds* of Erivan, Elisavetpol and Tiflis governorates and Kars *oblast*.

These survivors had walked long distances; many died from starvation, exhaustion and diseases: others were attacked en route by Kurdish gangs that did not spare women and children.[25] A number of survivor testimonies recount Russian soldiers and Cossacks who showed initiative and helped the desolate and exhausted refugees to survive. Srbouhi Mouradian reflected on her experience of flight from Bitlis. Her brother was killed, and her mother, Kakav, was so terrified that when she heard horses approaching, she thought Turks were attacking again, and threw herself and her daughters into the river. 'But the horsemen were Russian soldiers', Srbouhi lamented. 'They had felt that the woman had thrown herself into the water in despair; they jumped into the river, saved us and took us to the Russian general.'[26]

First responders

Reports and testimonies describing the first retreat of Russian troops and the population movement toward the Caucasus in December 1914 hold that it did not result in a major humanitarian crisis, first, because many refugees could soon return back home, and, second, because the local Armenian population mobilised all their resources towards the organisation of relief work for the displaced Armenians.[27] Karo Sassouni described the work of what he referred to as Armenian 'activists' in Basen and Alashkert, in early 1915.[28] He emphasised the villagers' efforts to organise relief work by making lists of the refugees, establishing how many of them were very poor and disabled, and in need of urgent assistance. 'January and February were the relief work months. The refugees were not abandoned', he assured.[29] These local efforts demonstrate that Armenians during the war and Genocide were not simply victims dependent upon external actors' mercy and assistance: they were self-reliant, willing and able to self-organise.[30]

More than three quarters of the refugees found shelter in Armenian villages. Dr Samuel G. Wilson, a Presbyterian missionary from the American Committee for Armenian and Syrian Relief (the organisation which would later become Near East Relief, NER), reported from Erivan: 'Many of the Armenian villagers have taken in and cared for the destitute refugees. Others have given them the use of their spare rooms, bake-houses, stables and barns ….'[31] Reporting to the Viceroy of the Caucasus, Samson Harutyunyants from the Armenian Benevolent Society, emphasised that the Armenian peasantry of the governorate, on their own, had provided products and monetary support worth up to 500,000 rubles.[32] His comments reflect the way in which the decentralised efforts of 'ordinary people' are often neglected in a historiography which has largely focused on major agencies.[33]

The ongoing provision of basic relief, however, constituted a major challenge for the locals. Because of the lack of labour force and draft animals during wartime, the peasantry could not cultivate the land. In addition, scarcity of supply transports from Russia resulted in unprecedented price jumps of bread and basic necessities, exerting immense strain on the local communities' resources.[34] The looming winter threatened disaster. Thus, relief efforts of local villagers were important, yet unsustainable. The need for more organised, structured and substantial assistance was evident.

Imperial responses

While the local population was responding to the arrival of thousands of Armenian refugees, reports about Turkish atrocities against Armenians in the Ottoman Empire and the humanitarian crisis emerging in the Caucasus quickly began to reach the imperial Russian authorities. Russia's joint declaration with Great Britain and France in May 1915 is perhaps the best known of the documents of the time. The Great Powers defined the atrocities against the Armenians in the Ottoman Empire as a 'crime against humanity' and promised to hold members of the Ottoman government and those 'implicated in massacres personally responsible' for those crimes.[35] Sergei Sazonov, the Foreign Minister of the Russian Empire, played a central role in the drafting of this declaration. He proposed public condemnation of the Ottoman government and engaged British and French diplomats in this process.[36]

A series of undertakings followed. Mikhail Papadjanov [Papajanian], the (Armenian) Russian State Duma representative for the Baku, Elisavetpol and Erivan governorates, claimed in his speech in the Duma (20 July 1915) that Turks targeted

Armenians in the bordering regions of the Caucasus front before the Russian troops had even entered, annihilating them as 'an element having close ties with Russia'.[37] Papadjanov, like many other statesmen in the Russian Empire, thus attempted to bring the Turks' violence against Armenians to wider attention. Pavel Miliukov, a prominent representative of the Constitutional Democratic party in the Duma, assessed: 'Assisting Armenian refugees not only saves lives of individuals, but we also ensure the survival of a nation, whose existence is a key to the success of our cultural mission in Turkish regions ....'[38]

Miliukov's statement demonstrates the complexity of the problem of humanitarian assistance on the Caucasus front of the First World War. Since the Treaty of Küçük Kaynarca (1774), the Russian Empire was regarded as 'protector of Christians in the Ottoman Empire'.[39] Thus, saving lives of Armenians fleeing the hostile Ottoman state was not merely an act of philanthropy but was seen as Russia's responsibility. At the same time, Russian military and civil authorities were responsible for defending the imperial interests in the region, which, among others, included successful military operations against the Turkish forces and probable establishment of some sort of Russian control in occupied eastern Ottoman provinces. Miliukov did not see a contradiction between imperial interests and assistance to Armenians in distress. Like Miliukov, many Russian political and public figures not only protested against Ottoman violence, they also pressed for relief work in order to confront this emergency.

Relief organisations

As the political response evolved, a number of committees and organisations, both Russian and Armenian, were already engaged in the Armenian refugee relief effort, in Transcaucasia and the Russian interior, as well as in eastern Ottoman regions occupied by Russian troops. The majority of Armenian national committees focused on emergency assistance to the Ottoman-Armenian refugees and to the displaced persons from the Ottoman–Russian borderlands from the very first days of war on the Caucasus front. Meanwhile, imperial Russian organisations, such as the Tatiana Committee and the VSG, were engaged with refugee humanitarian activity throughout the vast empire and at the frontlines.

Two of the first and most prominent organisations in the Russian Empire to address the Armenian refugee crisis from within the Armenian community were the Caucasus Armenian Benevolent Society and the Armenian Central Committee in Tiflis. The former had a long history of advocacy and assistance on behalf of Armenians in the Russian Empire and by 1915 coordinated the work of its seventy-two branches within the Caucasus.[40] The Armenian Central Committee for the Assistance of Victims of War, established in September 1914 in response to the outbreak of war, acted under the aegis of the Catholicos of all Armenians.[41] These two committees mostly worked together, and soon grew into a joint institution.[42]

The problem of refugee assistance was discussed on 9 November 1914 at the Central Committees' regular session, emphasising such important issues as the necessity to raise funds and send delegates to the refugees' temporary shelters and settlements for investigation of urgent needs of those desolate people. The Benevolent Society and the Central Committee established hospitals and food stations in Kars, Erivan, Nakhichevan, Julfa, Alexandropol, Van, Manazkert, Igdir and other places.[43] They sent medical squads to assist the refugees and organised labour assistance, by opening labour bureaus, workshops and laundries.[44] United, these organisations appealed to prominent and wealthy Armenians, banks and public institutions, urging them to donate. Due to this intensive work and continuous calls for help, a number of towns, Moscow, Petrograd, Nakhichevan on Don (Nor Nakhichevan) and many others, launched fundraising campaigns and collected monetary donations, as well as clothes and linen to send to the refugees.[45] Another organisation, the Moscow Armenian Committee of the Red Cross, was mostly supported by the donations of the Armenian community in Moscow. It operated in the Erivan governorate from April 1915, opening a hospital, a depot of flour and food, three orphanages and a school for 110 orphan-students in the village of Ashtarak, in Etchmiadzin *uezd*, and elsewhere.[46]

The Committee of Brotherly Aid was established in Etchmiadzin – chaired by the Catholicos of all Armenians – and extended its branches to Erivan, Alexandropol, Igdir, Nakhichevan, Nor Bayazet, Kars and Karakilisa.[47] It opened hospitals and medical and food stations, sent flying squads, and organised shelters and orphanages. Brotherly Aid also assisted with the distribution of official rations assigned by the government.[48] Furthermore, while in villages the refugees were sheltered in the houses of the peasants in an improvised manner, in towns housing was organised by the Brotherly Aid. There were functioning military hospitals, infirmaries and pediatric infirmaries inside the Etchmiadzin monastery and other buildings in the town, funded by the Committee of Brotherly Aid, the Caucasus Committee of VSG and others.[49]

Financial and professional support to promote and accelerate the implementation of life-saving operations by the Central Committee, the Benevolent Society and other Armenian committees, was provided also by major Russian humanitarian and benevolent organisations, which were coordinating and implementing relief across the Empire, in particular the Tatiana Committee and the VSG. The Tatiana Committee had tight connections with the government circles, shared the values of the monarchy and the monarch, and was hence trusted and supported by him. Its work included providing one-time financial support for refugees, refugee registration, responding to inquiries from relatives of the refugee-survivors, employment and housing assistance. Of the 300,000 rubles spent on needs of refugees in Transcaucasia by 1 March 1915, 200,000 rubles were provided by the Armenian institutions, and 100,000 rubles by the Tatiana Committee.[50] The Committee also deployed the power of the press and placed appeals in newspapers to raise money.[51]

The VSG, founded in August 1914 to aid the wounded and sick on the front, quickly grew into a large organisation.[52] With the escalation of war and opening of the Caucasus front, VSG's responsibilities expanded to refugees who streamed into the Russian Empire in great numbers. A branch, the Union of Caucasus Towns (Caucasus Committee of VSG), was founded in Tiflis under the auspices of the Caucasus Viceroy.[53] All the major towns in the region became members of the Caucasus Committee of VSG, and Aleksandr Khatisyan, the mayor of Tiflis, was to coordinate the work of the committee.

This organisation was responsible for collection of donations, transportation of the refugees from the frontline to the interior, establishment of food stations on routes of mass population movement, and sanitary-medical assistance to the displaced and the refugees (particularly prevention of epidemics during humanitarian operations).[54] The Caucasus Committee opened food and tea stations, as well as medical stations on the Igdir–Etchmiadzin–Erivan–Yelenovka–Dilijan–Aghstev route for refugees coming from Turkey.[55] At the beginning they aided refugees transported to and sheltered in the Erivan and Elisavetpol governorate. Khatisyan, the head of the Caucasus Committee, was delegated to Etchmiadzin to investigate condition of refugees, and to evaluate the emergency situation. His report made for grim reading: 'Number of refugees [in Etchmiadzin] is 30,000; [daily] death toll is above three hundred. Five hundred corpses remain not buried. Healthy refugees have scattered in panic', reported Khatisyan (28 August 1915).[56]

The VSG worked in cooperation with the All-Russian Union of *Zemstvos* (*Vserossiĭskiĭ Zemskiĭ Soiuz*, VZS), established on 30 July 1914, chaired by Prince Georgy Lvov, and was comprised of a main or central committee (in Moscow), as well as committees of governorates and *uezds*.[57] According to initial regulations and plans of the unions, refugee issues were the responsibility of the VSG, and the VZS was supposed to take care of the needs of local populations and communities of towns and villages flooded by refugees. By the middle of 1915, the VZS had also turned to the welfare of large numbers of refugees at the Caucasus front. The cooperation between these two unions lasted until 1916, when the VZS ceased refugee operations because of strained relations with government officials.[58]

Unlike the Tatiana Committee, a benevolent organisation sponsored and supported by the imperial government, VSG and VZS were seen as central actors in the Russian Empire's public (*obshchestvennyi*) life, the only initiative allowing Russian society to participate in the social developments of the imperial state.[59] Historian Galina Ulianova sees charity-benevolence, its structure, mechanisms and motivations as a 'means of self-organisation for the progressive layers of Russian society'.[60] Ulianova's analysis explains the imperial government's disapproval of the unions and their activity and the growing competition between the two major actors, the Tatiana Committee and the VSG, for dominance in humanitarian work in the Empire.

While the Armenian Benevolent Society and other national Armenian committees, as well as individual activists, were more focused on saving the remnants of the Armenians from the disaster of unfolding war and genocide, with a hope for a revival of the nation in Transcaucasia, the Russian benevolent organisations competed for dominance in the field of humanitarian relief work throughout the Empire. It would be easy to assume, given these aspects, that there was a sharp divide between imperial and emerging Armenian national agendas. Yet, my research shows that the boundaries between the two were blurred and we cannot make generalisations. Despite their differing agendas and relationships to the Tsarist regime, the goals, responsibilities and tasks of these humanitarian organisations, be it national Armenian or imperial Russian committees, funded by individual donors, compassionate communities or governmental credits, greatly overlapped and, frequently, required cooperation.

At the same time, the correspondence between the various agencies and institutions demonstrates that sometimes there were also misunderstandings and miscommunications, which led to delays in financial transfers, and inefficiency in relief work. Therefore, when M. M. Novikov, member of the State Duma, handed over to Aleksandr Khatisyan a donation worth 30,000 rubles from the Moscow City Duma, the following letter, stressing the need for clear cooperation was attached to the credit: 'I want to express my wish that the distribution and use of the funds be discussed with the VZS, as the latter has also received funding for the same purpose. It would also be preferable if the mentioned question could be discussed with the representatives of benevolent organisations of Tiflis working for and pursuing the same goals.'[61]

From improvisation to standardisation? The Special Council for Refugees

Almost all refugees from the Ottoman Empire and the bordering regions fled for their life and did not manage to carry anything with them. Once arriving at the temporary settlements or shelters, they were in desperate need of help. The imperial government had assigned an allowance for refugees on the Caucasus front – 15 kopeks per person – and provided them with some basic medical assistance.[62] The *ad hoc* measures to support the arriving refugees were crucial, yet, not very well coordinated. The Viceroy of the Caucasus in Tiflis and the governors of major provinces and towns did not suspect that within weeks thousands upon thousands of displaced people would flood the area. Exhausted, undernourished refugees, packed in towns and villages of Transcaucasia, were falling prey to disease and epidemics at an alarming rate.

By late summer 1915 the problem of population movement and the refugee crisis was alarming the authorities not only in the Caucasus, but also in the entire Russian Empire. Plenipotentiary Shchepkin, chair of the Department for Refugees of Union of Towns and *Zemstvos*, wrote, 'refugees are the natural consequence of the enemy's advance into our territories'.[63] Then referring to the unprecedentedly large-scale and disastrous population movement that began in the Russian Empire in July–August 1915, he added, 'the tragedy and horror [of the refugee movement] is impossible to convey ... The enormous crowds of refugees walk through dirt roads, like a solid wall, covering those roads with corpses.'[64] The German advance in spring and summer 1915 had resulted in tremendous losses for Russian troops, in the fall of Warsaw in July, and in an 'enormous wave of civilian displacement'.[65] Describing the influx of hundreds of thousands of refugees into Belorussia during this period, Peter Gatrell notes how 'provincial towns and villages were transformed overnight into feeding stations.'[66]

To confront the growing emergency, the Russian imperial authorities attempted to move beyond the improvised and fragmented measures that had characterised relief thus far. To this end, the Decree Meeting the Needs of Refugees was issued on 30 August 1915, establishing the Special Council for Refugees (*Osoboe soveshchanie po ustroĭstvu bezhentsev*) under the supervision of the Ministry of Interior.[67] The Special Council was to ensure the efficiency of refugee humanitarian activities: it disbursed funds for refugee relief; oversaw the registration and relocation of refugees; assisted in the return of refugees to their place of permanent residence; arranged loans for refugees; ascertained the value of property refugees had been forced to abandon; compensated refugees for losses incurred as a result of military action and for property that had been requisitioned; and addressed the spiritual and educational needs of refugees.[68]

The decree defining 'refugee' status that was also issued on 30 August 1915 stated that 'Individuals who left their localities threatened or already occupied by the enemy, or were displaced from the military zones at the command of either military or civil authorities, as well as individuals originating from Russia's enemy states are to be identified as refugees.'[69] The decree created a new legal basis for the humanitarian operations. All individuals identified as refugees were supposed to be issued a refugee card or book, which accorded them privileges (access to soup kitchens, financial and medical assistance). Those books helped the authorities register the refugees, keep track of their travels and workplace changes, record the number of surviving family members, and identify the male or female head of refugee households.[70]

The refugee decree and the creation of the special council marked an important shift in the relationship and balance of power between the government and non-state, as well as local and central organisations. This is seen clearly in the matter of registering refugees. From the very beginning of the population displacement in the Caucasus, local relief agents, municipal organisations and representatives of Russian public organisations, such as VSG and VZS, and the Tatiana Committee had been engaged with refugee registration. The reports about the size of the refugee population they provided proved to be inconsistent. Centralisation under the auspices of the Special Council for Refugees was supposed to overcome such issues.

In November 1915, in an effort to improve the efficiency of the system, the Special Council centralised the responsibility for registering refugees with the Tatiana Committee. The official reasoning of the Special Council was that the Tatiana Committee, located in Petrograd, was 'better connected with the local national organisations' (that were conducting the work at local level and providing the collected information to the centre) than VSG and VZS, whose headquarters were in Moscow. But this explanation did not sound credible to the unions. They insisted that the Special Council should have considered the already existing cooperation between the local *zemstvos* and towns and the Unions' Statistical Committee registering the refugees. They were very critical about this meeting of the Special Council, which made such an important structural decision at a session without the presence of their representatives.[71]

The decision to grant this responsibility to the Tatiana Committee reflected the fact that registering refugees was a politically sensitive matter on which the Tsarist authorities were unwilling to compromise. As Ulianova has assessed, 'independent philanthropic institutions in the highly centralized empire acted as elements of an emerging civil society'.[72] Thus, the government was not prepared or willing to trust the public organisations, VSG or VZS, with more tasks and responsibilities, seeing their empowerment as a political threat to the monarchy. They were more supportive of the Tatiana Committee's work in this direction, as the latter did not represent any threat to the imperial structure of the state and the society, on the contrary, it served as a tool for the state to reassert its power through claiming authority over the refugee population.

Nonetheless, reports from organisations providing relief in the months that followed showed that these questions were not comprehensively clarified. Away from the centres of power, confusion and overlapping roles and responsibilities persisted. For instance, in early January 1916, Plenipotentiary Khatisyan wrote to the Refugees Department of the VSG, asking for clarifications, whether they could conduct registration, or whether it was solely 'the duty of the Tatiana Committee'. To which the Department responded: 'in the view of the committees of both Unions, that question must be reconsidered, and an announcement/appeal about this has been made accordingly'.[73] Thus this attempt at centralisation, efficiency and greater political control was, at best, only partially successful. Misunderstanding and competition would continue into the coming months.

Conclusion

Hundreds of thousands of Ottoman Armenians as well as Russian Armenians living in the bordering regions of the two empires were forced to abandon their homes, and flee towards the villages and towns of Transcaucasia, because of the war unfolding on the Caucasus front and the genocide implemented by the Ottoman state. Many of the refugees, forced into flight, had lost their property, homes, family members and, finally, they had lost hope. Immediate mobilisation of local villagers, and activists, timely reaction of relief committees and establishment of new ones, made the organisation of humanitarian assistance for those desperate people in need possible. With the influx of the first waves of Armenians refugees into the Russian Empire, the imperial government assigned funds and rations for them to confront the emergency. Major organisations initially founded to assist the wounded and sick soldiers, VSG and the Tatiana Committee, among others, evolved into refugee relief institutions. Countless new committees emerged from within Armenian communities, like the Committee of Brotherly Aid and the Moscow Armenian Committee, taking responsibility for and saving the lives of thousands of Armenians, left without home and hope. Those villagers, the individual activists, the governmental and public organisations, local and other national committees, strengthened the 'third army' of humanitarians that Tumanyan was so concerned about.

From late August 1915 the imperial authorities strived to improve the organisation of refugee relief in the Empire. The formation of the Special Council for Refugees and the creation of a legal basis to meet the needs of refugees were giant steps towards the realisation of that goal. The Council's major task was to oversee and coordinate the work of all the actors and institutions already deeply involved in this tremendous humanitarian initiative, instead of starting campaigns and charities from scratch. This centralised model of relief work did not satisfy the public organisations, such as VSG and VZS, because they craved more independence and authority in refugee assistance, which the imperial government could not afford in wartime. Moreover, the official governmental attempts to control and coordinate the humanitarian efforts did not always ensure the success envisioned by the authorities, especially in 'peripheral' regions of the Empire like the Transcaucasian borderlands. However, in a number of cases the centralised and coordinated work-style could spark cooperation between institutions and organisations that might have been expected to have differing agendas. By paying close attention to the autumn 1914–summer 1915 period and the responses to the refugee and humanitarian crises, we do not see a top-down response by the Russian Empire in Transcaucasia that is simply aimed at promoting colonial agendas. Instead, we have a picture of a complex set of interactions between local and imperial agendas, practices and organisations. As the refugee crisis persisted through revolution and imperial collapse, the landscape of relief in Transcaucasia would be transformed. Imperial attempts to manage relief would collapse and local Armenian relief organisations would become crucibles for the articulation of new *national* solutions to the refugee problem.

Notes

1 See N. Tumanyan, *Husher yev zruyts'ner* (Yerevan: Luys, 1987), pp. 123–4.
2 H. Tumanyan, *Yerkeri zhoghovatsu*, Vol. 6 (Yerevan: Haypethrat, 1959), p. 213.

3. M. Aksakal, *The Ottoman Road to War in 1914: The Ottoman Empire and the First World War* (New York: Cambridge University Press, 2008), p. 17.
4. K. Ulrichsen, *The First World War in the Middle East* (London: Hurst, 2014), p. 30. Laycock suggests this is a product of post-war developments in Russia and Turkey: 'In Russia and the USSR, the significance of the First World War in popular memory and collective identity was displaced by the Russian Revolution and the Civil War. In the Turkish Republic it was overshadowed by the War of Independence and the foundation myth of the Turkish nation.' In J. Laycock, '"The Whole of War Is an Atrocity": Morgan Philips Price and First World War Reporting in the Ottoman/Russian Borderlands', in A. Einhaus, K. Baxter, and C. Dawson (eds), *The Edinburgh Companion to the First World War and the Arts* (Edinburgh: Edinburgh University Press, 2017), pp. 288–304, p. 297.
5. See for example T. Akçam, *Young Turks' Crime Against Humanity: The Armenian Genocide and Ethnic Cleansing in the Ottoman Empire* (Princeton, NJ: Princeton University Press, 2012); V. Dadrian, *The History of the Armenian Genocide: Ethnic Conflict from the Balkans to Anatolia to the Caucasus* (Providence, RI: Berghahn Books, 1995); R. Kevorkian, *The Armenian Genocide: A Complete History* (New York: I.B. Tauris, 2011).
6. Kevorkian, *The Armenian Genocide*, p. 220.
7. C. Semine, *Tragediia Russkoĭ Armii Pervoĭ Velikoĭ Voĭny 1914–1918* (New Mexico, 1963), p. 136.
8. For the American response, see: S. Payaslian, *United States Policy Toward the Armenian Question and the Armenian Genocide* (New York: Palgrave Macmillan, 2005); K. D. Watenpaugh, *Bread from Stones: The Middle East and the Making of Modern Humanitarianism* (Oakland, CA: University of California Press, 2015); for the British response, see: M. Tusan, *The British Empire and the Armenian Genocide: Humanitarianism and Imperial Politics from Gladstone to Churchill* (London: I.B. Tauris, 2017); for the German response, see: S. Ihrig, *Justifying Genocide: Germany and the Armenians from Bismarck to Hitler* (Cambridge, MA: Harvard University Press, 2016); for the Scandinavian response, see: M. Bjørnlund, '"When the Cannons Talk, the Diplomats Must be Silent" – A Danish Diplomat in Constantinople during the Armenian Genocide', *Genocide Studies and Prevention* 1:2 (2006), 197–223.
9. Peter Gatrell's work is an exception, though his analysis of the presence of national Armenian committees in relief is relatively brief and focuses on the role the Armenian elite and political activists played within Russian public organisations without examining in depth the implementation of humanitarian programmes on the ground. See P. Gatrell, *A Whole Empire Walking: Refugees in Russia During World War I* (Bloomington, IN: Indiana University Press, 2005).
10. L. Kelly, *British Humanitarian Activity in Russia, 1890–1923* (London: Palgrave Macmillan, 2017).
11. A. Harutyunyan, 'Ts'arizmi gaghutayin k'aghak'akanutyunĕ Arevmtyan Hayastanum (1914–17)', *Baikar Armenian Monthly* 4:5–6, (1996), 30–1. Criticism of Russian imperialist aspirations and anti-Armenian policy is also a central argument in Manoug Somakian's work. See M. Somakian, *Empires in Conflict: Armenia and the Great Powers, 1895–1920* (London: Tauris Academic Studies, 1995).
12. P. Holquist, 'The Politics and Practice of the Russian Occupation of Armenia, 1915–February 1917', in R. G. Suny, F. M. Göçek, and N. M. Naimark (eds), *A Question of Genocide: Armenians and Turks at the End of the Ottoman Empire* (Oxford: Oxford University Press, 2011); P. Holquist, 'Forms of Violence During the Russian Occupation of Ottoman Territory and Northern Persia (Urmia and Astrabad), October 1914–December 1917', in O. Bartov and E. Weitz (eds), *Shatterzone of Empires: Coexistence and Violence in the German, Habsburg,*

Russian, and Ottoman Borderlands (Bloomington, IN: Indiana University Press, 2013). See also H. Akarca, 'Imperial Formations in Occupied Lands: The Russian Occupation of Ottoman Territories During the First World War' (unpublished dissertation, Princeton University, 2014).
13 National Georgian Archives, Tbilisi (NGA), 520/1/204, Letter by Bishop Mesrop, 22 October 1915, p. 5. For a copy of the same letter also see, National Archives of Armenia, Yerevan (NAA), 28/1/128, pp. 21–5 (ob.).
14 A. Harutyunyan, 'Pervaia mirovaia voĭna i armianskie bezhentsy (1914–1917)', unpublished dissertation (Yerevan: Institute of History of Academy of Sciences of Armenian SSR, 1989), p. 17. For military developments on the Caucasus front in general see: A. Arutyunyan, *Kavkazskiĭ front, 1914–1917* (Yerevan: Hayastan, 1971); W. Allen and P. Muratoff (eds), *Caucasian Battlefields: A History of the Wars on the Turco-Caucasian Border, 1828–1921* (New York: Cambridge University Press, 1953).
15 M. Reynolds, *Shattering Empires: The Clash and Collapse of the Ottoman and Russian Empires 1908–18* (Cambridge: Cambridge University Press, 2011), p. 125.
16 K. Sassouni, *Tachkahayastanĕ Rusakan Tirapetut'ian tak (1914–1918)* (Boston, 1927), pp. 45, 48.
17 NGA, 519/1/47, Journals of VSG Caucasus Committee, 1915, pp. 60–3. Some of the sources differentiate between Armenian and other refugees, as the following text demonstrates, while others give general number of refugees (like Harutyunyants' report). Samson Harutyunyants represented the Central Committee in Tiflis and the Caucasus Armenian Benevolent Union and was also the plenipotentiary of the Caucasus Committee of VSG.
18 Yerevan, the capital of the current Republic of Armenia, was spelled Erivan in contemporary official documents of the First World War era.
19 *Odnodnevnaia perepis' bezhentsev iz Turtsii, Persii i iz mest, pogranichnykh s Turtsieĭ (armian, aĭsorov, grekov i pr.) 1914–15g* (Erivan: Statisticheskaia Kommissia, 1915), p. 39.
20 For more on military developments at the Caucasus front in spring–summer 1915 see: A. Arutyunyan, *Kavkazskiĭ front 1914–1917*, pp. 174–202; Allen and Muratoff (eds), *Caucasian Battlefields*, pp. 293–306.
21 Allen and Muratoff (eds), *Caucasian Battlefields*, pp. 307–8.
22 H. Barby, *Sarsap'i Yerkrin Mej: Nahatak Hayastan* (Constantinople: Y. Asaturean yev vordik, 1919), p. 110.
23 'Dispatch from the Special Correspondent of the Armenian Journal "Arev" of Bakou', in A. Toynbee (ed.), *The Treatment of Armenians in the Ottoman Empire, 1915–16: Documents Presented to Viscount Grey of Falloden, with a Preface by Viscount Bryce* (London: Hodder and Stoughton, 1916), p. 198.
24 Joint report prepared by Bishop Mesrop, Honorary chairman of the Armenian Central Committee, and Samson Harutyunyants on 22 October 1915, disclosed that 208,888 refugees arrived from Turkish territories in Transcaucasia in July 1915: 15,518 people came from the Basen region of Turkey; 6,050 refugees, from Abagi and Akbag; 180,000 arrived from Van, Bitlis, Mush, Manazkert, Patnos, Aintap and Alashkert; 7,320 refugees were from Olti, Ardahan and Ardanuch (NGA, 520/1/204, Letter by Bishop Mesrop, 22 October 1915, p. 5). According to Henry Barby, French journalist, the number of Armenian refugees that arrived in the Caucasus in summer 1915 was 207,473. See Barby, *Sarsap'i Yerkrin Mej*, p. 110.
25 About 10,000 people died during the retreat from Van from starvation, disease and attacks on the way (NGA, 520/1/204, Letter by Bishop Mesrop, 22 October 1915, p. 5 (ob.)). In his speech delivered at the State Duma (in spring 1916), Mikhail Papadjanov reflected on the immense suffering of the Ottoman Armenian refugees fleeing towards the Russian Empire because

of the Russian army's retreat in summer 1915 and claimed: 'the cost was 40,000 victims' (*Hambavaber*, Tiflis, No. 15 (3 April 1916), p. 460).

26 Srbouhi Mkrtich Mouradian (born in Bitlis, in 1911), her two sisters, and their mother, Kakav Mouradian, were taken to Van and then walked their way to Etchmiadzin. See V. Svazlian, *The Armenian Genocide: Testimonies of the Eyewitness Survivors* (Yerevan: Gitutiun, 2011), pp. 118–19.

27 See VSG plenipotentiary Kishkin and Caucasus Committee Chairman Khatisyan's reports in: *Kratkie svedeniia o volne bezhentsev iz Turetskoĭ Armenii v iiule 1915g. i o merakh, priniatykh Kavkazskim Komitetom Soiuza Gorodov dlia bor'by s epidemieĭ sredi nikh* (Tiflis, 1915) and *Bezhentsi i vyselentsi. Otdel'nie ottiski iz No17 Izvestiĭ Vserossiĭskogo Soiuza gorodov* (Moscow, 1915); Karo Sassouni's eyewitness account in: Sassouni, *Tachkahayastanĕ Rusakan Tirapetut'ian tak*.

28 Karo Sassouni, originally from the Sasun region in the eastern Ottoman Empire, was among those Armenians who played an active role in the provision of assistance to the refugees during the mass population movements as well as to those sheltered in Transcaucasia. His use of the word activist is significant here as it hints that programmes for relief and rehabilitation of refugees were also connected to emerging Armenian political goals for towns and villages in bordering regions, and the hope they would be 'liberated' from Ottoman rule.

29 See Sassouni, *Tachkahayastanĕ Rusakan Tirapetut'ian tak*, p. 52.

30 For a parallel argument about Armenian humanitarian action among survivors in Syria, see K. Mouradian, 'Genocide and Humanitarian Resistance in Ottoman Syria, 1915–1917' (unpublished dissertation, Clark University, 2016), pp. 11, 35.

31 'Letter Dated Erivan, 29 December 1915, from Rev. S. G. Wilson to Dr Samuel T. Dutton, Secretary of the American Committee for Armenian and Syrian Relief', in Toynbee (ed.), *The Treatment of Armenians in the Ottoman Empire*, p. 216.

32 NGA, 520/1/204, Letter by Bishop Mesrop, 22 October 1915, p. 6.

33 B. Little, 'An Explosion of New Endeavors: Global Humanitarian Responses to Industrialized Warfare in the First World War Era', *First World War Studies* 5:1 (2014), 1–16.

34 N. Nercessian, *The City of Orphans: Relief Workers, Commissars and the 'Builders of the New Armenia' Alexandropol/Leninakan, 1919–1931* (Hollis, NH: Hollis Publishing, 2016), pp. 10–12.

35 Kevorkian, *The Armenian Genocide*, p. 763.

36 As P. Holquist notes, 'The dynamic of internal reporting on the massacres [of Armenians] caused the Russian government to initiate the joint Allied note', in 'The Origins of "Crimes Against Humanity:" The Russian Empire, International Law, and the 1915 Note on the Armenian Genocide', unpublished paper, presented to the conference 'From the Armenian Genocide to the Holocaust: The Foundations of Modern Human Rights', University of Michigan, Ann Arbor, 2–4 April 2015.

37 Y. Barseghov (ed.), *The Genocide of Armenians: The Responsibility of Turkey and the Obligations of the World Community. Documents and Commentary*, Vol. 1 (Moscow, 2002), p. 251.

38 As cited in L. Osherovskiĭ, *Tragedia Armian-bezhentsev* (Piatigorsk, 1915), p. 23.

39 R. Davison, 'Russian Skill and Turkish Imbecility: The Treaty of Kuchuk Kainardji Reconsidered', *Slavic Review* 35:3 (1976), 463–83.

40 The Armenian Benevolent Society was established in January 1881, starting its work in Tiflis, as the Caucasus Armenian National Society. For more on activities of the Benevolent Society see: NAA, f. 28 (Caucasus Armenian Benevolent Society in Tiflis).

41 NAA, 28/1, introduction, NGA, 520/1/204, Letter by Bishop Mesrop, 22 October 1915, p. 6 (ob.).

42 A. Harutyunyan, 'Hay gaghtakanakan komiteneri gortsuneut'yunn Arajin ashkharhamarti tarinerin', *Etchmiadzin* (June–July 1994), p. 111.
43 NGA, 520/1/204, Letter by Bishop Mesrop, 22 October 1915, p. 7; A. Sharafeants, 'Internal Review', *Hambavaber*, Tiflis, No. 4 (17 January 1916), p. 102.
44 NGA, 520/1/204, Letter by Bishop Mesrop, 22 October 1915, p. 7.
45 *Ibid*. An identifiable and enduring Armenian diaspora began to take shape in the eighteenth century in Russia, see The 100 Years Facts Project, 'The Formal Armenian Presence in Russia Dates Back to the 18th century', http://100years100facts.com/facts/formal-armenian-presence-russia-dates-back-18th-century/ (accessed 23 November 2019).
46 NGA, 520/1/197, Report by General Tamamshev, 20 November 1915, p. 3.
47 *Ibid*, p. 1.
48 Brotherly Aid provided each person with 1.5 pounds of flour and 3 kopeks. See *ibid.*, p. 2.
49 *Ibid*, p. 2 (ob.).
50 *Odnodnevnaia perepis' bezhentsev*, p. 41.
51 GARF (Gosudarstvennyĭ Arkhiv Rossiĭskoĭ Federatsii), 651/1/39, Report by A. Neidgardt, p. 1.
52 *Kratkiĭ otchët o deyatel'nosti Kavkazskogo otdela Vserossiĭskogo soiuza gorodov pomoshchi bol'nym i ranennym voinam* (Tiflis, 1915), p. 1.
53 The Union of Caucasus Towns was incorporated into the Caucasian Department of the VSG (or Caucasus Committee) on 9 November 1914. See *Kratkiĭ otchët o deyatel'nosti Kavkazskogo otdela Vserossiĭskogo soiuza*, p. 11.
54 *Ibid.*, pp. 18, 37–9.
55 *Kratkie svedeniia o polozhenii bezhentsev na Kavkaze*, p. 11.
56 As quoted in *Bezhentsi i vyselentsi. Otdel'nie ottiski*, p. 91.
57 *Zemskoe Delo*, No. 3 (5 February 1915), p. 159. Prince Lvov was an activist and reformer, and he became the first Prime Minister of the Provisional Government established after the 1917 February Revolution.
58 GARF, 5913/1/2a, Nikolai Ivanovich Astrov's monograph/report, 1924, p. 352.
59 *Zemskoe Delo*, No. 2 (20 January 1915), p. 91.
60 G. Ulianova, *Blagotvoritelnost' v Rossiĭskoĭ imperii. XIX – nachalo XX veka* (Moscow: Nauka, 2005), p. 401.
61 *Kratkiĭ otchët o deiatel'nosti Kavkazskogo otdela za Fevral'i Mart 1915g., VSG pomoshchi bol'nym i ranennym voinam, Vypusk II, Aprel'* 1915 (Tiflis, 1915), pp. 80–1.
62 Not all refugees received the allowance of 15 kopeks: it varied from area to area and depended on the age and status of each refugee. For instance, the able-bodied men were expected to find a job and were not provided with the allowance, while finding employment right after the displacement was extremely challenging (NGA, 520/1/197, Report by General Tamamshev, 20 November 1915, p. 4 (ob.)).
63 *Bezhentsi i organizatsia pomoshchi im v sviazi s rabotami Osobago Soveshchania: Doklad Glavnym Komitetam Upolnomochenago, predsetatelia Otdela M.M. Shchepkina*, Mart 1916g (Moscow, 1916), p. 1.
64 *Ibid*.
65 Gatrell, *A Whole Empire Walking*, p. 20.
66 *Ibid.*, p. 21.
67 *Rukovodiashchie polozheniia po ustroĭstvu bezhentsev* (Petrograd, 1916), p. 1.
68 *Zakony i raspolozheniia o bezhentsakh*, Vol. 1 (Moscow, 1916), p. 5. For a history of requisition and appropriation of property, see E. Lohr, *Nationalizing the Russian Empire: The Campaign Against Enemy Aliens During World War I* (Cambridge, MA: Harvard University Press, 2003).

69 *Ibid.*, p. 2.
70 The structure of Armenian refugee families changed since the male members were targeted and destroyed during the Genocide.
71 *Bezhentsi i organizatsia pomoshchi im v sviazi s rabotami Osobago Soveshchaniia*, pp. 40–1.
72 Ulianova, *Blagotvoritelnost' v Rossiĭskoĭ imperii*, p. 401.
73 RGVIA (Rossiĭskiĭ Gosudarstvennyĭ Voenno-istoricheskiĭ Arkhiv), 13273/1/156, Telegram, 19 January 1916, pp. 8–9 (ob.).

5

'Making good' in the Near East: The Smith College Relief Unit, Near East Relief and visions of Armenian reconstruction, 1919–21

Rebecca Jinks

In a quiet moment on board the SS *Leviathan* in February 1919, four days into their journey from New York to Constantinople, Alice Moore typed an update on the Smith College Relief Unit. All five women were well, she reported back to Smith College's War Service Board, busy with Armenian classes and meetings, as tentative plans were made for their deployment with Near East Relief (NER).[1] 'We all feel more and more thrilled every day to think that we are part of such an expedition', Alice wrote. 'We will try to get word to you ... as often as we can, but we are probably going to some very wild wilds, and all being adventurous spirits are immensely pleased with the prospect.'[2]

The five women – Alice Moore, Justina Hill, Esther Greene, Elma Guest and Ruth Henry – were all graduates of Smith, a liberal women's college in Northampton, Massachusetts. Each had a different specialism: Justina was a bacteriologist, Esther a social worker, Elma a nurse, Ruth a teacher and Alice an agriculturalist.[3] Under the aegis of the Smith War Board – which was formed by Smith graduates in 1917, to facilitate Smith's participation in the war effort – the five signed up as volunteer workers with NER, and travelled to the crumbling Ottoman Empire for relief and reconstruction work.[4] Since 1915, NER had been raising huge sums for relief: now, in 1919, NER enlarged its operations, and the *Leviathan* was the first relief ship to sail, crammed with supplies and 250 relief workers. Some were missionaries of the American Board of Commissioners for Foreign Missions (ABCFM), returning to the stations they left in 1917, when America entered the war. The majority, though, were volunteers – some, like the Smith women, with particular skills (doctors, nurses, engineers), others members of organisations like the Young Men's Christian Association (YMCA).[5] These 'adventurous spirits' were mostly young and college-educated, and seizing the opportunity to travel the world, as well as do some good in it. The sheer variety of backgrounds, professions, affiliations and worldviews among the relief workers on board the *Leviathan* represented a microcosm of the shifts underway within humanitarianism at this time. These relief workers – the Smith women included – were among those who would begin reshaping the practices of humanitarianism in the Near East.

Historians have recently begun to explore the 'explosion of new endeavours'[6] that accompanied the war's violence in Europe and the Near East, and the contemporary transformations in humanitarian policies, practices and personnel.[7] As is clear, the war and its aftermath saw a shift away from the nineteenth-century 'civilising mission', and a gradual infusion of new policies, practices, personnel, and organisations into the humanitarian landscape. Within the Ottoman Empire, aid itself became a battlefield during the war, as the Ottoman state and Entente powers sought legitimacy and loyalty, and mission stations sought their own survival and that of the populations they worked among.[8] After the war, the League of Nations, the mandate powers and humanitarian organisations – including NER – provided emergency aid, and also sought to 'reconstruct' society in ways that went 'beyond relief'.[9] These organisations became increasingly bureaucratised and professionalised, and portrayed their work as neutral, expert-driven humanitarian interventions into suffering.

However, these shifts were not a case of the simple 'replacement' of missionary with 'modern' humanitarianism.[10] Rather, as historian Davide Rodogno observes of NER, 'different visions of humanitarian aid coexisted and clashed' within the organisation.[11] Yet despite recognising this, most recent works over-generalise about what '[all] NER workers' believed, or did.[12] In order to explain the coexistence and clashes of different humanitarian visions, and – crucially – to avoid conflating the statements of NER executives with the worldviews and actions of relief workers, it is necessary to use accounts 'from the field' to differentiate between relief workers. This chapter focuses on the experiences and thoughts of the five Smith women, whose letters offer insights into NER operations across several theatres of relief and embody some of the changes underway within humanitarianism.

First, hired as skilled or semi-skilled college graduates, the Smith women were harbingers of the professionalisation of humanitarianism. This was, however, a gradual and uneven process: most NER workers in 1919 were relief workers with professions, not professional relief workers.[13] In this they joined the thousands of other temporary volunteers staffing the Red Cross, the American Relief Administration, the Commission for Relief in Belgium, and many others.[14] This chapter thus begins the work of conceptualising the meaning, role and impact of temporary volunteer workers in these years.

Second, as Progressive Era women, with a liberal college education rather than missionary training, they approached Armenian relief and reconstruction from a standpoint that emphasised scientific, expert-led social reform, rather than the reforms of the 'social gospel'.[15] Building on the experiences of Progressive Era reforms in American cities, 'reconstruction' described diverse efforts to effect change within society through 'scientific' and 'rational' reforms.[16] This conception of reconstruction was nevertheless, of course, highly gendered – and while the Smith women aided all who were in need, in the Progressive Era vein of 'women's work for women', their imagination was particularly caught by the idea of helping other women.

Finally, the Smith women exemplify the gendered shifts occurring within contemporary humanitarianism (and Western society). Not only did women constitute three-fifths of the 250 relief workers on board the *Leviathan*, they were agriculturalists, bacteriologists and social workers as well as nurses and missionary wives. Charitable work – including missionary work – had long provided middle- and upper-class women with opportunities for respectable work and independence outside the home.[17] Now, volunteering as relief workers (with a small monthly salary) provided these women with valuable professional experience, intended to ease their path into employment *outside* the charitable sector. In her anthropology of present-day Finnish Red Cross workers, Liisa H. Malkki draws attention to a 'coeval, co-present neediness ... *the neediness of the helper*'.[18] For Malkki's interlocutors, international relief work fulfilled their sense of international obligation, allowed them to participate in occupational solidarities and professional teamwork, and satisfied their desire to travel.[19] For the Smith women, a century earlier, volunteering for NER fulfilled a different set of needs – which certainly included overseas travel (likely unaffordable to them before the war) and the opportunity to participate in internationalist visions of reconstruction, but more importantly, the need for professional *experience*.

Thus, what particularly distinguishes the Smith women is their desire to 'make good', as they themselves wrote in several letters home. To 'make good' is to be recognised as having worked hard and achieved individual success; it is also to 'make something happen', to organise and carry out (or indeed bankroll) a project or promise to completion. 'Making good' on the challenges of relief work would help the Smith women 'make good' in life, and on the promises of the Progressive Era – even as that dream was slipping through the fingers of American progressives back home.[20]

Preparations

On the journey, the Smith women got to know each other. Besides having different specialisms, they had graduated in different years: Esther in 1901, Ruth in 1908, Alice in 1912, Justina in 1916, Elma in 1917. Esther, in a characteristically blunt letter home, described Justina as 'nice ... a very sophisticated manner but so naïve really'; Alice as 'fearfully charming' and a 'bravura office hand'; Ruth, she thought, had 'less personality or initiative than any of the others'.[21] Elma was not yet officially part of the Smith Unit, but hoped to join: 'She would be a valuable member', wrote Justina: she was 'congenial' and with 'the right character and physique to put through good work'.[22]

Despite their differences, the women had Smith and their white, middle-class, Progressive Era background in common. Smith College was founded in 1872, one of a proliferating number of women's colleges, which sought to prepare young women for intellectual leadership outside the home.[23] By the time these five graduated, American public resistance to women's higher education had subsided, and this generation of 'college girls' 'looked to a future allowing them to combine political reform, professional achievement, and personal fulfilment'.[24] Following in the tradition of women's volunteerism, these five now took the opportunities brought by the war to extend Progressive Era reforms beyond America, to embrace populations devastated by war and genocide in the Near East.

The women were also hoping to emulate a much larger Smith College Relief Unit (SCRU), which had been based at Grécourt in northern France since 1917, undertaking relief and reconstruction in villages devastated by successive war fronts.[25] The French SCRU, famous among Smith students and alumnae, would hover as both model and challenge for these five throughout their time in the Near East. Thus, they happily reported from the SS *Leviathan* that they were in high demand: the leaders of the Caucasus, Aleppo and Harput relief stations all wanted the Smith Unit, so they felt 'quite set up'.[26] It was finally decided to assign them to Harput, a former missionary station in Anatolia – the 'wild wilds' Alice's letter had described.[27]

After arriving in Constantinople, however, the women's eagerness to get to Harput was quickly frustrated. One month earlier, a Commission of NER executives had begun surveying the ABCFM stations, which were to serve as relief stations. Until the Commission's return, the relief workers were stuck at the port of Derindje outside Constantinople, unloading the ship and preparing relief teams with equipment and supplies. Here another frustration arose, and the women were blunt in reporting to Smith their concerns with the NER leadership. The Commission had not thought about storage, and instead of being unloaded methodically, the ship's contents were dumped haphazardly in hastily rented warehouses at Derindje.[28] 'As we see it', wrote Esther, the Commission was 'without doubt perfectly serious and well-meaning ... [but] spends its time wandering about Asia Minor in box cars instead of making plans for us'.[29] Alice contrasted NER's official 'very business-like estimates' of the resources necessary to get Turkey on its feet – including seed and agricultural implements – with the Commission's refusal to consider an increasingly urgent agricultural survey of the country.[30] 'Whatever good work may be accomplished in the field', she argued, would 'be due entirely to the fact that the individual workers make good, and not to any executive ability on the part of the Commission'.[31]

Alice's letters also evidence a growing distance between the volunteer workers and the missionaries working under NER's umbrella. From the warehouse, she observed that 'every missionary and doctor is trying to get the supplies and personnel that he wants for his particular station': everywhere else, including Derindje, was ignored.[32] The other Smith women seem to have shared her concern: apart from one or two medical missionaries, mentioned admiringly, missionaries are largely absent from their letters. Instead, the Smith women found more common ground with other volunteer workers. At this stage, the unity found on the boat seemed to be dissipating, and the Smith women were uneasy about the potential of NER's disorganisation to disrupt their goals.

Nevertheless, they threw themselves into 'making good', keen to demonstrate their organisational skills. Elma, Esther and Justina spent weeks in the warehouses, sorting boxes; Esther was 'quite proud and puffed up' from reorganising one warehouse 'after three men had given up in despair'.[33] Ruth was helping in the canteen, and running the post office 'like a professional post-mistress'.[34] Justina started lab work, and Alice began ploughing nearby fields.[35] Thus, Ruth wrote, 'we are all doing actual work right here and don't feel so discontented, perhaps'.[36]

The women started planning their work in Harput. A letter arrived in Derindje from Maria Jacobsen, a Danish missionary who had remained in Harput throughout the war, describing the need for food, clothing and bedding, and the many Armenians leaving the Muslim households in which they had spent the war.[37] The Smith women had already visited a home for 'rescued' Armenian girls, run by the Armenian Red Cross in Constantinople, and were impressed with its 'lovely' Armenian manager and programme of schooling and teaching basic trades.[38] 'We are anxious to get in as soon as possible', wrote Justina, after receiving Jacobsen's letter: 'It is hoped that some interest can be roused at Smith in the girls' school at Harput.'[39]

However, the unit's plans were suspended in early May, after two months at Derindje, when Ruth volunteered for an excursion to the Caucasus, to provide relief to the thousands of refugees in the independent Republic of Armenia, founded after the Russian imperial collapse in 1918. 'So the unit is broken, temporarily you see', she wrote to Smith. 'I still plan to join the crowd at Harpoot in the Fall ... but I first want to have made my mark here.'[40] Shortly after, Justina and Elma were sent to Aleppo, to organise lab work among the thousands of Armenian refugees who had survived deportation to the desert. Justina regretted leaving the others, but was glad 'to graduate from the warehouse and get back to my own pet work'.[41] Finally, in late May, Alice and Esther left for Harput, packing the final freight car with supplies. By that point, Alice had relented and was participating in the missionary 'game of grab': 'by getting all we can to go out with we feel quite in it'.[42]

Relief

After long journeys, the Smith women arrived at their three relief stations. All new to relief work, they were initially overwhelmed by the scale of suffering confronting them. Ruth arrived in Yerevan (then known as Erivan), capital of the independent Republic, with twelve doctors, nurses and relief workers.[43] 'The reports were not exaggerated', she wrote: 'here under the shadow of Mount Ararat, are the thousands of sick and starving people'. Her team was responsible for 26,000 orphans, and helping scattered refugees return home. After a tour, she wrote, 'I was *weak* both physically and mentally from it all.'[44] Nevertheless, the enthusiasm in her letters suggested she soon found her feet, first managing an orphanage in Yerevan, then another at Etchmiadzin.⁴⁵ She reported success in achieving 'some semblance of order' and having things done her way, and enjoyed opening a new shelter outside Etchmiadzin.⁴⁶ She was, however, troubled by having 'to make myself over into a machine always', and admitted sometimes bending the rules.⁴⁷ After a frustrating bout of dengue fever, in October she was 'honored' to become the Yerevan district orphanage manager, which she found '*so* absorbing and so much larger than I ever dreamed ... and I'm so eager to make good in new capacity!'⁴⁸ Demonstrating that she had indeed 'made good', her letters tell of successfully 'straightening' the orphanages, and 'grow[ing] steadier with it all' despite the increasing complexity of the problems.⁴⁹

Meanwhile, Justina and Elma reported that there were five thousand refugees in Aleppo, with thousands more passing through.⁵⁰ Although eager to join the others in Harput, Justina was 'happy to linger a little in Aleppo' running the laboratory: 'Relapsing fever, tuberculosis, malaria, venereal work, and even typhus are there and my fingers and my mind dance to be at it.'⁵¹ Elma was working as an operating-room nurse, and helping with 500 orphans. Just as they received news that they could leave for Harput, Elma was asked to take charge of 2,400 orphans for a few months. It was a difficult decision not to join the unit – which had now moved to Malatya, 60 miles from Harput – but, she wrote, 'I hope the Smith War Board would want me to do the immediate job rather than wait for ideal "unit conditions"'. Her training, she decided, meant she could achieve much in that short time: 'You can imagine I am excited about it, as Dr. Lambert's giving me this big job means I've made good so far.'⁵² Justina left without her, arriving in Harput in early September. Tied to the Harput laboratory, she hoped Elma would come soon, 'to relieve the strain Esther and Alice are under' in Malatya.⁵³

Esther and Alice had arrived in Harput in early June. They, too, were daunted: Esther confided to her mother that the prospect of thousands of orphans made her 'badly frightened'.⁵⁴ Once they arrived, Alice was given the accounting and Esther the making of bedding: 'at first I felt absolutely at sea', she wrote to her mother, 'but I am gradually getting hold'.⁵⁵ However, they soon sent news to Smith of their transfer to Malatya, and Esther's letters recovered their business-like tone. At Harput, they were 'mere spokes in the wheel': Malatya, by contrast, was 'distinctly our work. We are the whole thing ... we have worked frightfully hard.'⁵⁶ Shortly after they arrived at Harput, an NER team investigated Malatya, and found the German orphanage 'in a very bad way'; another orphanage, Esther reported luridly, was run by 'the worst Armenians hereabouts – all but two had turned Moslem to save themselves and were a drunken immoral lot'.⁵⁷ Maria Jacobsen helped them take over in July, and they 'began sorting and cleaning and organizing and now we are pretty well arranged. Big boys in one place; children – girls to 15 and little boys in another; and the older girls, the ones who have come from Turkish homes, in another.'⁵⁸ She and Alice expressed pride at having sole charge of 600 orphans, and Esther – completing a narrative of redemption and transformation – described how after three months the children, once silent 'bundles of bones and sores', were 'now shouting and playing and rosy, quite normal, and happy … [they] will grow up to be the leaven of the nation'.[59] This transformational narrative involved overlooking the traumas and challenges the orphans still faced, but served well as evidence of 'making good'. Elma, who arrived in October, confirmed to Smith: 'The girls have done a splendid piece of work here. But how could it be otherwise?'[60] Malatya was now 'a real Smith unit', 'a small edition of Grécourt'.[61]

However, the Smith women's narrative of pioneer-like independence, hard graft and success concealed the evolving and sometimes discordant relationships between NER workers. Sometimes these were differences of personality: as Ruth remarked, 'Aren't a lot of people thrown together intimately a perplexing problem! Why – I discover a brand new aversion or a keen appreciation every hour out here!'[62] She also hinted at rifts caused by differences in age and gender: 'The men of our unit are all young and alive and it hurts some of the older women dreadfully to have to take suggestions from them.'[63] (Conversely, Alice remarked – with the confidence of a younger generation of women – that among the Harput team were two American men, 'both of them rather young and probably easily managed'.[64])

Far more significant were the NER workers' varying approaches to relief and reconstruction, whose clashing and coexistence within NER reflected the shifting grounds of humanitarianism. Although the volunteers recognised and were to some extent dependent on the missionaries' long experience, the missionaries' understanding of relief as a means to (re)create a spiritually, morally and culturally 'pure' Armenian nation jarred with the reformist visions of volunteer workers like the Smith women. These differences made for 'amusing cross currents in the organisation', as Ruth phrased it, between 'relief workers, medical units, and the missionaries, but one has to keep sane and smile, I find!'[65] Ruth's approach was to steer a conciliatory course through the divisions and changes of 'regime' in the Caucasus, as the American Relief Administration arrived and took control of the relief operations. Justina, far less kindly disposed toward missionaries, outlined a more stark situation at Harput: 'We relief workers have royal battles with the missionaries on such questions as the expenditure of [NER] money on education, while children are starving, etc. We usually compromise by an unhappy medium.'[66] The missionaries, for their part, sometimes felt brushed aside: NER surveyors noted that at one station, 'All work [is] under control of new personnel with no representation of missionaries, who feel that the old timers' knowledge and experience are being overborne and neglected.'[67]

The missionaries, then, found themselves unable to impose their relief norms on the volunteer workers, who – as they found their feet – increasingly tried to put their own ideas into practice. Nevertheless, it is important to understand the practical limits on the volunteers' agency to substantially shape the relief work, especially in this first 'emergency' stage. The Smith Unit was, after all, reliant on the Harput missionaries for their relief budget, and indeed to assign them Malatya in the first place.⁶⁸ They were reliant, too, on the missionary-trained Armenian staff sent with them from Harput, who were central to the work and the orphans' daily experiences of it. The Smith women's organisation of general relief at Malatya also conformed to NER norms – particularly the division of orphans by age and sex, which reflected American moral and bureaucratic preferences.

However, in other ways, the Smith women exercised the latitude their distance from Harput afforded them. This could be in entirely quotidian matters: Esther, for example, resolved that 'I can't possibly get cloth to dress the children alike and wouldn't if I could. I do not want them to look institutional or military'⁶⁹ – suggestive of the Progressive Era emphasis on individuality, rather than the missionary insistence on uniformity within the community.⁷⁰ With more far-reaching consequences, the Smith women's perspective on Armenian women 'rescued' from Turkish, Kurdish and Arab households is also an illuminating site of difference. 'Rescuing' these Armenians was core NER policy, but most missionaries were suspicious of what they perceived as the women's sexual, moral and religious impurity, and thought them unfit to be part of Armenian national renewal: instead, they focused on the orphans.⁷¹ Some NER volunteers tried to help these women; others avoided them. From the beginning, the Smith women expressed interest in helping these women: 'it is one of the greatest questions here', wrote Esther.⁷² From Aleppo, where her laboratory colleague Stanley Kerr was 'rescuing' Armenians from Arab villages at the weekends,⁷³ Justina noted that this 'enormous problem' 'interests me especially ... I hope that perhaps we Smith girls can help these especially unfortunate victims when we get together'.⁷⁴ In Malatya, Esther recorded a number of dramatic stories of taking in Armenian women, and while the Smith women found these women's experiences 'frightful',⁷⁵ in general they did not view them as 'problematic', or shun them, as some missionaries did.⁷⁶

The Smith women were perhaps unusual among the volunteer workers in the degree of autonomy they wielded – with Ruth as orphanage district manager in Yerevan, and the others relatively unsupervised in Malatya. But while they certainly disagreed with other NER workers on several fronts, the core outcomes of their emergency relief were not substantially different. Rather, in those first months, their primary focus was on 'getting hold' of the work and demonstrating via narratives of success and transformation that they had 'made good'.

Reconstruction

After a summer of hard work, and with Elma due from Aleppo in November (Ruth stayed in Yerevan), the Smith Unit's thoughts turned more fully to reconstruction work. Although aware of the increasing tension as the Greco-Turkish war broke out in May 1919 and the Turkish National Movement was galvanised, they were hopeful that America would accept a mandate over Armenia, and sought to begin the reconstruction work they expected America would oversee. They pursued various ideas: Alice, the agriculturalist, planned to develop the orphanages' land, and asked Smith to send several pounds of a dry-land bean she thought suitable for Malatya.[77] Convinced of the power of education to generate progress, educational schemes were also key to the Smith women. A second request went to Smith for boys' building sets, and Esther was overjoyed to find pre-war school supplies in Malatya's market.[78] Unsurprisingly, they also advocated college education, diverging from NER's emphasis on industrial and vocational training. The Smith women consistently spoke of the American college graduates among the Armenians as the 'leaven in the lump' and future leaders,[79] and tried to nurture and train their young women staff.[80] They suggested a sponsorship scheme, where Smith alumnae would fund promising young Armenian women's education through the American missionary colleges.[81]

However, when Smith suggested funding a larger project, they proposed a hospital. The Malatya orphanages had only a small infirmary, with an Armenian doctor named Krikor Yardumian (who they valued highly) employed part-time. Now, with winter (and the threat of typhus) looming, and the news that an American doctor, Emily MacLeod, was being assigned to Malatya, expansion was both necessary and possible. They also suggested far more ambitious plans to Smith. 'We think it would be wonderful to make this a permanent Smith center', wrote Esther: 'There must be doctors and nurses among [our] graduates [who] would like to come out for a time.'[82] The women were jubilant when Smith granted them $3,000 for the hospital, and Alice's letter of thanks made clear their ambition. 'You see, we have been rather a step-child of [NER], being a sub-station', she wrote: now, they would 'take the pick' of the older girls, and train them as quickly as possible.[83]

However, they quickly reported – with some alarm – that the new Dr MacLeod was 'not panning out'. 'She is proving herself a person of no executive ability', wrote Esther, 'and no desire to help generally'[84] – offending against the Smith women's pride in being able to turn their hands to any job. More worryingly, 'She has ridden rough-shod over our native nurses and even Dr. Krikor ... entirely upsetting the morale ... [and] insists on regarding them as lazy stupid slovens, which they are not'.[85] The Smith women of course arrived in the Near East convinced of their own racial and educational superiority, but their attitude towards Armenians was perhaps less peremptory than that of other relief workers.[86] Their letters were full of praise for Dr Krikor and their other staff, and frank about their dependence on them.[87] MacLeod's attitude thus jarred with the Smith women's own, and the realities of organising relief. 'All this has made us modify our ideas as to a hospital as we did not want to start anything to be turned over to her',[88] they wrote – fearful, it seems, that having 'made good', their hard work would be ruined.

In their letters to Smith in December, when the hospital officially opened, MacLeod appears as the catalyst for the radical reduction in their plans. But a number of other factors were crystallising, which led them to jettison the idea of a permanent hospital. First, the disparity between their initial, romanticised idea of relief work 'at the hardest station', and the wearying reality of life in Turkey's harsh interior, did not augur well for a permanent Smith Unit. Second, malaria was a constant threat: during the Genocide, the drainage system (and many houses) in Malatya's Armenian quarter was destroyed, and the mosquitos hovering around the stagnant water made Malatya 'too unhealthful'. Finally, most of their orphans were not from Malatya but passing through, and soon 'the work' would reduce to a small permanent orphanage.[89] Thus, a permanent centre seemed unviable – a view that dovetailed with their growing belief that reconstruction should be left to the Armenians themselves (and diverged sharply from the views of NER executives and missionaries).

Thus, Elma now wrote to Smith, 'the need [for the hospital] is immediate and, we hope, temporary'.[90] They would run it for a few months, and 'in the spring or summer the orphanage work in Malatia [sic] can be left to a committee of [the] Armenians who work so well with us'.[91] This was a mark of confidence in their Armenian staff, but also a particular vision of how reconstruction – and social progress – should happen. As Justina wrote:

> Frankly, I see the need for relief work here now, and over this winter, but not after that. ... The hundred-year failure of the missionaries here to accomplish any visible progress has taught me that these people must help themselves ... I don't think the Armenians are 'hopeless' and 'no good', etc., as many of our people do, but that they have ability and power to make their own way when the time comes.[92]

Here Justina was articulating the contemporary American social reformist view that in a society full of opportunities, the poor and immigrants (particularly whites) should – and could – pull themselves up by their bootstraps, in the pursuit of individual and collective progress.[93] With their own hard work of educational 'self-improvement' a cornerstone of their identities, the Smith women perhaps believed this more fully than some NER workers. They thus shared the worldview of the educational experts, social workers and infrastructural engineers employed by NER later in the 1920s, who aimed to bring about social progress through scientific intervention, rather than religion. As Esther put it, 'It would be easy to rid [Malatya] of all stagnant water ... Please send us sanitary engineers not clergymen.'[94] A permanent Smith hospital would have been the Unit's contribution to reconstruction and development. But in the face of so many structural difficulties in Malatya, and the possibility of failure to 'make good', the Smith women retreated.

Departure

The harsh winter intensified the women's reluctance to establish a permanent Smith Unit. Alice, Elma and Esther all contracted malaria, confirming their argument that Malatya was 'too unhealthful'. Although they described frustration at having to rest – replicating the image NER publications constructed of heroic relief workers who refused to stop, despite suffering serious disease – a certain weariness also pervades their letters from this time.[95] As spring (and the end of their year's contract) approached, their letters began to display an increasing disconnection from 'the work'. As volunteer workers, they had always intended their time in the Near East to be temporary. While they enjoyed the work, the opportunities it brought, and felt sorry to leave their staff and orphans, none of those four wanted to stay another year. Nevertheless, they insisted they would stay 'until the first stage in our work is over', meaning the winter emergency relief.[96] Their need (in Malkki's terms) to 'make good' – to be able to say that they had successfully completed the task of emergency relief – required that they stay a few extra months.

In Yerevan, a second type of neediness – 'being needed' – was driving Ruth's decision to stay. She decided she would remain if the work 'really needs me'; regardless, she *was* certain that she wanted to continue relief work, and wrote to Smith: 'If there is any chance of a transfer to another country for Relief Work and you need a person – here am I! … I'm willing to be sent anywhere.'[97] Shortly after, though, NER was suddenly evacuated from the Caucasus, as Bolshevik forces closed in on the briefly independent Armenia. Safely in Constantinople, Ruth wrote of the wrench of leaving, and her deliberations over what to do – but decided to accept the position of Director of the Adana unit, 'with a very good salary and a very big work ahead'.[98] In May 1920, before Ruth left Constantinople, Justina and Elma passed through, en route home; just as she left, Alice and Esther arrived from Malatya.

All three – Esther, Alice and Ruth – stayed on with NER for a few months, past their initial expectations. For Alice, it was too late to return to America for the farming season, so she transferred to Samsoun on the Black Sea, joining a friend she'd made in Derindje.[99] There, she wrote far less about relief work, and more about recuperating from malaria and conjunctivitis, and 'enjoying a good time'.[100] She returned home in November 1920. Esther remained in Constantinople, managing a NER needlework factory that employed 300 Armenian women refugees. Once again, she took pride in turning around the 'hopeless tangle' left by an elderly missionary: 'it nearly killed me getting it systematized and straightened but now it is inventoried and stock-sheeted completely'.[101] Her letters indicate care and concern for the refugee women and, again, her better-educated Armenian staff. Although intending to leave after three months, she repeatedly deferred her departure (each time due to 'need'), eventually leaving in March 1921.[102] In Adana, Ruth began work as fighting broke out between the French occupying forces and the Turkish nationalist forces surrounding the city. Although initially glad that the fighting kept the missionary in charge in Adana – so that he could show her the ropes – she also looked forward to his departure so that she could run things her own way.[103] She described providing for the swelling numbers of refugees while resisting budget cuts, and her unease at the 'levelling, mechanical routine of this Relief Work'.[104] She left, after six months, on a less assured note. As the Turkish War of Independence engulfed the interior stations, and 'heart-rending reports' came from the Caucasus, she found herself wondering: 'What are we doing out here anyway – you and I, and our strange, foreign ideas?'[105]

The mix of reasons Ruth, Esther and Alice gave for staying – not so different from those which brought them – indicate the evolution of the volunteer workers' motivations. Their letters still discuss 'the work' and relief needs, but place far more emphasis on the value of staying to themselves. Partly they stayed for travel and fun: Esther enjoyed Constantinople, and described herself as an 'adventurous spirit' (staying longer was also a pay-off for 'settling down' upon her return home);[106] Alice was 'enjoying a good time' after the hardships of Malatya; Ruth, under siege in Adana, exclaimed that 'life at home will be *so* drab in comparison'.[107] More tangibly, this value came in the form of an increased salary (an incentive to stay that NER offered). But more important seems to have been the value of further 'opportunities' (a word Esther used frequently) for opening up employment at home. As Ruth wrote in Etchmiadzin: 'It is a liberal education this "manager of a district" game and I feel sure I shall be more fit for service in the States after this year.'[108] This pull of extra work experience, more money, and travel, kept them in the Near East a little longer.

Conclusion

'We've done the country, with Ruth Henry in the Caucasus, Esther and Alice in Armenia, Justina and I in Syria; and I think we have made good and shown again what Smith spirit is', wrote Elma from Aleppo.[109] 'Making good' was of the utmost importance to the five Smith women. Like Malkki's Finnish Red Cross workers, these women also had 'needs': as Malkki carefully emphasises, her interlocutors are not generic 'global citizens' but 'specific social persons with homegrown needs, vulnerabilities, desires, [and] multiple professional responsibilities'.[110] It was as Progressive Era, college-educated, American women that the Smith women needed to 'make good' in their personal, social and professional lives in the US. Signing up to NER offered them the opportunity to prove themselves, and to advance through the gendered minefield of American employment. The public role charity work brought was no longer an end in itself: now, it provided a springboard for the Smith women to enter the public sphere *outside* charity work – as a noted bacteriologist (Justina), a teacher (Elma), a social worker (Esther), an agriculturalist (Alice) and a teacher (Ruth).[111]

This professional advancement was one of the 'radical' goals of Progressive Era women, and one they were quite clear about. Notably, though, NER promotional materials stuck closely to the traditional representation of relief workers as selfless, self-sacrificing heroes – an image the Smith women rejected.[112] In its 1924 roll-call of NER workers' achievements and current occupations, NER also, quite literally, 'domesticated' these women: many, including Elma Guest, were listed as 'attending to her duties as a housewife' (entirely ignoring Elma's career in education).[113] The Smith

War Board, unsurprisingly, did its own sculpting of the women's experiences and achievements. On the women's archived original letters, often sections are marked out, in pencil, to be omitted from official Smith publications – always passages in which the women discuss disagreements or incompetence within NER ranks, or express disillusionment. The extracts marked for *inclusion* in Smith's publications – those which describe needy refugees, the women's achievements and 'Smith spirit' – always confirmed and completed the women's own efforts to 'make good'.

By focusing on the particular experiences, worldviews and contributions of NER's temporary volunteer workers, we can hone our understanding of the entire organisation's evolution at what was a distinct point in its development. For 1919–21 was the period when NER's workforce was mainly composed of temporary volunteer workers,[114] both like and unlike the Smith women – and also the period before declining donations and successive crises (the evacuation of the Caucasus, the Turkish War of Independence, the Smyrna fire) drastically curtailed NER's operations in the former Ottoman Empire. Despite their own relative transience in the field, these volunteer workers were the harbingers of longer-term changes in perspectives and practices within the humanitarian sphere. Different humanitarian visions did indeed 'clash' and 'coexist', but the story is also a more complicated one, in which the volunteer workers were sometimes reliant on the missionaries and in general followed NER's structures, but at other times used what latitude they had to pursue their own reformist visions. Hence the necessity of differentiating between relief workers as far as possible – since generalisations about what 'NER workers' thought or did obscures the sometimes sharp differences that shaped the provision of relief, and the recipients' experiences of it.

Notes

1 On NER's background, see the Introduction to this volume.
2 Smith College Archives, Northampton, Mass., 12. War Service Collection, WWI, 1914–1918, Near East Relief Unit, Box 30, Alice Moore to Florence Snow, 20 February 1919. Box 30 contains all of the Near East Unit's archive (except for Ruth Henry's photograph album in Box 31). Unless stated otherwise, all subsequent archival references are to this collection and box.
3 *Smith Alumnae Quarterly*, November 1918, p. 67; February 1919, p. 127; February 1918, p. 164. Very little information is available on their lives before 1919 (or after 1921).
4 The archive contains no information on the process by which the NER Smith Unit was formed. The Smith War Board remained ultimate sponsor of the Unit (financially and organisationally), and the five Unit members sent regular letters to Board members, primarily May Lewis, Florence Snow, Helen Thayer and Helen Whitman.
5 See A. D. Krikorian and E. L. Taylor's data compilation and analysis, 'Ninety-six Years Ago Today', *Armenian News Network*, 16 February 2015, www.groong.org/orig/ak-20150216.html (accessed 20 March 2020).
6 B. Little, 'An Explosion of New Endeavours: Global Humanitarian Responses to Industrialized Warfare in the First World War Era', *First World War Studies* 5:1 (2014), 1–16.

7 For example, special issue of *First World War Studies* 5:1 (2014); D. Rodogno, 'Non-state Actors' Humanitarian Operations in the Aftermath of the First World War: The Case of Near East Relief', in F. Klose (ed.), *The Emergence of Humanitarian Intervention: Ideas and Practice from the Nineteenth Century to the Present* (Cambridge: Cambridge University Press, 2015), pp. 185–207; R. Jinks, '"Marks Hard to Erase": The Troubled Reclamation of "Absorbed" Armenian Women, 1919–1917', *American Historical Review* 123:1 (2018), 86–123; B. Cabanes, *The Great War and the Origins of Humanitarianism, 1918–1924* (Cambridge: Cambridge University Press, 2014); K. D. Watenpaugh, *Bread from Stones: The Middle East and the Making of Modern Humanitarianism* (Oakland, CA: University of California Press, 2015); D. Kévonian, *Réfugiés et diplomatie humanitaire: Les acteurs européens et la scène proche-orientale pendant l'entre-deux-guerres* (Paris: Publications de la Sorbonne, 2004).

8 M. Tanielian, *The Charity of War: Famine, Humanitarian Aid, and World War I in the Middle East* (Stanford, CA: Stanford University Press, 2018); S. Jackson, 'Transformative Relief: Imperial Humanitarianism and Mandatory Development in Syria-Lebanon, 1915–1925', *Humanity* 8:2 (2017), 247–68.

9 Rodogno, 'Non-state Actors', p. 190; Watenpaugh, *Bread from Stones*.

10 Watenpaugh, *Bread from Stones*, p. 2. For a critical discussion see Jinks, '"Marks Hard to Erase"', 91–3.

11 Rodogno, 'Non-state actors', p. 178.

12 *Ibid.*, pp. 194–5, 198; Watenpaugh focuses primarily on two NER workers in *Bread from Stones*, pp. 91–123; A. Lapidot-Firilla, '"Subway Women" and the American Near East Relief in Anatolia, 1919–1924', in H. Herzog and A. Braude (eds), *Gendering Religion and Politics: Untangling Modernities* (Basingstoke: Palgrave Macmillan, 2009), pp. 153–72.

13 See F. Piana, 'The Dangers of "Going Native": George Montandon in Siberia and the International Committee of the Red Cross, 1919–1922', *Contemporary European History* 25:2 (2016), 253–74.

14 Little, 'Explosion of New Endeavours'.

15 D. Ekbladh, *The Great American Mission: Modernization and the Construction of an American World Order* (Princeton, NJ: Princeton University Press, 2010), pp. 17–18.

16 *Ibid.*, p. 17.

17 D. Williams Elliott, *The Angel Out of the House: Philanthropy and Gender in Nineteenth-Century England* (Charlottesville, VA: University of Virginia Press, 2002); B. Reeves-Ellington, *Domestic Frontiers: Gender, Reform, and American Interventions in the Ottoman Balkans and the Near East* (Amherst, MA: University of Massachusetts Press, 2013).

18 L. H. Malkki, *The Need to Help: The Domestic Arts of International Humanitarianism* (Durham, NC: Duke University Press, 2015), p. 8.

19 *Ibid.*, p. 24.

20 M. E. McGerr, *A Fierce Discontent: The Rise and Fall of the Progressive Movement in America, 1870–1920* (New York: Free Press, 2003).

21 Esther Greene to family, 2 February 1919.

22 Justina Hill to May Lewis, 5 April 1919.

23 McGerr, *Fierce Discontent*, pp. 50–1.

24 L. D. Gordon, 'The Gibson Girl Goes to College: Popular Culture and Women's Higher Education in the Progressive Era, 1890–1920', *American Quarterly* 39:2 (1987), 211–30, 225.

25 R. Gaines, *Ladies of Grécourt: The Smith College Relief Unit in the Somme* (New York: E. P. Dutton, 1920).

26 Esther Greene to May Lewis, 25 February 1919; Ruth Henry to Florence Snow, 19 March 1919.

27 *Smith Alumnae Quarterly*, May 1919, p. 246. 'Harpoot' (today Mamuret-ul-Aziz) is the Americanised spelling of the western Armenian Kharpert.
28 Esther Greene to mother, 9 May 1919.
29 *Ibid*. However, the Commission's aims went beyond merely distributing NER supplies and workers, since it intended to influence the peace settlement and potential American mandate. J. L. Grabill, *Protestant Diplomacy and the Near East: Missionary Influence on American Policy, 1870–1927* (Minneapolis, MN: University of Minnesota Press, 1971), pp. 166–71.
30 Alice Moore to Helen Thayer, 27 April 1919.
31 *Ibid*.
32 *Ibid*.
33 Esther Greene to family, 4 April 1919.
34 Hill to Lewis, 5 April 1919.
35 Justina Hill to Helen Thayer, 26 April 1919.
36 Ruth Henry to May Lewis, 18 April 1919.
37 Hill to Lewis, 5 April 1919. On Armenians 'absorbed' into Muslim households, see Jinks, '"Marks Hard to Erase"'.
38 Alice Moore to May Lewis, 25 May 1919.
39 Hill to Lewis, 5 April 1919.
40 Ruth Henry to Helen Thayer, 25 May 1919; Ruth Henry to May Lewis, 16 July 1919.
41 Hill to Thayer, 26 April 1919.
42 Moore to Lewis, 25 May 1919.
43 Henry to Thayer, 25 May 1919.
44 *Ibid*.
45 Ruth Henry to Helen Thayer, 27 June 1919.
46 Ruth Henry to Helen Thayer, 24 August 1919.
47 Henry to Thayer, 27 June 1919; Ruth Henry to May Lewis, 22 December 1919.
48 Ruth Henry to May Lewis, 14 November 1919.
49 Henry to Lewis, 22 December 1919.
50 Justina Hill to May Lewis, 4 June 1919.
51 *Ibid*.
52 Elma Guest to mother, 25 August 1919.
53 Justina Hill to May Lewis, 7 September 1919.
54 Esther Greene to mother, 2 June 1919.
55 Esther Greene to mother, 12 July 1919.
56 Esther Greene to May Lewis, 11 October 1919 and 1 October 1919.
57 Greene to Lewis, 11 October 1919.
58 *Ibid*.
59 *Ibid*.
60 Elma Guest to Board, 2 December 1919.
61 *Smith Alumnae Quarterly*, February 1920, p. 125; Guest to mother, 25 August 1919.
62 Henry to Thayer, 27 June 1919.
63 *Ibid*.
64 Moore to Lewis, 25 May 1919.
65 Henry to Thayer, 25 May 1919.
66 Justina Hill to Helen Thayer, 4 October 1919.
67 American Research Institute in Turkey, Istanbul, ABCFM/Near East Relief Collection, 'Notes of Captain E. H. Niles and Mr. A. E. Sutherland taken on trip of investigation

July & August, 1919', p. 1, https://archives.saltresearch.org/handle/123456789/42841 (accessed 20 March 2020).
68 Hill to Thayer, 4 October 1919.
69 Esther Greene to Helen Thayer, 29 October 1919.
70 A. Durst, *Women Educators in the Progressive Era: The Women Behind Dewey's Laboratory School* (Basingstoke: Palgrave, 2010).
71 See Jinks, '"Marks Hard to Erase"', 100–1, 107–15.
72 Greene to mother, 9 May 1919.
73 Zoryan Institute, Toronto, Stanley E. Kerr Collection, 88, Kerr to mother, 25 May 1919.
74 Hill to Lewis, 4 June 1919.
75 *Ibid.*
76 Esther Greene to mother, 2 September 1919 and 28 September 1919; Greene to family, 20 November 1919.
77 Alice Moore to Helen Thayer, 14 June 1919.
78 Alice Moore to Florence Snow, 15 August 1919; Esther Greene to Mildred, n.d. December 1919.
79 Greene to mother, 12 July 1919.
80 Guest to mother, 25 August 1919.
81 Alice Moore to Helen Thayer, 16 November 1919.
82 Greene to Lewis, 1 October 1919.
83 Moore to Thayer, 16 November 1919.
84 Esther Greene to Ellen Emerson, 2 December 1919.
85 *Ibid.*, Greene to mother, 8 October 1919.
86 On Progressive Era attitudes to race, see McGerr, *A Fierce Discontent*, chapter 6; C. Fox, *Three Worlds of Relief: Race, Immigration, and the American Welfare State from the Progressive Era to the New Deal* (Princeton, NJ: Princeton University Press, 2012).
87 Esther Greene to Anne, 7 October 1919.
88 Greene to Emerson, 2 December 1919.
89 *Ibid.*
90 Guest to Board, 2 December 1919.
91 Moore to Thayer, 16 November 1919.
92 Justina Hill to May Lewis, 17 October 1919; c.f. Moore to Thayer, 16 November 1919.
93 Fox, *Three Worlds of Relief.*
94 Greene to family, 20 November 1919.
95 Lapidot-Firilla, '"Subway Women"', p. 161.
96 Guest to Board, 2 December 1919; Greene to Emerson, 2 December 1919; Moore to Thayer, 16 November 1919.
97 Ruth Henry to Helen Thayer, 15 February 1920.
98 Ruth Henry to Helen Thayer, 18 May 1920.
99 Alice Moore to Helen Whitman, 7 June 1920; Alice Moore to Helen Thayer, 28 June 1920.
100 Moore to Thayer, 28 June 1920.
101 Esther Greene to Board, 21 December 1920.
102 Esther Greene to mother, 25 July 1920.
103 Ruth Henry to Board, 11 July 1920.
104 Ruth Henry to Helen Thayer, 30 November 1920.
105 *Ibid.*
106 Esther Greene to mother, 7 June 1920.

107 Ruth Henry to Helen Thayer, 25 October 1920.
108 Henry to Lewis, 16 July 1919.
109 Guest to mother, 25 August 1919.
110 Malkki, *Need to Help*, p. 4.
111 See Justina's oral history interview: Smith College Archives, Northampton, MA, RG 12, Smith Centennial Study Oral History Project, Box 12. Elma: *Smith Alumnae Quarterly*, Winter 1988, p. 68. Esther: *Smith Alumnae Quarterly*, February 1923, p. 188. Alice: *Smith Alumnae Quarterly*, February 1931, p. 210. Ruth: Krikorian and Taylor, 'Ninety-six Years Ago Today'.
112 E.g. Ruth Henry to May Lewis, 22 December 1919; *cf.* Malkki, *Need to Help*, pp. 28–9.
113 Krikorian and Taylor, 'Ninety-six Years Ago Today'.
114 Most NER volunteer workers who travelled on the SS *Leviathan* left in May, June or July 1920.

6

Care and connections:
Orphans, refugees and Norwegian relief in the Soviet Armenian Republic, 1922–25

Inger Marie Okkenhaug

In the autumn of 1920 the independent Armenian Republic, established in 1918, was invaded by Turkish nationalist forces. As the Turks advanced towards the western part of the country, Soviet rule was established in the remaining areas. In addition to military occupation, this tiny, war-torn country experienced devastating famine and disease. The arrival of approximately 500,000 refugees worsened the chaotic situation; thousands of people suffered from starvation or died of hunger.[1] Since it was unable to meet the needs of its people, the Armenian government allowed the American Relief Administration to provide relief. The interventions of the American Relief Administration, which relied on funds mainly from the American government and charitable organisations, 'spared the people of Armenia absolute annihilation'.[2]

When the American Relief Administration closed down in the summer of 1919, American relief efforts shifted to the Near East Relief (NER), a private, non-political organisation with strong links to the American government.[3] The focus of this chapter is, however, the smaller European relief operations that worked alongside NER in the Armenian Republic. These included a Norwegian orphanage, established and run by the nurse, midwife and missionary Bodil Biørn. Biørn, who had arrived in Anatolia in 1905 in the employ of the German Deutscher Hülfbund's Mission, established an orphanage in Alexandropol (Leninakan/Gyumri) in the north-western part of Armenia in 1922.[4] Norwegian relief was small and unassuming compared to NER's humanitarian operation, and it was financed by private funds from Norwegian women. Even so, it aimed for modern, international standards, and for the children admitted to the home it often made the difference between life and death. This chapter, based on sources from the Norwegian Women's Mission organisation (Kvinnelige misjonsarbeidere, KMA) and the NER, as well as memoirs, focuses on Bodil Biørn's humanitarian work in the Armenian Republic from 1922 until the Soviet authorities closed the orphanage in 1925.

This chapter argues that Scandinavian welfare among Armenian refugees and orphans in the 1920s and 1930s exemplifies the complex interrelation between faith-based relief work and emerging 'modern' practices of relief, which presented themselves as 'scientific' or based on 'expert' knowledge. Historian Keith D. Watenpaugh has demonstrated the transition from religious to secular forms of Western humanitarianism during the inter-war period. However, this was not necessarily a linear phenomenon.[5] The complex processes of change in humanitarian practices during the inter-war period are exemplified by historian Rebecca Jinks' work on relief and Armenian Genocide survivors. Jinks suggests that the complexities of humanitarian practices 'are best captured by exploring the thoughts and initiatives of ordinary relief workers on the ground, since they themselves frequently embodied, and were agents of these changes ...'.[6] Investigating the aspirations, practices and priorities of Biørn and her Scandinavian colleagues who worked in Greece and Lebanon in the early 1920s provides one way to do so. This chapter claims that Scandinavian relief workers wished to combine a missionary vocation with humanitarian work among Armenian survivors. Biørn was convinced that God had a plan for the Armenian children who had survived the Genocide as well as plan for her, whose vocation and religious duty was relief work.[7] To do so, she combined religion with her scientific training in nursing and midwifery.

Second, this chapter claims that Biørn belonged to and created different networks that made her activities possible, both in Soviet Armenia and in Norway. Biørn succeed in creating and running a Christian-based relief operation in Armenia, which was managed by an anti-religious, communist regime, without the support of a state or a larger organisation. In order to do so, Biørn relied on connections with the Armenian community she had worked and lived with for more than ten years – first in Mezreh (Eläzig) and in Mush, in Eastern Anatolia.[8] There, she had accumulated vast experience in medical practice and in running an orphanage for Armenian boys. On the spot, Biørn cooperated with other Scandinavian and American missionaries, who, due to the Genocide, had turned into relief workers. Equally important was the network of women sponsors in Norway, who had an emotional (and needlework) bond with Armenia and supported their 'envoy' in Armenia with prayers as well as more tangible contributions.

Finally, the chapter argues that the visual representations that the KMA made of refugees and orphans was unique among other contemporary humanitarian organisations and associations. On this topic, Peter Gatrell claims that 'refugees tend to be portrayed as anonymous and timeless'. To him, 'the lack of context neither explains displacement nor illuminate refugees' strategies for survival'.[9] In contrast, KMA sources offer us a historical narrative centred on individual Armenians – with a name and biography – living as refugees in a specific time and place.

Scandinavian women's mission and humanitarian work

The KMA was the first independent women's mission organisation in Scandinavia. Established in Sweden in 1894, in Denmark and Finland in 1900, and in Norway in 1902, its aim was to improve the lives of women in 'foreign parts of the world'.[10] The KMA's founders were influenced by the numerous women's mission organisations in North America, Great Britain and Germany that had been established in the late nineteenth century.[11] The Scandinavian KMA missionaries belonged to the upper and upper middle classes, and they were to a large extent highly educated, professional women who all shared an understanding of a personal calling to mission work. The few women who chose to work in Turkish Armenia defined their missionary vocation as closely tied to the healing of suffering Armenians, after the Hamidian massacres in 1894–96. These women's deep Lutheran conviction linked them directly, in both spiritual and practical terms, to the German missions, and especially with the pietistic *Deutscher Hülfsbund für christliches Liebeswerk im Orient*. Even so, it did not prevent cooperation with other Protestant denominations, for example the American Board of Commissioners for Foreign Missions (ABCFM).[12]

Bodil Biørn was one of the women working for the KMA. Educated as a nurse in Christiania (Oslo) and Berlin, during her first year in Turkey, from 1905–6, she worked in both American and German institutions. At the same time she also learned Armenian. She then moved to Mush, one of the regions that had been worst hit by the massacres of the 1890s. In October 1914, when the Ottoman Empire joined Germany and Austria in the war, Biørn had already spent a long period of time in Mush. She was in charge of the *Deutscher Hülfbund's* polyclinic, an orphanage for boys and a school for girls. Because of the war, Biørn and her Swedish colleague Alma Johansson adapted their work and nursed Turkish and Armenian soldiers in hospitals established by the Red Cross. After the summer of 1915, when the Genocide began, she and her Scandinavian colleagues became part of the illegal relief network of Armenians and Western missionaries. The war led these Scandinavian women to become relief workers, war correspondents and part of the network that opposed the Ottoman Empire's war against its Armenian population.[13]

After the end of the First World War, many Scandinavian missionaries continued to live in the region and provided relief to Armenian survivors. These women, who were unmarried and without children of their own, felt a profound connection to the Armenian people.[14] After having lived with the Armenians through war and genocide, it was impossible to envision a quiet, secure and comfortable life in Scandinavia.[15] Biørn, Johansson and their Danish colleagues had originally planned to go back to the areas where they had formerly worked in Anatolia. Even so, an American special commission travelling to the interior of Turkey in 1919 reported that there were no refugees left in Van, Bitlis (the province that included Mush) and Erzerum.[16] Therefore, in 1920, Johansson left for Istanbul, and, a year later, Biørn joined her at a refugee camp in Scutari (Üsküdar) in Istanbul.

With no refugees left to care for in Turkey and the Turkish nationalist government banning missionaries' entry into the country, the Scandinavian missionaries followed Armenian refugees in their relocations in the Levant, Greece and the Armenian Republic. In 1922, the Danes Maria Jacobsen and Karen Marie Petersen established and ran what was to become the largest orphanage in Lebanon, 'The Bird's Nest', financed by the Danish KMA. Another Dane, Karen Jeppe, had been active before the war among the Armenians as a teacher, working for the German Orient Mission. From 1920, Jeppe played a crucial role in refugee aid in Aleppo, Syria, working for the secular organisation Armenien Vennen (Friends of Armenia) and in 1921, she joined the League of Nations' committee for the release of abducted Armenian women and children. Alma Johansson eventually left Istanbul for Greece, where she worked with relief among Armenians until she retired in 1941.[17] Bodil Biørn was the only one who chose to go to Armenia. She made her decision after spending time in refugee camps in Istanbul, where she gathered significant information from contacts made pre-genocide.[18]

Biørn and her colleagues soon realised that the catastrophe of war and genocide shattered the foundations of essentially all aspects of the life of Armenian survivors, as it was known before 1915. Most personal networks had been destroyed; formal institutions like churches, schools and political parties were also broken.[19] In Istanbul, Biørn was able to observe how old family structures had disappeared. Often, one person was the sole survivor of a family that had once consisted of twenty to thirty members.[20] Therefore, with their deep knowledge of Armenian language, culture, history and people from all different social classes of pre-genocide society, American and Scandinavian missionaries became crucial links in the social networks that Armenian survivors were re-establishing. These networks, linking the pre-genocide society with the post-war Armenians, were also vital for the missionaries in their relief efforts in the refugee camps. In Beirut, for example, Karen Marie Petersen and Maria Jacobsen hired Armenian women as employees. Eight *mayriks* (mothers) cared for the children in the Bird's Nest. These young women had a deep personal connection to the Danes and especially to Petersen. They were all orphans who had grown up in the Danish orphanage Emaus (Emmaus) in Mezreh, which was headed by Petersen before the war. During the Genocide, Petersen had managed to protect these eight and a number of other children and women by keeping them hidden in the orphanage. Arriving in Beirut as refugees, the young women were employed by their Danish *mayrik*.[21]

Biørn also depended on her pre-genocide network for planning aid for refugees. One of the refugees Biørn met in Istanbul was a survivor from Mush, who worked for an English aid organisation. He had recently returned from a mission in the Armenian Republic. His description of the dreadful situation in Armenia inspired Biørn to make her next move.[22] Unable to go back to Anatolia, Biørn decided that her new vocation would be relief among Armenian refugees in the Armenian Republic. It was also here that Armenian survivors from Mush, Van and Erzerum, and other Turkish Armenian provinces, had taken refuge hoping to return to their former homes in Anatolia.[23] When Biørn arrived in Erivan (Yerevan) in the spring of 1922, refugees from Mush were to play key roles in her humanitarian practice.

Humanitarian work for refugees and orphans in Armenia

As the chapter by Asya Darbinyan in this volume demonstrates, war on the Caucasus front and the Armenian Genocide had, by 1915, created a refugee crisis in the Russian imperial provinces of Transcaucasia. By 1918 an independent Republic of Armenia had been created in this territory. 'The burden of several hundred thousands of unsheltered and unemployed refugees was enough in itself to cause an economic maelstrom', writes historian Richard Hovannisian of the situation in the first year of the Republic's tumultuous existence.[24] By the summer of 1919, following a season of drought, 200,000 people – 20 per cent of the republic's population – had perished.[25] Both locally and internationally, the American NER was the only major reliable contributor of relief.[26] By 1921, by which time a Soviet state had replaced the independent Republic, the NER took care of a total of approximately 100,000 orphans in Armenia (including Persia and Mesopotamia), Syria and Palestine, Greece and Constantinople. A large number of these lived in the fifty-three orphanage centres but there were also at least 100,000 other needy, homeless orphans outside orphanages.[27]

Cooperation with the NER proved essential to Biørn. Since the Soviet government did not permit the presence of missionary organisations or individuals, the only way Biørn could be allowed to work in the Armenian Republic was through her contacts with the NER. She did not, however, want to be employed by the secular NER, but negotiated a special affiliation with the organisation that would allow her to continuing faith-based humanitarian work.[28] When Biørn arrived in Erivan in the early spring of 1922, the country was still ravished by famine. American aid workers reported that during the harsh winter months there had been several cases where people had become so desperate from hunger that they had resorted to eating human flesh. 'Officials said that they are doing all they can to prevent it but the people lost their senses from hunger.'[29] In April, the same year, NER workers based in Alexandropol reported terrible starvation among refugees and orphans in the mountain villages of central Armenia. Upon returning from a five-day horseback visit to twenty villages, NER worker K. A. Downer reported that foodstuffs throughout the area were exhausted. People attempted to make bread from all sorts of substitutes, including flax chaff and sawdust, and they were extracting undigested materials from old refuse and giving it their children. Due to malnutrition health conditions were critical, with one-fourth of the adults incapacitated and bedridden. Downer concluded that only one in fifty of the population was 'normal'.[30]

For Biørn it became imperative to organise relief as soon as possible. While native Armenians in the villages suffered starvation and sickness, the situation for refugees in the cities was, if possible, even worse. The Armenian government was not ready for that, however, and she spent the two first months in Armenia negotiating with government representatives as to where a Norwegian orphanage might be established. Biørn, who spoke (western) Armenian fluently and had lived among

Armenians for more than ten years, was able to negotiate with Armenian officials. The harsh conditions, however, influenced her health. An illness prolonged the negotiations for a suitable location for the orphanage. Even so, Biørn was able to begin working by distributing grain. Again, she used her pre-genocide Armenian network to decide whom the recipients of this relief should be, namely widows from Mush. These single women, old and young, had to support children and older relatives. During the difficult months before the grain was ripe, in April, May and June 1922, the food distribution financed by Norwegian women saved several families from starvation. Even so, there was a large number of children without homes, sleeping on the streets. Biørn wrote home about nights when abandoned children crying for bread outside her windows kept her awake. These reports moved Norwegian donors to fund one year's rent, 900 Norwegian *kroner*, for an orphanage.[31]

Eventually, lack of housing in the capital forced Biørn to look elsewhere for establishing the orphanage. When local authorities offered her a large, beautiful patrician house with a garden in Alexandropol, she accepted. The city was the centre of the NER's enormous relief operation in Armenia. Biørn knew several of the NER workers, who were formerly American missionaries during her time in Anatolia. These connections were important in the process of establishing the Norwegian orphanage. During the first months in Alexandropol, when the building was being renovated into an orphanage, Biørn was allowed to stay in one of the NER homes. This building was located a 30-minute drive outside the city. Biørn was still recovering and too weak to walk the distance. Now her old Mush connections volunteered to help. Two young men, who had grown up in the German orphanage in Mush headed by Biørn, lived in Alexandropol. They volunteered to drive Biørn to and from the city, in addition to inviting her for meals in their home.[32] These young men were probably motivated by a sense of reciprocity and maybe obligation to a carer from their orphaned childhood. As had been the case in Istanbul, besides her international network of present and former missionaries, Biørn's pre-genocide Armenian (Mush) network became a crucial factor in creating an orphanage.

The Norwegian orphanage

Alexandropol was the 'show' district of the NER. This was due to the good housing possibilities found in *Kazachee Post*, the former Russian military barracks, which housed over 5,000 children. This American orphanage and hospital, which was more like a village, was located about a mile from Alexandropol. It consisted of about forty stately and substantial stone houses, surrounded by extensive fields. The community also included schools and training courses in agriculture and crafts for older children.[33] In addition, there was another group of barracks situated on the opposite side of the city, *The Polygon*, where 20,000 refugees lived.[34] In his capacity as High Commissioner for Refugees of the League of Nations, Fridtjof Nansen – the Norwegian explorer and humanitarian – visited Leninakan (formerly Alexandropol) and *The Polygon* in 1925. Nansen found the facilities, where 11,000 orphans were taken care of, highly impressive.[35]

The children in the care of the NER were boys and girls – most of them under eleven years of age – who were in orphanages or were taken care of in local homes supported financially by the NER.[36] After the Genocide, according to historian Lerna Ekmekçioğlu, unmarried girls and boys, regardless of their age, were considered orphans if they had lost one parent, usually the father, and if they had no male relative on whom to depend. Orphanhood and the disintegration of the known family structures were closely related. To a certain extent, orphanhood meant an absence of the support of a family on whom one depended upon for everything before the catastrophe.[37]

Biørn's ideal for the Norwegian orphanage was the reconstruction of a family. Biørn wanted to establish a small-scale, personal and unhurried recovery process for the weakest children. It would be a qualitative addition to the NER's large and highly efficient refugee work. The American enterprise was invaluable, but their orphanages were much too large to be, in Biørn's view, real homes for the children. The large, luxurious villa she was renting made it possible for Biørn to create an orphanage after her own design. The house had ten rooms, two kitchens, and there were gardens both in the front and in the back. Biørn was practical and had running water installed – 'one of the most important things in an orphanage'.[38] She named the orphanage *Lyskilden* (Source of Light).

The Norwegian operation generated jobs for the local population. Biørn hired two 'kind and able' Armenian women: one cooked and one looked after the children. The cook's name was Asniv Djanercharian, she was from Bitlis where she had lived a comfortable life in a wealthy family before 1915. She was a faithful coworker and a quiet and good woman, who enjoyed hearing and reading God's word, according to Biørn. Djanercharian's faith was typical of the female refugee: her husband had been killed during the massacres, but her five children survived. As a widow having to support a large family, she was fortunate that several of her children stayed in the American orphanages and she managed to support the others working as a cook. Women could cook, but for purchasing foodstuffs at a public marketplace, a man was needed. Thus, Biørn employed a man to buy food and other necessities.[39]

The home could take up to thirty-six boys, aged between four and ten years. Some of the weakest children were found in the line outside one of the NER soup kitchens, by Biørn and her staff. In many cases, mothers or other relatives who lived in extreme poverty begged Biørn and her staff to take care of their children.[40] Soon there were thirty-five children in the Source of Light: all of them weak, sick and extremely undernourished.[41] Skin diseases as well as gastric and intestinal troubles prevailed among the local population in general, due to malnutrition. The American medical doctor Mabel Evelyn Elliott, who worked for the NER and for the American Women's Hospitals in Alexandropol from 1921 to 1923, reported that of the 40,000 orphans that were in the care of the Americans, there was not one healthy child.

All of them had the contagious diseases of favus and trachoma.⁴² Children at the Norwegian orphanage suffered from similar health issues, and many of them had very bloated stomachs, caused by a diet consisting of grass and 'greens'. Lack of food was a great threat to the existence of the Armenian orphans, and not only during the famine in the Armenian Republic. An Armenian orphan, Karnig Parnian, tells a similar story of hunger in his memoir of the orphanages of Anatolia and Lebanon, *Goodbye Antoura*.⁴³

In the Soviet Armenian Republic, the NER struggled to find enough foodstuffs to distribute and had strict rations of food. Even though there was supposed to be enough food for every child in their care, many of the older children went hungry. Biørn also had to ration food, but she seemed to have had enough provisions for the children. The social anthropologist Nefissa Naguib writes of food and food distribution among refugees today: 'whereas food deprivation breaks the human spirit, feeding others provides human meditation, caring, and healing others. Unpacking the many dimensions of humanitarian food distribution ... is an intricate process during which veracity and sentimentality must be constantly assessed. Nevertheless, something rich emerges when we examine the simple act of feeding others and the ripples of global moments it creates.'⁴⁴ Biørn did not cook or feed the children herself, that was taken care of by the Armenian women. However, she shared daily meals with the children and staff. The fact that Biørn – a foreign head of the orphanage – decided not to eat alone indicates that food was not only important as relief, it also speaks of the social interaction implied by shared meals in everyday life. Food was also a topic of the letters back to headquarters in Norway, where reports from Armenia were published. KMA members and other interested readers (to a large extent female) got a detailed picture of the orphanage's basement filled with food to last for a whole season: vegetables, potatoes, flour, fat, canned meat, beans and tomatoes.⁴⁵ This assured Norwegian women donors that their money was well spent on sound housekeeping and well-fed children.

Limiting the number of children, and admitting only the sickest and the weakest, was important to Biørn's vision, as maintaining a calm and enclosed environment, with proper food, was important to the healing process. During the stay at the orphanage, the children would be given nutritious food, medical treatment and care.⁴⁶ When they had regained their health, the children would return to their family or other carers. It was important to create a feeling of homeliness for the children who had lived on the streets. Staying warm during the winter months was part of this strategy. During his visit to the NER facilities, Fridtjof Nansen had not only observed children sharing bunk beds. There were several hundred children in large sleeping halls. These halls were clean and light, but not heated during the wintertime.⁴⁷ In a region with five months of snow, and winter temperatures of minus twenty degrees Celsius, even the polar explorer reacted to the fact that these halls were unheated. Biørn shared Nansen's concern about the cold winters and she wanted each child at the Source of Light to have their own bed.⁴⁸ Her solution to the problem reflected her personal approach to orphan care. Biørn and her staff washed and dried wool for the beds on the roof. Later the wool was stuffed and made into mattresses and quilts.

Care and connections

Biørn wrote at length detailing the work she and her staff devoted to creating the woollen bedding described above.[49] Her emphasis on this process was perhaps not surprising and reflected the way her personal background shaped her relief practices. In Norway, wool was essential to keeping people warm during long winters. Norwegian women knew how to knit; girls were taught knitting in school at an early age. Women supporting KMA's relief work knitted socks and sweaters for the children of the Source of Light. This voluntary needlework created an imagined connection between their own world and the Armenian world. In the words of anthropologist Liisa H. Malkki, in her study of female volunteers in Finland, knitting and sewing for a distant sufferer 'was a giving of one's skill, of time, and of oneself *in aid* of others, and linking it with other's skills and giving. It was a way of imagining oneself as a member of the lively world, and of something greater than oneself.'[50] On the receiving end, in the context of the Source of Light, hand-knitted socks and sweaters kept Armenian children and their relatives warm at a time when most Armenians, refugees and orphans, lacked clothing.

In 1919, the American Red Cross donated 754 metric tons of clothing to Armenia.[51] A few years later, many Armenians could still not afford winter clothing and old American clothes were 'far more valuable than money'.[52] Biørn encouraged Norwegian donors to send warm clothes to Armenia, specifying that the recipients would be forty families from Mush living in and around Alexandropol.[53] As we have seen, the Norwegian KMA had supported an orphanage and a health clinic in Mush before the war. Now they continued this transnational connection with strong links to the pre-genocide Armenian world. While the shipment of clothes (and toys) depended on assistance from the NER, the KMA volunteers packed and clearly marked their own boxes, in order for them not to disappear among all the other boxes transported to the NER.[54] By writing in detail of how Norwegian women should pack and address the packages to Alexandropol and the route the bulk transport would take, Biørn assured supporters that their gifts would arrive safely and helped to reinforce the sense of a personal bond between donor and recipient.[55]

These boxes with clothes and toys played a significant role both materially and psychologically in the transnational links between Norwegian supporters and the users of the orphanage. The clothes kept small bodies warm and at the same time reminded the children of the providers. Women in Norway 'adopted' Armenian children at the orphanage. Each person who donated money for the upkeep of a child was given the title 'foster mother'. Norwegian adoptive mothers not only sent funding, but also knitted socks, sweaters and hand-sewn clothes for 'their' child.

Miss Raaen in Bergen, for example, had sewn a winter coat for 'her' adoptive son Anuschvang.[56]

Why did this woman in Bergen and her fellow KMA members spend their money on buying yarn or textiles, and spend hours knitting and sewing? An unmarried woman in Norway in the 1920s would live a life without a spouse or children. Spending her free time sewing a warm coat for an Armenian boy might be motivated by a Christian belief in giving to fellow human beings in need, as well as by loyalty to the KMA. However, this generosity might also be driven by loneliness and a 'stark need' for a family of her own.[57] In the words of Malkki: 'Giving is often styled as emanating from abundance ...', but giving might also 'emerge out of stark need. ... the ethical generosity of "givers" and "helpers" overlay an intent *need for attachment*, and for living in social time'.[58]

The many photographs of children residing at the Source of Light also responded to donors' 'need for attachment', and the photographs were yet another vital factor in the creation of personal ties between 'mothers' in Norway and the children in Armenia.[59] Many of the children were photographed when they were accepted at the home: emaciated, dirty and clothed in rags.[60] After a few months, Biørn photographed the children again and these 'after' photos became proof of the difference the donors made. The KMA printed the photographs in their magazine. In addition to printed reports in the KMA magazine, Biørn also wrote letters to each donor. This was not a one-way process. Biørn asked each foster parent to send photographs of herself to 'her' child. Biørn talked to the children about the foster mothers and showed the children where the benefactors lived on a map of Norway. The children also sent greetings to their 'mothers' in Norway.

The clothes knitted for a specific child, the long distance adoption, and the exchange of photographs, letters and parcels of clothes were all part of what Watenpaugh calls 'unstrangering the object of humanitarianism'.[61] He argues that at the centre of modern humanitarian reason is a process whereby the subject of humanitarianism's actions are less about assisting those who are strange and different, and more about helping those found to be knowable, similar and deserving. The aim of humanitarian reason is effectively to make the 'victims of war, famine, and disaster seem familiar' and make these victims' problems into a problem for humanity.[62] By presenting the children as individuals and creating personal ties between them and their donors, Biørn was making the orphans familiar to a specific, female Norwegian audience.

Short biographies published for potential Norwegian donors were also part of this process of 'unstrangering'. While the helplessness and suffering of female refugees common to representations of Armenian victimhood at this time is a feature of these biographies, they present a more complex picture. This was also the case with the story of a widow who had twice walked long and strenuous distances to ask Biørn to take care of her five-year-old son. In order to support herself the woman resorted to begging, but this was not enough to support the son. She had been married twice and both husbands had been murdered, the first one in the massacres in Mush in 1915, and the second one in Tabriz in Persia in 1918. The boy was born while she was fleeing Mush for Russian Armenia. Both of the parents were Protestants and the woman asked for work at the orphanage. Biørn was not able to give her work, but the boy stayed.[63] Although this woman was clearly grieving and suffering, she was not portrayed as helpless and passive. Rather, her story emphasises that she was determined to get help from Biørn and was willing to walk long distances in order to do so. In addition, she was seeking work. This refugee woman is portrayed not as an archetypal victim, but as an individual with a religious and geographical identity. These facts – she is Protestant and from Mush – create a familiar link for the Norwegian donors who had supported Biørn's health and educational work in Mush before the war.

In his seminal study of the history of the modern refugee, Gatrell argues that the 'images of refugees are unidentified and de-contextualized. Only on rare occasion are people identified.'[64] Biørn's work is an exception. By identifying the orphans and their relatives, the refugees in Biørn's published texts and photographs were given a historical context. In addition, by identifying children, parents and other carers by name and age, and narrating their unique, individual stories of survival, Biørn did not portray Armenian children and women refugees as anonymous, passive receivers of aid. On the contrary, in the narratives very young children actively seek to escape destructive situations in order to seek better lives. Armenian female refugees and children were portrayed as dislocated, starving and sick victims, but also as personifications of 'will and courage'.[65] In addition, by supplying a context – giving names, family and geographical belonging to individual survivors – Biørn's eyewitness reports from the orphanage contributed to an individualisation of the 'Armenian refugee'. This is a contrast to the prevailing tradition of portraying refugees as unnamed individuals merged into 'a collective category of concern'.[66]

Conclusion

In 1924 Biørn became seriously ill and was forced to go back to Norway. She employed a Protestant Armenian woman from Bitlis, educated at the American Board Mission, and felt confident that this Armenian woman would run the orphanage in the spirit of the KMA.[67] However, the Soviet government was not willing to tolerate this Christian institution any longer. When Biørn, after regaining her health, tried to return to Armenia in 1925, she was denied permission. Soviet authorities asked the NER to take the children from the Norwegian orphanage. If the Americans were not willing to take the children, they would end up in the care of the Armenian state. We do not know what happened to the children of the Source of Light. The NER began to wind up their work in the Armenian Republic in 1927, while Bodil Biørn established an orphanage for Armenian children in Aleppo. She and her female Armenian co-worker also offered relief and education to women refugees. In 1934, at the age of 63, Biørn retired and lived in Oslo with her Armenian adopted son and his family; writing and publishing on the lives of Armenian refugees until her death in 1960.

Biørn's deep knowledge of Armenian language and culture, and her experience as a relief worker during the Genocide, were also decisive elements in explaining her success in Soviet Armenia during the early 1920s. By relying on pre-genocide Armenian networks, especially from the region of Mush where she had lived for seven years, Bodil Biørn was able to operate as a humanitarian worker independent of the American relief operation in the Armenian Republic. Survivors from Mush advised as to where she should establish a relief operation, and they helped in practical matters when she had arrived in Armenia, which was new territory for this Norwegian woman. Biørn also focused her relief on refugees from Mush, some of whom came to her seeking assistance for their children and themselves. The network from Mush created a familiar sphere in an unfamiliar political and geographical context.

In addition to this pre-genocide personal network, Biørn could take advantage of her connections with former American missionaries now working for the NER in the Soviet Republic, while remaining apart from their wider operation and thus preserving the particular character of her work. Her network of Norwegian sponsors, from much further afield, also played a crucial role in facilitating her relief work. Through photographs and biographical narratives focusing on children at the orphanage and surviving Armenian parents, Biørn created personal links between Armenian children and female benefactors in Norway. Through donating money and time, writing to and knitting and sewing for 'the needy', the latter created imagined connections between their own world and that of the Armenians.

These bonds were reinforced through the sharing of KMA texts and photographs about the refugees. These texts, which gave refugees identities and biographies, emphasising survival strategies as well as victimhood, are a reminder that prevailing representations of refugees as 'anonymous and timeless' should not be taken for granted.[68] Gatrell has demonstrated that the anonymisation of refugees is in part to blame for the general absence of refugees in historical scholarship.[69] These KMA sources offer us a chance to begin to write the refugee into history.

Notes

1 R. G. Hovannisian, *The Republic of Armenia. Volume 1. The First Year, 1918–1919* (Berkeley, CA: University of California Press, 1974), p. 126.
2 *Ibid.*, p. 144; F. M. Surface and R. L. Bland, *American Food in the World War and Reconstruction Period: Operations of the Organizations under the Direction of Herbert Hoover, 1914 to 1924* (Stanford, CA: Stanford University Press, 1931), p. ix.
3 See K. D. Watenpaugh, *Bread from Stones. The Middle East and the Making of Modern Humanitarianism* (Oakland, CA: California University Press, 2015) and M. D. Peterson, *'Starving Armenians': America and the Armenian Genocide, 1915–1930 and After* (Charlottesville, VA: University of Virginia Press, 2004).

4   See I. M. Okkenhaug 'Refugees, Relief and the Restoration of a Nation: Norwegian Mission in the Armenian Republic, 1922–1925', in H. Nielssen, I. M. Okkenhaug and K. Hestad Skeie (eds), *Protestant Mission and Local Encounters in the Nineteenth and Twentieth Centuries* (Leiden: Brill, 2011), pp. 207–33.
5   Watenpaugh argues that 'while many of the individuals in the theater of humanitarian action had their origins in the region as missionaries, as did most of the organizers of the humanitarian project of NER, collectively they stood at the culmination of a secular movement in the missionary project, in which the goals and methods of evangelism gave way almost entirely to addressing the suffering of human beings and developing institutions for their care, social development and higher education.' Watenpaugh, *Bread from Stones*, p. 18.
6   R. Jinks, '"Marks Hard to Erase": The Troubled Reclamation of "Absorbed" Armenian Women, 1919–1927', *The American Historical Review* 123:1 (2018), 86–123, 121–3. See also R. Skinner and A. Lester, 'Humanitarianism and Empire: New Research Agendas', *The Journal of Imperial and Commonwealth History* 40:5 (2012), 729–47.
7   National Archives (Riksarkivet), Oslo, PA 699, Kvinnelige misjonsarbeidere (hereafter KMA), 0028, *Kvartalshilsen*, nr. 2, 1922, p. 17.
8   See N. Migliorini, *(Re)constructing Armenia in Lebanon and Syria: Ethno-Cultural Diversity and the State in the Aftermath of a Refugee Crisis* (New York: Berghahn Books, 2008).
9   P. Gatrell, *The Making of the Modern Refugee* (Oxford: Oxford University Press, 2013), p. 10.
10 E. Bockelund, *Høsten er stor. KMA's historie gennom 50 år* (København: Kvindelige missions arbejdere, 1950), p. 7.
11 I. M. Okkenhaug, 'Women on a Mission! Scandinavian Welfare and the Armenians in the Ottoman Empire, 1905–1917', in N. Naguib and I. M. Okkenhaug (eds), *Interpreting Welfare and Relief in the Middle East* (Leiden, Brill, 2008), pp. 57–81.
12 I. M. Okkenhaug 'Scandinavian Missionaries, Gender and Armenian Refugees During World War One: Crisis and Reshaping of Vocation', *Social Sciences and Missions* 23:1 (2010), 63–93.
13 M. Småberg, 'Witnessing the Unbearable: Alma Johansson and the Massacres of the Armenians, 1915', in K. Aggestam and A. Björkdahl (eds), *War and Peace in Transition: Changing Roles of External Actors* (Lund: Nordic Academic Press, 2009), pp. 107–27; M. Bjørnlund, 'Before the Armenian Genocide: Danish Missionary and Rescue Operations in the Ottoman Empire, 1900–1914', *Haigazian Armenological Review* 26 (2006), 141–64, and M. Bjørnlund, 'Karen Jeppe, Aage Meyer Benedictsen, and the Ottoman Armenians: National Survival in Imperial and Colonial Settings', *Haigazian Armenological Review* 28 (2008), 9–43.
14 During the war Biørn adopted a boy who was a few months old at the time. She named him Fridtjof and brought him to Norway in 1917. During Biørn's stay in Armenia, Fridtjof lived in an orphanage in Norway. This might be a reason for Biørn's choice to establish an orphanage for boys only. Maybe there was simply a need for a boys' orphanage. See I. M. Okkenhaug *En norsk filantrop: Bodil Biørn og armenerne, 1905–1934* (Kristiansand: Portal Forlag, 2016).
15 See A. Johansson, *Ett folk i landsflykt: ett år ur armeniernas historia* (Stockholm: Kvinnliga missionsarbetare, 1930/1979).
16 Hovannisian, *The Republic of Armenia*, p. 135.
17 M. Småberg 'Mission and Cosmopolitan Mothering: Saving Armenian Mothers and Orphans, 1902–1947', *Social Science and Missions* 30 (2017), 44–73; M. Småberg 'Witness Narrative as Resistance and Recovery: Alma Johansson and the 1915 Armenian Genocide', in A. Ahlbäck and F. Sundevall (eds), *Gender, War and Peace: Breaking Up the Borderlines* (Joensuu: University Press of Eastern Finland, 2014), pp. 136–63.
18 National Archives, Oslo, PA 699, KMA, 0028, *Kvartalshilsen*, nr. 3, 1920, p. 20.

19 Migliorini, *(Re)constructing Armenia in Lebanon and Syria*, p. 45.
20 National Archives, Oslo, PA 699, KMA, 0028, *Kvartalshilsen*, nr. 2, 1922, p. 14.
21 In 1922–23 these young women, together with more than 20,000 other Christian Armenians, Greeks and Assyrians, mostly women and children, had been forced to leave Anatolia by Mustafa Kemal Atatürk's regime. M. Bjørnlund, *På Herrens mark: Nødhjælp, mission og kvindekamp under det armenske folkedrap* (Viborg: Kristelig Dagblads Forlag, 2015), p. 193.
22 National Archives, Oslo, PA 699, KMA, 0028, *Kvartalshilsen*, nr. 2, 1922, p. 17.
23 Hovannissian, *The Republic of Armenia*, p. 363.
24 *Ibid.*, p. 130.
25 *Ibid.*
26 Rockefeller Archive Center (hereafter RAC), LSRM, 104–111/3, 104, telegram to (executive secretary) Vickrey, Near East, NY, signed Peet, Huntington, Maccullum, Jaquith, 1 March 1922.
27 RAC, LSRM, 104–111/3, box 9, 104, letter to the Laura Spelman Rockefeller Memorial, from the Executive Committee of the Near East Relief, on behalf of the Board of Trustees, of Near East Relief, James L. Barton, Chairman Board of Trustees, Edwin M. Bulkely, Chairman Executive and Finance Committees, John H. Finley, Vice-Chairman Board of Trustees, Cleveland H. Dodge, Treasurer, Charles V. Vickrey, General Secretary. In December 1923, in the Armenian Republic, the NER had 28,748 Armenian children in their care, of these 17,469 were in orphanages. RAC, LSRM, 104–111/3, box 9, 104, Near East Relief Graphic, 1923.
28 National Archives, Oslo, PA 699, KMA, 0028, letter from KMA board to 'Armenien-venner', Oslo, December, 1926.
29 RAC, LSRM, 104–111/3, 104, telegram from Jaquith to Near East Relief, Vickrey, New York, 2 April 1922. See also Hovannisian, *The Republic of Armenia*, p. 139.
30 RAC, LSRM, 104–111/3, 104, telegram from Jaquith to Near East Relief, Vickrey, New York, 2 April 1922.
31 National Archives, Oslo, PA 699, KMA, 0028, *Kvartalshilsen*, nr. 1, 1923, p. 2.
32 *Ibid.*, p. 39.
33 *The New Near East*, January 1920, p. 11.
34 *The New Near East*, Vol. IV, No. 8 (7), February 1920, p. 5.
35 F. Nansen, *Gjennom Armenia* (Oslo: Aschehoug, 1962), pp. 118–22, 123–4.
36 RAC, LSRM, 104–111/3, box 9, 104, letter to the Laura Spelman Rockefeller Memorial, from the Executive Committee of the Near East Relief, on behalf of the Board of Trustees, of Near East Relief, James L. Barton.
37 L. Ekmekçioğlu, *Recovering Armenia: The Limits off Belonging in Post-Genocide Turkey* (Stanford, CA: Stanford University Press, 2016), p. 28.
38 *Ibid.*, p. 8.
39 National Archives, Oslo, PA 699, KMA, 0028, *Kvartalshilsen*, nr. 1, 1923, p. 2
40 National Archives, Oslo, PA 699, KMA, 0028, *Kvartalshilsen*, nr. 1, 1923, p. 4.
41 *Ibid.*, p. 2.
42 M. E. Elliott, *Beginning Again at Ararat* (New York: Fleming H. Revell Company, 1924) (2007), pp. 176–7.
43 K. Parnian, *Goodbye Antoura: A Memoir of the Armenian Genocide* (Stanford, CA: Stanford University Press, 2015).
44 N. Naguib, 'Middle East Encounters 69 Degrees North Latitude: Syrian Refugees and Everyday Humanitarianism in the Arctic', *International Journal of Middle East Studies* 49 (2017), 645–60, 645.
45 National Archives, Oslo, PA 699, KMA, 0028, *Kvartalshilsen*, nr. 1, 1923, p. 2.

46 *Ibid.*, p. 7, letter from B. Biørn, Alexandropol, 9 November 1922.
47 Nansen, *Gjennom Armenia*, p. 122.
48 *Kvartalshilsen*, nr. 1, 1923, p. 7.
49 Wool 'is a compelling metaphor for warmth – and not simply a metaphor: its social warmth is linked to its … physical warmth', writes L. H. Malkki. L. H. Malkki, *The Need to Help: The Domestic Arts of International Humanitarianism* (Durham, NC: Duke University Press, 2015), p. 161.
50 *Ibid.*, p. 161.
51 Hovannisian, *The Republic of Armenia*, pp. 142–3.
52 Elliott, *Beginning Again at Ararat*, p. 175.
53 National Archives, Oslo, PA 699, KMA, 0028, *Kvartalshilsen*, nr. 1, 1923, p. 7, letter from B. Biørn, Alexandropol, 9 November 1922.
54 *Ibid.*
55 Malkki, *The Need to Help*, p. 159.
56 National Archives, Oslo, PA 699, KMA, 0028, *Kvartalshilsen*, nr. 1, 1924, p. 2.
57 Malkki, *The Need to Help*, p. 164.
58 *Ibid.*
59 Bodil Biørn's photographs, see: https://commons.wikimedia.org/wiki/Category:Photographs_by_Bodil_Bi%C3%B8rn (accessed 19 November 2019).
60 On Armenian refugees and humanitarian photography, see P. Balakian, 'Photography, Visual Culture, and the Armenian Genocide', in H. Fehrenbach and D. Rodogno (eds), *Humanitarian Photography: A History* (Cambridge: Cambridge University Press, 2015), pp. 89–114.
61 Watenpaugh, *Bread from Stones*, p. 19.
62 *Ibid.*
63 National Archives, KMA, PA 699, nr. 0028, *Kvartalshilsen*, nr. 1, 1923, p. 2.
64 Gatrell, *The Making of the Modern Refugee*, p. 10.
65 N. Maksudyan, *Orphans and Destitute Children in the Late Ottoman Empire* (Syracuse, NY: Syracuse University Press, 2014), p. 152.
66 Gatrell, *The Making of the Modern Refugee*, p. 10.
67 National Archives, Oslo, PA 699, KMA, 0028, *Kvartalshilsen*, nr. 3, 1925, p. 2.
68 Gatrell, *The Making of the Modern Refugee*, p. 11.
69 *Ibid.*

7

Humanitarian diaspora? The AGBU in Soviet Armenia, 1920–30s

Vahé Tachjian

The early 1920s were pivotal years for the emerging post-genocide Armenian diaspora. After the destruction of Armenian collective existence in the Ottoman Empire (with the exception of Istanbul), inter-war attempts to create a new homeland for Armenian Genocide survivors within the frontiers of the former Ottoman Empire failed. Tens of thousands of refugees were therefore forced to start new lives in the Middle East, Europe and the Americas, facing many challenges of reconstructing community life and identity.[1]

These processes coincided with the fall of the First Republic of Armenia after barely two and a half years of existence and, in December 1920, the establishment of a Soviet regime in its place. A considerable number of members of the short-lived Republic's apparatus – most of them members of the Armenian Revolutionary Federation (ARF, or Dashnaktsutiun) – fled the country and took refuge in the Armenian communities of the diaspora.[2] There, they continued their political struggle against Soviet rule. These circumstances meant that the 1920s were also decisive for the politicisation of the new diaspora and attitudes to the Soviet Armenian regime became the main source of inter-community oppositions and conflicts.[3]

The new diaspora faced fundamental challenges of existence, survival and identity. This was manifested on the ground by the need to build houses and shelters for tens of thousands of refugees in the Middle East and Greece, among them many orphans. The construction of schools and churches was also undertaken in order to renew community life. Nonetheless, an ideological and political battle emerged within the new diaspora between those in favour of cooperation with the Soviet Armenian regime and those who were determined to fight against it, work for its downfall and create an independent state.[4] Thus, before the emergence of the Cold War, a similar situation already existed in the Armenian diaspora of the 1920s, where political bi-polarity became the rule and the dividing line between groups was their attitude vis-à-vis the regime in Soviet Armenia.

The Armenian General Benevolent Union (AGBU) was one of the most active and dynamic Armenian diaspora organisations in the 1920s and was deeply involved in the post-genocide national reconstruction process. It became a pioneer in cooperating with the Soviet Armenian regime and was transformed into the main coordinator of diasporan efforts to send aid to Armenia and contribute to its economic, cultural and social development. The close relationship between the AGBU and the Soviet regime might be seen as a paradox, given the bourgeois-liberal and in many respects elitist nature of the organisation.[5] Founded in Cairo in 1906 by elite members of the Egyptian Armenian community, the aim of the AGBU was initially to ameliorate the conditions of the Armenians of the Ottoman Empire in the socio-economic and educational spheres, especially in the countryside. In the declaration of its first general assembly in 1909, it was stated that the objective of the organisation was to promote trade and the agricultural development of Ottoman Armenians.[6]

However, exceptional conditions within the Ottoman Empire, the outbreak of the First World War and the Armenian Genocide forced the AGBU to shift its activities considerably. In the immediate aftermath of the Genocide it concentrated mainly on refugee and orphan issues, as well as supporting schools that were newly established in diaspora communities. In the early 1920s, the AGBU began a new chapter in its history, directing its efforts towards mainly humanitarian and development projects in Soviet Armenia. These efforts lasted more than a decade before their brutal rupture by the Stalinist regime.

This chapter draws on materials from the AGBU archives located in Cairo and Paris in order to analyse relations between the AGBU and Soviet Armenia in the inter-war years. By doing so it expands and challenges the existing historiography on humanitarianism in the aftermath of the Armenian Genocide by drawing attention to the neglected role of diaspora actors. The way the AGBU established relations with Yerevan constitutes one of the most turbulent and fascinating episodes in its history. The fate of Armenian orphans, refugees in Syrian, Lebanese and Greek camps, the development of Armenia and the reinforcement of the Armenian state were all major preoccupations for the AGBU leaders who were persuaded that their strategy working hand-in-hand with the Soviets would open up new opportunities on these fronts. As this chapter argues, cooperation with the Soviet regime was not an easy task and required flexibility and restraint from the AGBU leaders, as failure risked having fatal consequences for the relationship. First, I examine the reasons for the cooperation between the AGBU and the Soviet authorities. Then I analyse the negotiations behind the construction of the Nubarashen (Nuparashen) village and the settlement of Armenians in Soviet Armenia in the 1920s and 1930s. Finally, I consider how changing political agendas in the Soviet Union impacted the work of the AGBU. Examining these episodes provides a reminder that diaspora humanitarian and development interventions are not simply a phenomenon of the post-Cold War world, but also have a long and understudied history.

Why cooperation?

In the 1920s, when hundreds of thousands of Armenian orphans and refugees were scattered in the Middle East and Greece, the AGBU was responsible for many of them living in Syria, Palestine, Lebanon, and even Greece.[7] As chapters in this volume by Jinks, Okkenhaug and Damousi show, the AGBU was just one of several organisations involved in assisting these uprooted Armenians. Nevertheless, it saw itself as bearing the primary responsibility for what became of them. The AGBU was concerned not only with the orphans' education and eventual integration into society, but also with the environment in which they would end up living. For the orphans and refugees were housed, in the eyes of the AGBU's leaders, in an alien world, on Greek, Syrian, Lebanese or Palestinian soil, where they were condemned to assimilation and, sooner or later, loss of their national identity. These issues were crucial for the AGBU leaders and were raised several times during the inter-war period. For example, in 1920, the AGBU complained about the way an Armenian orphanage in Adana was run by a French administration 'relying on a mostly foreign staff and providing the children an education with nothing Armenian about it'.[8]

In these circumstances, it was perhaps hardly surprising that the alternative represented by Soviet Armenia should monopolize the attention of the AGBU's leaders. They became convinced that the small state in the south of the Caucasus constituted a homeland, where 'the nation was being conserved and advanced', regardless of the political regime there.[9] This idea was predominant across all diasporan Armenian political tendencies, whether in favour of or hostile to the Soviet regime. For the AGBU leaders, the settlement of Armenian refugees and orphans in Soviet Armenia was considered a 'humanitarian mission', as well as a way to find for them a homeland, which would secure their national identity.[10]

The most significant contacts between the Soviet regime and the AGBU were forged in Moscow, where a member of the AGBU's central board, Mikayel Papajanian, arrived in December 1922, as the representative of the Armenian National Delegation.[11] Papajanian met with Lev Karakhan, an ethnic-Armenian and a high-ranking Soviet diplomat, and the Soviet Armenian representative, Sahag Ter Gabrielian as well as with Lukashin (Sargis Srapionian) chairman of the Armenian Council of People's Commissars, and Ashot Hovhannisian, the first secretary of the Communist Party of Armenia. The future of the orphans and refugees dominated the agenda. For the first time, an AGBU officer heard Soviet politicians express a desire to see the refugees and orphans resettle in Soviet Armenia. Papajanian even reached agreement with them on the 'repatriation' of the oldest male orphans from the Beirut, Aleppo and Jerusalem orphanages.[12]

Settling young Armenian men was more than a humanitarian mission; it also coincided with the Soviet leaders' political and economic goals for Armenia. Presumably with this idea in mind, they stressed that there was a shortage of arable land for the newcomers and suggested that the AGBU '[take] charge of draining swampland and irrigating uncultivated land, [build] villages to accommodate [them], and [supply] them with seed, livestock and agricultural machines'.[13] On these conditions, the Soviets agreed to work with the AGBU to find a solution to the orphan and refugee problem. They very clearly stipulated, however, that this cooperation must exclude all organisations affiliated with the ARF or individual ARF members.[14]

As soon as Papajanian returned to Paris, the central board of the AGBU began a careful examination of the Soviet proposals. The organisation was interested in finding the orphans agricultural employment, since it too had plans to found a model farm and agricultural school for them.[15] Certain AGBU leaders – very likely unaware of the real situation in Soviet Armenia – even thought that, after the orphans had been trained in the agricultural school, they could buy land and become independent farmers.[16] While their willingness to found farms and schools is indicative of the blurred boundaries between the provision of relief and what might now be more readily termed 'development', the organisation's leaders did not feel ready to take on major projects like the draining of swamps or irrigation of uncultivated land. Therefore, after evaluating Papajanian's report the AGBU mobilised another expert: the central board asked the agronomist Tigran Aslanian to go to Yerevan and assess first-hand the possibility of founding a demonstration farm and agricultural school.[17]

Aslanian (originally from the Ottoman Empire) arrived in Yerevan in August 1923 and met with Lukashin and several other leaders. Based on his experience he wrote a lengthy report entitled *An Excursion to the Communist Paradise* (Une Excursion au Paradis Communiste). The report reads more like travel literature than a serious field study, describing all the Soviet cities that Aslanian travelled through on his way to Yerevan, as well as numerous issues of administration, accommodation and food that he encountered in the Soviet world.[18] Although the AGBU representative's account was not overly critical of the Soviet regime in Armenia, certain points are indicative of the contradictory reactions of Soviet leaders to the prospect of cooperation with the AGBU and the various risks that work in Armenia might entail. One example cited in the report was an article published in Yerevan in the Armenian Party's official organ, *Soviet Armenia (Sovetakan Hayastan)*, during his stay in which the AGBU was critically referred to as an organisation composed of 'obscure individuals', 'Egyptian planters' and 'fugitive ministers'. Moreover, during his negotiations in Moscow with Armenian representatives, Aslanian also noticed that the local authorities did not support the establishment of agricultural settlements and schools, as the AGBU leaders suggested. Indeed, Lukashin was vocal in stressing that, first and foremost, Soviet Armenia needed foreign capital and financial contributions in order to build irrigation canals and industrial enterprises. According to the Soviet Armenian leader, these steps were necessary before cooperation on other issues could begin.[19]

The lack of 'concrete conclusions' in Aslanian's report did not please the AGBU central board, the more so as Yesayi Garigian, another AGBU member, returned from a short stay in Yerevan around the same time.[20] In October 1923, Garigian had participated in the Congress of the Committee for Armenian Assistance (the Hayastani Ognutian Komite, or HOK, founded in Yerevan in 1921), during which Soviet Armenian leaders confirmed that they had put their stamp of approval on the idea of resettling the orphans in Armenia.[21] Reporting on his positive impressions before the central board, Garigian seemed to have convinced the AGBU leadership to cooperate with the Soviets in resolving the problem of the orphans. He even convinced the Soviets to grant the AGBU about 2.702 acres of land in Yeghvard (north of Yerevan) and Dalma (on the right bank of Hrazdan river, in present-day Yerevan).[22]

On top of this agreement, Garigian secured Yerevan's approval of a plan to resettle 2,000 orphans on Armenian territory, on condition that the AGBU met their traveling expenses and transferred $100 for the upkeep of each orphan.[23] In the first phase of the plan, the Soviet authorities would make all necessary arrangements for the resettlement of between 150 and 200 AGBU orphans.[24] The central board accepted Yerevan's conditions and decided, in May 1924, to send a delegation to Armenia to relocate the orphans and bring the land that the Soviet authorities had ceded to the AGBU under cultivation. Levon Pashalian and the engineer Gevorg Asatur headed the delegation and reported to the AGBU. In October 1924, 250 AGBU orphans from AGBU's Jerusalem, Aleppo and Beirut orphanages boarded a Soviet ship in Jaffa, Palestine and set sail for Armenia.[25]

The AGBU's participation in Soviet Armenian development projects

The most important AGBU project in Soviet Armenia was the construction of the village of Nubarashen, a southern suburb of present-day Yerevan. The central board of the AGBU, based on the report of the Pashalian-Asatur delegation, ultimately decided to drop the Dalma and Yeghvard projects and take on only another one suggested by the Soviet Armenian authorities, this time localised in Shengavit (a southern suburb of Yerevan), where the AGBU pledged to build a residence for 250 orphans as well as an irrigation canal, at a cost that Asatur estimated at £6,000.[26] The official agreement was signed with a Soviet Armenian representative on 10 January 1925 in Paris. On this occasion, Boghos Nubar made a personal donation of £4,000 to the AGBU towards the construction of the Shengavit orphanage. It was to be called the 'Marie Nubar Foundation', in memory of Boghos Nubar's late wife.[27] After that, the AGBU became a major donor to many development projects in Soviet Armenia.[28]

The Nubarashen project was inspired by the repatriation of a few thousand refugees to Soviet Armenia, mainly from Greece, in 1925 and the prospect of a further wave of immigration, discussed in more detail in the following part of the chapter.[29] At its annual congress, in 1926, the AGBU's American Central Committee decided to launch a fundraising campaign to finance the reclamation of land to facilitate resettlement in Soviet Armenia.[30] The funding drive had the goal of raising

$250,000 by the AGBU's twenty-fifth anniversary in 1931. If the goal was fulfilled, Boghos Nubar pledged to contribute another $100,000.[31]

On the Central Committee's suggestion, it was also decided that a new village planned for some of the new arrivals would be called Nubarashen. The Soviet authorities soon expressed reservations about the name; their tendency was to name Armenia's cities and villages after Communist luminaries. From his end, Boghos Nubar minimised the question around the village's name and encouraged the pursuit of fundraising.[32] Indeed, despite the ongoing discussions about the village's name, the real problem with the Nubarashen project was money, as early success gave way to a sharp drop in contributions after the 1929 stock market crash. It was not until May 1930 that the final agreement was signed with Soviet authorities and preliminary work on the site began.

As stipulated in the agreement, around 7,400 acres of land were set aside for Nubarashen. It lay to the south-west of Yerevan, fewer than four miles from the capital, on the Hrazdan plateau east of Nor Gavit and Aghamzalu (today's Marmarashen). The AGBU and the local Armenian authorities had to cooperate in order to irrigate the land, build, and equip the settlement with basic structures and services.[33] Nubarashen's streets would bear the names of the native towns and villages of its inhabitants, all of them from the Ottoman Empire. This clause of the agreement was calculated to encourage compatriotic associations in the diaspora to invest in the project.[34] Funds were also used to construct the village's basic institutions, such as schools, daycare centres, workshops, a hospital and a theatre. The AGBU further agreed to sponsor construction of a spinning mill and carpet factory. In 1931, it sent 32,000 feet of steel pipe to Yerevan for the transport and distribution of water, together with a number of tank trucks.[35]

The construction work was supervised by a committee formed in Yerevan and headed by the architect Alexander Tamanyan, later replaced by Sergo Khanoyan, who was also appointed president of the HOK.[36] Construction began in 1931 and progressed slowly. By September 1936, no more than 100 houses had been erected and only 1,000 refugees, mostly from Greece and France, had moved to Nubarashen.[37] The construction of schools, a hospital and textile shops had also been finished.[38] By July 1936, the AGBU had invested $417,000 (£83,452) in the Nubarashen project.[39]

Repatriation of refugees in the 1920s and 1930s

In parallel with its involvement in infrastructure and development projects in Soviet Armenia, the AGBU had continued to engage in negotiations for repatriation of Armenian refugees in the Soviet Republic on a larger scale. In February 1923, as we have seen, Soviet Armenia's leaders had agreed to the relocation of Armenian refugees from the Near East and Greece to Armenia. At the request of the Armenian National Delegation, the League of Nations (LON) decided, in September 1923, to share the responsibility for the transfer of 50,000 Armenian refugees from Greece and also to meet the costs of reclaiming land in Armenia's Sardarapat district, where the newcomers were to live.[40]

For this purpose, the LON created, in 1924, a group of experts under the direction of its High Commissioner for Refugees, the Norwegian delegate Fridtjof Nansen. Nansen proceeded to write a report in which he noted that the authorities in Yerevan were willing to cede a tract of land and that £900,000 would be required to make it habitable for the 15,000 refugees from Greece and Istanbul who were to be settled on it, along with another 10,000 existing inhabitants of Soviet Armenia. The AGBU and its president, Boghos Nubar, were also engaged in the negotiations aimed at the realisation of this major project. However, the project failed as it faced political opposition from Western states not eager to invest in the Soviet Union.[41]

Despite of the collapse of the large-scale repatriation project, convoys of refugees – 3,199 from Greece and 700 from Istanbul – left for Soviet Armenia late in 1925. The AGBU agreed to bear the costs of these transfers, for a total of £5,000.[42] 1,081 refugees of rural background were settled in villages on the Araztayan plain, in Armash, Yeraskh, Arvash and Amo.[43] In 1927, a second transfer of refugees to Armenia was organised, again with financial support of £11,910 from the AGBU.[44] That year, only 1,609 refugees, mostly from Greece and Istanbul, were transferred.[45] The Greek government helped defray their travel expenses, in spite of its own desperate economic plight, so as to lighten the burden on a country overflowing with hundreds of thousands of Greek Ottoman refugees.

In 1930, although the Nansen plan had already been dismissed, Greece asked the LON to transfer 30,000 Armenian refugees still living on its territory, many in catastrophic conditions, to Armenia, promising to help meet their travel expenses.[46] The Greek authorities agreed to bear the costs of transporting the Armenians as far as Batumi. The AGBU and the former High Commission for Refugees (which had by then become the Nansen International Office for Refugees after Nansen's death) agreed, for their part, to pay related travel expenses.[47] The first group of 1,923 refugees, 135 of them orphans who had received their schooling in AGBU institutions in Nicosia, Jerusalem and Beirut, boarded ship in Piræus on 30 December 1930.[48] Between then and July 1932, four more convoys, a total of 6,242 refugees (about 1,000 of whom had been living in Bulgaria), left Greece for Armenia.

In 1930 Calouste Gulbenkian assumed the presidency of the AGBU and relations with the Soviet Union regressed, which had a direct impact on the repatriations. Only one more transfer took place, in May 1936. This brought 1,801 refugees from France to Armenia. The AGBU paid the transportation costs, including the refugees' board, as far as Marseille, spending a total of £2,000.[49] 267 members of this convoy were settled in Nubarashen.[50]

The same principle adopted by the AGBU leaders during the initial transfer of orphans in 1924 remained entrenched in their minds when it came to these repatriations of refugees. Along with all the Armenian political parties, they continued to believe that repatriation to Soviet Armenia, notwithstanding its political orientation, was the best means of preserving their national identity. However, Soviet Armenia proved not to be socially or economically prepared to welcome and resettle a massive number of compatriots. Despite difficulties and shortcomings, the ABGU joined the Soviet propaganda to portray repatriation as the best solution to the post-genocide dispersion of Armenians. Although the Armenian organisations, the AGBU included, were not misinformed of the realities of Armenia of that time, nevertheless they simply considered repatriation as the ultimate and unequalled solution to the Armenian identity preservation issue. In this case, it could be said that the thousands of refugees repatriated to Armenia were used as 'cannon fodder' for the identity agenda by diasporan leaders – mostly those of the AGBU – who rarely followed the same path of repatriation and remained in the diaspora.

From the art of dealing with the Soviet Armenian regime to the presidency of an 'imperialist agent'

The fifteen years during which the AGBU played an active part in constructing Soviet Armenia were a painful experience, as it encountered many problems and rarely experienced full cooperation with local authorities. The AGBU leaders faced an ambivalent Soviet administration, concerned with refugees, yet jealous of its national sovereignty and little inclined to leave any margin of manoeuvre to foreign organisations wishing to operate on its territory.

The creation of the HOK in 1921 and the subsequent development of its activities in the diaspora had proved to be another handicap. Members of this committee were, in the Soviets' view, trustworthy partners whose official mission was to help Soviet Armenia. While these efforts to harness the support of the diaspora were not altogether in vain, support for the HOK did not match the Soviet leadership's expectations. Given the limited reach of the HOK, if they wanted to be able to use diaspora resources in the socialist development of Armenia, the Soviet leaders had little choice but to continue to collaborate with the AGBU. Even so, they continued to pressure it in various ways, forcing it to accept their own working methods.

After sending several fact-finding missions from the early 1920s onwards, the AGBU's officers were persuaded that the most effective way of operating in Soviet Armenia was to maintain a local delegation to oversee the realisation of its projects. In the early 1920s, Samson Harutyunyan, a former member of the Armenian Populist Party and a former minister during the first Armenian Republic, had acted as the AGBU's informal representative in Armenia. Eventually, however, the AGBU central board wished to have an official Yerevan representative with direct affiliation to their organisation.

At stake in the question of a permanent AGBU representation in Yerevan was countering the HOK's influence over AGBU projects in Armenia. The HOK had become a Soviet propaganda tool and strove to centralise and monitor all the relief work performed by individuals or organisations in the diaspora for the benefit of Soviet Armenia.[51] Indeed, the local authorities preferred to entrust fundraising to an organisation like the HOK that was wholly under its thumb and could be relied upon to promote Soviet ideologies abroad.[52] However, it was a source of resentment that, while the AGBU cooperated with the HOK, it was not subordinate to it and rather pursued its own projects. The HOK did not hesitate to criticise the AGBU openly and accused it of failing to use all available funds for the reconstruction of Armenia.[53] This strategy of publicly maligning the AGBU was one means of pressuring it to invest more in the country. Therefore, the AGBU sought to keep its distance from the HOK and rely upon its own intermediaries in Armenia in order to maintain the independence that the HOK tried to restrain.

The Nubarashen project is symptomatic of the tensions between the AGBU and the HOK. In early 1926, the HOK had launched its own worldwide funding drive in order to build houses for thousands of Armenian refugees who had been resettled in Armenia. However, the diaspora's largest donors were already closely connected to the AGBU. Its American Central Committee, supposedly the richest in the world, declared that it was ready to participate in the HOK's campaign but the AGBU central board was reluctant. As Boghos Nubar saw it, the HOK's attitude was not 'such as to encourage us to strike down the same path'.[54] The AGBU therefore decreed that the funds raised by the new drive should not be channelled through the HOK but rather 'centralized in the treasury of [its] New York chapter' and that 'the funds should then be transferred to Armenia by the AGBU's executive board'.[55] Thus began the Nubarashen project.

However, the controversy between the AGBU and the HOK continued. In October 1927, Arshag Karaguezian, chairman of the fundraising drive and the AGBU's future president, angrily condemned the actions of the HOK:

> it [was] no secret for anyone that the HOK, which [was] without a doubt inspired by Yerevan, [was] doing everything it can to obstruct the AGBU's operations. We must make the Armenian government understand that, if it continues to behave in this fashion, it will force us to participate less fully than we should in the work of reconstructing Armenia ... It is highly desirable that we reach a clear, frank understanding with the Armenian government; Yerevan must be brought to see that Armenia will be the first to benefit from it.[56]

The Nubarashen project represented the AGBU's biggest investment in Armenia and consequently called for systematic supervision of the way its funds were used. The AGBU accordingly made plans to create a corporation, whose capital would be independent of its own, for the sole purpose of financing its construction projects in Soviet Armenia.[57] By doing so the AGBU hoped to keep a more methodical watch over its project manager, the Soviet state. But this plan, like others designed to supervise the utilisation of the funds sent to Yerevan, was unceremoniously rejected.

In June 1928, the central board designated Haykaz Garakeuzian as 'the AGBU's representative in Armenia', in the hope that it could thereby get around its problems.[58] His appointment does not seem to have led to concrete changes. The construction work at Nubarashen continued to elude the AGBU's control. Their official representative sent the central board regular, detailed reports about how the work financed by the AGBU was coming along; yet the funds continued to be received directly by Soviet officials, who would not tolerate interference with their methods of managing them.

As the AGBU struggled to maintain its autonomy in its work with the Soviet regime, a further question arose – were the funds that AGBU dispatched to Yerevan in fact being utilised for the intended purposes? Here too, examining the Nubarashen project provides the beginnings of an answer. The AGBU allocated over £83,000 ($417,000) to the construction of this settlement. This was a great deal of money; yet, by autumn 1936, less than 100 buildings had been erected and some 1,000 people had moved to Nubarashen.[59] This suggests that the funds raised for the Nubarashen project were often diverted to other ends. A few concrete examples confirm that this was the case. In December 1932, the Soviet Armenian Council of People's Commissars decided to acquire four Ford automobiles. An official memorandum sent to Haykaz Garakeuzian made clear that the cost of the automobiles was to be charged to the Nubarashen fund.[60] The cars were rapidly expedited to Yerevan. They were obviously not for the construction site, since the order was for three convertibles and a 'Ford Lux sedan'. This form of embezzlement did not escape the attention of the AGBU's officers, and it is plain that certain orders which Yerevan charged to the Nubarashen account were in fact intended for private use. But the central board preferred to close its eyes and process the orders without protest; the AGBU, which had become familiar with the practices of the Soviet apparatchiks, probably regarded this kind of corruption as inherent in the situation.

After the death of Boghos Nubar, Calouste Gulbenkian was appointed as the new president of the AGBU in 1930. Such an appointment led to an unmistakable shift in the organisation's stance toward Soviet Armenia.[61] Although the new president wished to continue working with Yerevan on projects in progress, he intended to prioritise building Armenian neighbourhoods in Syria, Lebanon and Greece. It should be noted that during the post-genocide presidency of Boghos Nubar, Gulbenkian's predecessor, humanitarian work for Armenian refugees in Syria, Lebanon and Greece was not at all neglected by the central board. This suggests that the AGBU had been engaging with multiple humanitarian solutions for the Armenian refugees, but priority was now shifting from the Soviet Armenian to other options.

Gulbenkian was not inclined to continue a policy of unconditional cooperation with Soviet Armenia. His new policy naturally irritated the Soviet leaders, who had become accustomed to seeing Armenia prioritised and to dealing with an organisation tolerant of working procedures that were rather less than transparent. The Soviet leadership was not slow to react. On 16 October 1931, the newspaper *Soviet Armenia* published an attack on Gulbenkian in a speech by Aghasi Khanjian, general secretary of the Central Committee of the Communist Party of Armenia. As Khanjian saw it, Gulbenkian's project was designed to discourage 'the Armenian working masses' from emigrating to Armenia; it aimed at the creation of an Armenian national home on Syrian soil, thus serving French imperialist interests in Syria.[62] Khanjian attacked Gulbenkian *ad hominem*, accusing him of developing the strategy of settling Armenians in Syria in order to assure himself of a source of cheap, easily exploitable labour for his Syrian oil pipeline project.[63]

Khanjian's broadside was the beginning of a campaign that the Soviet press waged against Gulbenkian in the following months. Via Gulbenkian, the Soviet leaders were targeting the AGBU's new orientation. But it is also possible that different factions in the Soviet Armenian establishment were settling their own scores by way of these attacks. During this period, Stalin was moving to reinforce his positions in the Soviet hierarchy, and conducting purges of all those likely to contest his power. The Armenian Communist Party was not unaffected by this context. Eduard Melkonian analyses changing attitudes to the AGBU in the context of a struggle between Ter Gabrielian and Khanjian, leaders of rival factions in the Armenian Party. He points out that First Secretary Khanjian's 1931 diatribe against the AGBU was an implicit attack on his rival Ter Gabrielian who had met with the 'imperialist agent' Gulbenkian a few weeks earlier in Paris. Melkonian contends that this represented Khanjian's attempt to 'bolster his position vis-à-vis the country's other leading politicians' at a time when every Soviet leader was at pains publicly to affirm his loyalty to Soviet ideology and to Stalin.[64] The resignation of the AGBU's president followed the next year. On 22 April 1932, he sent the central board a letter announcing that he was laying down his post. All efforts of the AGBU's officers to persuade him to reconsider proved in vain.

Conclusion

After this *coup de théâtre*, Yerevan's criticisms of the AGBU seem to have petered out. The Soviet Armenian regime was probably conscious that it was not possible to control the diaspora and its resources through its overseas agents, in particular the HOK committees. Attempts made in this regard in the 1920s failed, and the AGBU continued to constitute the wealthiest Armenian association maintaining solid relations with potential donors. The central board of the AGBU, for its part, monitored the development of projects in Armenia, for it continued to believe that reconstructing the country called for sacrifices on its part. Thus, the cooperation between these two sides was very likely based on such considerations.

From the outset, the AGBU had been ready to seek compromises in order to meet Soviet requirements and to continue its relations with this unusual partner. While the AGBU during the post-genocide period focused its activities in the Middle East and Greece on relief to refugees and orphans, in Soviet Armenia it complied with Soviet conditions and started to invest in other development projects too, like building new villages, city districts, irrigation canals, etc. Some well-publicised successes in the fields of culture, industry and agriculture in Armenia strengthened the conviction of AGBU leaders that they had chosen the right line of action.

This conviction is clearly reflected in the report submitted by two AGBU representatives, Léon Guerdan and Arshak Chopanian, on their return from a mission to Yerevan late in 1932, where they had taken part in the election of the new Armenian Catholicos of Echmiadzin. Guerdan described his meetings with Khanjian and Ter Gabrielian as 'extremely interesting', and called the Party's First Secretary, who had launched his unrestrained polemic against Gulbenkian a year earlier, a 'forceful personality' and 'the Armenian Stalin', an epithet that, in the USSR of the early 1930s, counted as a high praise.[65] Guerdan concluded with a summary of Ter Gabrielian's comments on the AGBU's role in the reconstruction of Armenia: 'With or without us', said Guerdan, 'this work will go on; we will be the more honoured if it goes on with our help'.[66]

The two AGBU representatives had doubtless been unable to make a thorough assessment of Armenia's socio-economic situation in the course of their short stay in the country. There is every reason to believe that these two high-ranking AGBU officials' travels in Armenia were closely monitored, and that they were given the kind of guided tour reserved for the many 'friends' of the USSR who had to be convinced of the existence of a Soviet miracle. These and many other reports that arrived on the desks of the central board in Paris were characterised by their conformity to the Soviet order and by their lack of critical reflections on the local situation. They thus contrasted sharply with the disappointment and anger expressed by other visitors to the Soviet Union, for example, André Gide in *Retour de l'U.R.S.S.*[67] Probably, in AGBU representatives' eyes the preservation of Armenian identity in this last segment of the Armenian homeland overshadowed all other concerns, including emerging patterns of state violence.[68] It is interesting to note here that, in contemporary politics, this same attitude of consent and acquiescence was to become in many regards the rule among all the classical diasporan political parties and associations (ironically both the AGBU and the ARF) vis-à-vis their relations with the Republic of Armenia.

In 1936, the shock waves of the purge reached Soviet Armenia. Khanjian, the first victim, was executed in July 1936. Mass arrests and the execution of the Party's old elite began the following year. The construction programme initiated by the AGBU in Armenia was soon brought to a halt. On 7 October 1937, the Party leadership in Yerevan even decided to dissolve the HOK and the local AGBU chapter. On 8 December, this decision was made public in the Party organ *Soviet Armenia*. It was now clear that the AGBU could no longer engage in any activities whatsoever in Soviet Armenia. Haykaz Garakeuzian, its official representative in Yerevan, was arrested and murdered in July 1938.[69] Such a murder was the last message the Soviet regime sent to the ABGU Paris.

Notes

1 See M. Hovanessian, *Le lien communautaire: Trois générations d'Arméniens* (Paris: Armand Colin, 1992); R. Panossian, *The Armenians: From Kings and Priests to Merchants and Commissars* (London: Hurst, 2006); R. Kévorkian, L. Nordiguian and V. Tachjian (eds), *Les Arméniens 1917–1939: La quête d'un refuge* (Beirut: Presses de l'Université Saint-Joseph, 2006); N. Migliorino, *(Re)constructing Armenia in Lebanon and Syria: Ethno-Cultural Diversity and the State in the Aftermath of a Refugee Crisis* (New York: Berghahn Books, 2008).
2 The Dashnaktsutiun party was the dominant force in the First Republic of Armenia. It was established in 1890 in Tiflis. It became the most significant Armenian political party operating mainly in the Ottoman Empire, Tsarist Russia and Persia, as well as having branches worldwide.
3 K. Tololyan, 'Exile Governments in the Armenian Polity', in Y. Shain (ed.), *Governments-in-Exile in Contemporary World Politics* (New York: Routledge, 1991), pp. 166–87; K. Tölölyan, 'Rethinking Diaspora(s): Stateless Power in the Transnational Moment', *Diaspora: A Journal of Transnational Studies* 5:1 (1996), 3–36; Panossian, *The Armenians*, pp. 294–95, 301–3, 366–71; V. Sahakyan, 'Between Host-Countries and Homeland: Institutions, Politics and Identities in the Post-Genocide Armenian Diaspora (1920s to 1980s)' (PhD dissertartion, University of Michigan, 2015), pp. 171–3.
4 For details see A. Ter Minassian, *La République d'Arménie: 1918–1920* (Bruxelles: Éditions Complexe, 1989); C. Mouradian, *De Staline à Gorbatchev. Histoire d'une république soviétique, l'Arménie* (Paris: Éditions Ramsay, 1990); T. Ter Minassian, *Colporteurs du Komintern: L'Union soviétique et les minorités au Moyen-Orient* (Paris: Presses de Sciences Po, 1997); Panossian, *The Armenians*.
5 See R. Kévorkian and V. Tachjian (eds), *The Armenian General Benevolent Union: One Hundred Years of History, volume I (1906–1940) and volume II (1941–2006)* (Paris: AGBU Central Board of Directors, 2006).
6 *Ibid.*, pp. 17–20.
7 According to a report of July 1923, there were 1,327 orphans living in establishments directly administered by the AGBU. AGBU Central Archives, Cairo. Report sent by Boghos Nubar to the AGBU Cairo office from Paris, 25 July 1923.
8 Archives Bibliothèque Nubar/Paris. Letter from the head office in Cairo to Boghos Nubar in Paris, 29 November 1920, Correspondence of the head office, vol. 42, Cairo, f. 166.
9 Panossian, *The Armenians*, p. 370. See also: T. Nalbantian, 'Understandings of "Repatriation" in the Armenian Literary Scene in Lebanon (1945–1947)', in C. Babikian Assaf, C. Eddé, L. Nordiguian and V. Tachjian (eds), *Les Arméniens du Liban: Cent ans de présence* (Beyrouth: Presses de l'Université Saint-Joseph, 2017), pp. 85–105.
10 Such a discourse echoed the 'repatriation plans' that took place after the Second World War. As Jo Laycock shows, even though the majority of orphans and refugees were originally from former Ottoman territory and had never before set foot in Armenia, this process was, for the most part, referred to as 'repatriation' rather than settlement. This was also true of later movements of diaspora Armenians to the Soviet Republic. J. Laycock, 'Armenian Homelands and Homecomings, 1945–9: The Repatriation of Diaspora Armenians to Soviet Union', *Cultural and Social History* 9:1 (2012), 103–23, 112.
11 Papajanian (1868–1929) was an Armenian from the Caucasus who had served as a member of the Russian Duma; he settled in Paris when the Soviets took power. He had previously been involved in the relief of refugees on the Caucasus front (see Chapter 4). The Armenian

National Delegation (AND) was established in 1912 in order to lobby the European Powers to defend the reform programme in the Eastern provinces of the Ottoman Empire. Boghos Nubar was appointed head of the delegation by the Catholicos Kevork V of Echmiadzin. The AND continued during and after the First World War to operate as a political representation of the Armenians.

12 Arch. Bibl. Nubar/Paris, Archives of the AND, no. 13, Report on Papajanian's mission to Moscow, submitted to the AND, Paris, 16 March 1923.
13 Arch. Bibl. Nubar/Paris, Minutes of the Central Board Meetings (hereafter MCBM), 33rd meeting, 26 May 1923, f. 147.
14 Report on Papajanian's mission to Moscow.
15 Arch. Bibl. Nubar/Paris, MCBM, 34th meeting, 4 May 1923, ff. 152–3.
16 Ibid., f. 153.
17 Arch. Bibl. Nubar/Paris, MCBM, meeting of 26 May 1923, ff. 149–50.
18 In this respect his report echoes the published narrative of Nansen, League of Nation's High Commissioner for Refugees, on his visit to Armenia in 1925. F. Nansen, *Armenia and the Near East* (London: G. Allen & Unwin, 1928).
19 AGBU Archives, Arch. Bibl. Nubar/Paris. Tigran Aslanian, 'Une excursion au paradis communiste: Petrograd, Tiflis, Érivan. Description de voyage, des principes et de leur application, projets d'entreprise', 14 October 1923, Paris, pp. 31–3.
20 Arch. Bibl. Nubar/Paris, MCBM, meeting of 23 November 1923, f. 197.
21 Ibid.
22 Arch. Bibl. Nubar/Paris, MCBM, 45th meeting, 21 December 1923, f. 212.
23 Arch. Bibl. Nubar/Paris, MCBM, 46th meeting, 1 February 1924, ff. 218–19.
24 Arch. Bibl. Nubar/Paris, MCBM, 47th meeting, 25 February 1924, f. 221.
25 Anon., 'H. B. Ě. Miut'yun ev Hayastan (verashinut'yun, nergaght' ev mshakoyt')' [The AGBU and Armenia: Reconstruction, repatriation and culture], *Miutyun*, 13/101, September–October 1924, pp. 65–6; AGBU Archives, Arch. Bibl. Nubar/Paris. Letter no. 23448/46 of 12 April 1924 from the Cairo Executive Committee to B. Nubar, Correspondence of the head office, vol. 62, f. 106.
26 Arch. Bibl. Nubar/Paris, MCBM, 56th meeting, 28 November 1924, f. 256.
27 Arch. Bibl. Nubar/Paris, MCBM, 69th meeting, 1 December 1925, ff. 316–17. Marie Nubar (1855–1925) was the deceased wife of Boghos Nubar.
28 For details on these projects see V. Tachjian, 'The AGBU and Soviet Armenia: The Difficult Task of Working with the Soviet Regime to Reconstruct Armenia', in Kévorkian and Tachjian (eds), *The Armenian General Benevolent Union*, pp. 179–86.
29 Many Armenians were living at that time in extremely precarious conditions in refugee camps across Greece. Few of them had become Greek citizens, a circumstance that, to say the least, left them in an uncertain situation, especially after the Greco-Turkish Exchange of Populations.
30 On this issue, and also on the humanitarian projects undertaken by the League of Nations in Soviet Armenia in close coordination with Fridtjof Nansen, see: C. Skran, *Refugees in Inter-War Europe: The Emergence of a Regime* (Oxford: Clarendon Press, 1995); D. Kévonian, *Réfugiés et diplomatie humanitaire: Les acteurs européens et la scène proche-orientale pendant l'entre-deux-guerres* (Paris: Publications de la Sorbonne, 2004); K. D. Watenpaugh, *Bread from Stones: The Middle East and the Making of Modern Humanitarianism* (Oakland, CA: University of California Press, 2015); N. N. Nercessian, *The City of Orphans: Relief Workers, Commissars and the 'Builders of the New Armenia', Alexandropol/Leninakan, 1919–1931* (Hollis, NH: Hollis Publishing, 2016).

31 Arch. Bibl. Nubar/Paris, MCBM, 82nd meeting, 23 July 1926, f. 377.
32 Arch. Bibl. Nubar/Paris, MCBM, 127th meeting, 12 October 1928, ff. 169–70.
33 Arch. Bibl. Nubar/Paris, MCBM, 171st meeting, 17 April 1930.
34 Associations (*hayrenaktsakan mioutyun*) established in the diaspora each one representing formerly Armenian inhabited towns and villages of the Ottoman Empire. Exiles and their descendants from these places regrouped within such associations and were involved in cultural and educational activities.
35 AGBU Archives, Arch. Bibl. Nubar/Paris. Anon., Nubarashen.
36 Anon., Nubarashen.
37 *Husharar* (organ of the AGBU), 23/168, October 1936, pp. 58–9.
38 Arch. Bibl. Nubar/Paris, MCBM, 319th meeting, 8 October 1936.
39 *Husharar*, 24/171, January 1937, p. 4.
40 Arch. Bibl. Nubar/Paris. Harold Buxton (secretary of the Lord Mayor's Fund), letter from London to H. Morgenthau, 26 March 1924.
41 On this subject see: Kévonian, *Réfugiés et diplomatie humanitaire*; J. Laycock, *Imagining Armenia: Orientalism, Ambiguity and Intervention, 1879–1925* (Manchester: Manchester University Press, 2009), pp. 207–9.
42 Arch. Bibl. Nubar/Paris, MCBM, meeting of 1 December 1925, f. 318.
43 Anon., *H.B.Ĕ.M. Teghekagir kedronakan varzhakan zhoghovi 1926 tareshrjani* [Report of 1926 from the AGBU's Central Board], *Miutyun*, 16/120, November–December 1927, Paris, p. 93.
44 Anon., 'Secours au profit des réfugiés', Arch. Bibl. Nubar/Paris.
45 *Miutyun*, 18/127, January 1929, Paris, p. 104.
46 Arch. Bibl. Nubar/Paris, MCBM, 187th meeting, 10 October 1930, f. 1047.
47 Arch. Bibl. Nubar/Paris, MCBM, 215th meeting, 17 September 1931, f. 1209.
48 Arch. Bibl. Nubar/Paris, MCBM, 226th meeting, 21 January 1932, f. 1258.
49 Arch. Bibl. Nubar/Paris, MCBM, 317th meeting, 15 May 1936.
50 *Miutyun*, 25/179, May–June 1936, p. 35.
51 Panossian, *The Armenians*, p. 368.
52 About the role of the HOK as a Soviet political agent in the diaspora see Mouradian, *L'Arménie*, pp. 309–11; Sahakyan, 'Between Host-Countries and Homeland', pp. 183–6.
53 K. Mikayelian, *Hay zhoghovrdakan harstut'iunnern artasahmanum (ktakner, nuiratwut'iwnnerĕ ev hasarakakan kumarner)* [*The People's Wealth in the Diaspora (Legacies, Donations, Public Funds)*] (Moscow, 1928), p. 41 (cited in G. Dallakian, *H. B. Ĕ. Miut'yun nakhagah C. Gulbenkiani hrazharakani harts'I shurj*) [*On the Resignation of K. Gulbenkian, President of the AGBU*] (Yerevan: Publisher unknown 1996), p. 27; A. Hovhannisian, *Gaghut'ahay khndirner* [*Diasporan Armenian Problems*] (Yerevan: Pethrat, 1925), p. 22; V. Hamazaspian, *Haykakan Baregortsakan ĕndhanur Miut'yun ev Hayastanĕ* [*The AGBU and Armenia*] (Yerevan: Tigran Medz Publisher, 2001).
54 Arch. Bibl. Nubar/Paris, MCBM, 79th meeting, 19 May 1926, ff. 353–4.
55 Ibid.
56 Arch. Bibl. Nubar/Paris, MCBM, 103rd meeting, 14 October 1927, f. 525.
57 Arch. Bibl. Nubar/Paris, MCBM, 95th meeting, 11 May 1927, ff. 450–1.
58 Arch. Bibl. Nubar/Paris. MCBM, 119th meeting, 22 June 1928, f. 114. We have little biographical information on Garakeuzian. He was born in 1882 to a wealthy Trebizond family involved in the tobacco trade, moved to Odessa very early in life and settled in Yerevan with his family in 1923 (E. Melkonian, *Haykakan Baregortsakan ĕndhanur Miut'yun Khorhrdayin Haystanum*

1923–1937 [*The Armenian General Benevolent Union in Soviet Armenia, 1923–1937*] (Yerevan: Noyan Tapan Publisher, 1999), p. 173).
59 *Husharar*, 23/168, October 1936, New York, pp. 58–9; *Husharar*, 24/171, January 1937, p. 4.
60 Arch. Bibl. Nubar/Paris, I. Karapetian, Secretary of the Council of commissars, note of 10 December 1932 from Yerevan to Haygaz Karageuzian; Karageuzian, telegram no. 328, 10 December 1932 from Yerevan to Maleziann.
61 Born in Istanbul in 1869 and died in Lisbon in 1955, Gulbenkian was one of the most important figures of the oil industry in the early 1920s. He was also a philanthropist.
62 Dallakian, *On the Resignation of K. Gulbenkian, President of the AGBU*, p. 48.
63 *Ibid*.
64 Melkonian, *The Armenian General Benevolent Union in Soviet Armenia*, p. 103.
65 Arch. Bibl. Nubar/Paris, MCBM, 244th meeting, 7 December 1932, f. 1348.
66 *Ibid.*, f. 1351. See also: Léon Guerdan's Personal Papers.
67 A. Gide, *Retour de l'U.R.S.S., suivi de retouches à mon retour de l'U.R.S.S.* (Paris: Gallimard, 1950).
68 The Stalinist purges in Soviet Armenia remain understudied, for an overview see R. G. Suny, *Looking Toward Ararat: Armenia in Modern History* (Bloomington, IN: Indiana University Press, 1993), pp. 150–61. See also the new research project, *Armenia Totalitaris*, www.armeniatotalitaris.am/?lang=en (accessed 23 March 220).
69 Melkonian, *The Armenian General Benevolent Union in Soviet Armenia*, pp. 305–8.

8

Tremor and change: Humanitarian interventions after the 1988 earthquake in Armenia

Katja Doose

In 'terms of value, the range of donors, and the scale of the logistics' the Armenian earthquake that shook the earth on 7 December 1988 and took about 25,000 lives was considered by the International Federation of Red Cross and Red Crescent Societies as 'one of the largest international relief operations ever staged'.[1] The Soviet and international response to the earthquake opened a new era in the humanitarian age, in quasi-anticipation of the subsequent post-Cold War developments.[2] In the medical literature the earthquake 'has become a code word for disaster only second to the attack on the World Trade Center'.[3] Taking the assumed 'turning point' issue aside, this chapter questions how the Soviet state and international actors dealt with the novelty of openness and how they engaged with the newly found 'humanitarian space'.[4] In the Armenian case this space served as a ground for the Soviet state to claim influence and international recognition and for the Armenian diaspora to reshape its ideas of the Armenian 'homeland'.

This chapter will first explore why the Soviet government allowed Western humanitarian aid into the Soviet Union and how it was framed by domestic political communication. Following this, it will look into the motives of the West, in particular of the Armenian diaspora, for getting involved in humanitarian aid. Finally, the chapter explores how the Armenian diaspora shaped the path of Armenia's independence. Based on archival sources and interviews from Russia, Armenia and the United States, I argue that the disaster offered the diaspora the opportunity to regain agency and to break the re-enactment of victimhood. This empowerment resulted in a power transfer at local level through the involvement of the Armenian diaspora in local politics prior to the demise of the Soviet Union, which happened despite the fact that allowing Western aid was originally aimed at boosting the image of the Communist Party and at preventing the collapse of the Soviet empire.

The politics of aid during the Cold War

The emerging history of humanitarian aid has shown that the humanitarian space is not devoid of politicisation, although humanitarianism often claims to be apolitical.[5] Much is known already about the way industrialised countries have provided humanitarian aid to countries in Africa, Latin America, Asia and, after 1991, to the countries of the former Eastern Bloc.[6] However, there is still insufficient research on the Eastern side of the narrative, on how humanitarian aid was used or refused by the two superpowers before and during the Cold War. While Soviet aid to its citizens continued throughout the whole existence of the Soviet Union, the provision of aid from the USA and Europe to the Soviet Union came very quickly to a halt in the late 1920s, briefly resumed during the Second World War and then entirely stopped until the 1988 earthquake in Armenia.

The history of Western aid to the new Communist empire was short-lived and highly political. In the early 1920s, when Russia experienced famine, many Western governments organised famine relief for Russia with the intention to weaken the new Soviet regime by undermining communist ideology.[7] In the end, however, the opposite effect was achieved, because the Bolsheviks used Western humanitarian aid as a cement for their own legitimacy. Trotsky denounced the American relief effort as a way for the US government to dump US grain surpluses and to protect the Russian bourgeoisie.[8] In the years that followed, Stalin completely distrusted foreign philanthropy, which he considered as spying. As a result, when an earthquake struck Armenia in October 1926, the Soviet government refused foreign offers of assistance and barely tolerated the activities of organisations already present in Armenia in response to the Genocide such as the American Near East Relief.[9] By 1927, all Western relief aid to Armenia had definitely stopped.[10] In the meantime, the Soviet government itself invested heavily in the provision of aid to other countries, especially as the Cold War emerged. From 1945 on, both superpowers were involved in development aid and later humanitarian aid. Aid became an instrument of rivalry and ideological reward between the superpowers and their sphere of influence.[11]

From 1921 on, humanitarian aid was managed and distributed by the national societies of the Red Cross and Red Crescent of each Soviet Republic, which eventually formed the 'Union of Red Cross and Red Crescent Societies of the USSR' (Soviet Red Cross) in 1923. It set up long-term hospitals, provided medical experts such as in Ethiopia, but also provided short-term medical aid in the case of epidemics in North Korea and China in 1947.[12] At the beginning of the 1960s, when television increased worldwide interest in disaster response, the Soviet Red Cross also sent medical teams to Somalia, Congo and other countries to treat disaster victims, but its main mode of intervention consisted of sending goods, not rescue teams.[13] Twice the Soviet Red Cross also intervened, although marginally, with material assistance after floods in the West: in 1953 for the 'Big Flood' in Great Britain and in 1962 in

Spain.[14] In general, both the United States and the Soviet Union avoided intervention in the enemy's disaster zones and preferred to invest in their own perceived or potential allies. Yugoslavia's non-alignment led to the first Cold War competition in humanitarian aid on the same soil since both the USSR and the USA intervened in response to the 1963 earthquake in Skopje.[15]

This political economy of aid gained further momentum during the 1970s as a result of a combination of several factors, among them the emergence of a 'third world' of newly independent states and of new actors representing a civil society with global ambitions. These emerging relationships between relief agencies, governments and journalists during the 1980s constituted what came to be known as the 'development and aid industry'.[16] It is in this context one should view the humanitarian aid provided to the victims of the 1988 Armenian earthquake.

Receiving help from the enemy: Soviet motives and framing of Western aid

The reforms of Mikhail Gorbachev laid the foundation for what would become a turning point for international humanitarian aid as well as for the response to natural disasters in the Soviet Union.[17] Previous Soviet leaders had responded to disasters but without revealing details to the Soviet public or admitting to any wrongdoings that led to the vulnerability of the victims. Understanding that disasters may harm ruler legitimacy because the origins and consequences of disasters reveal the weaknesses and ineptitude of the state, Soviet censorship strictly controlled most information regarding disasters of all kinds.[18] However, from 1985 onwards, disasters occurring on Soviet territory were shown on Soviet TV and, for the first time, the voices of victims were made public.[19] This change was politically necessary for the new leadership. In order for his economic and political reforms of *glasnost* and *perestroika* to be accepted by his fellow party members and by the Soviet public, Gorbachev wanted to expose some of the weaknesses of the regime so that they could be tackled. By 1988, this meant showing that the Soviet Union not only needed help from within, but also from abroad.[20]

However, most help arrived from other Soviet Republics. When earthquakes had struck Armenia in 1926, the Turkmen capital Ashgabat in 1948 or Tashkent in 1966, medical staff from the neighbouring Soviet Republics had come upon official request to treat victims.[21] For the Armenian earthquake, the Soviet state organised about 1,000 relief flights, packed 27,000 train waggons full of food, clothes and other relief goods and mobilised some 19,500 employees from 500 different institutions for the rescue efforts.[22] Blankets or food were collected from Soviet citizens and sent to disaster zones. But before 1988 the disaster zones remained a restricted territory with defined access rules for Soviet journalists as well as for foreigners. Normal Soviet citizens could not have visited a disaster zone and provided aid individually without permission. This was considered and desired to be the government's task only.

While this still held true for the Chernobyl accident in 1986, it changed completely with the earthquake in Armenia, only two years later.[23] Hobby mountaineer clubs came from Ukraine and elsewhere and people from all over the Soviet Union queued to donate blood.[24] Other private individuals sent food, clothing, blankets or money. It was not the magnitude of the disaster that made this possible. Rather, the Soviet regime had changed its attitude towards philanthropy. Throughout the late 1920s and 1930s, all private and religious charities in the Soviet Union had been outlawed. The state considered charity as a remnant of the capitalist system and substituted private or religious efforts with centrally organised solidarity campaigns.[25] Taking care of its citizens was the task of the Soviet state only. As Boris Ionov from the Russian Red Cross remembered in an interview: 'In the Soviet Union, everything was regulated. Even the feelings of private goodwill.'[26] However, after decades of interdiction, private charity organisations had been allowed to work again in summer 1987.[27] Allowing citizens to participate in philanthropy and humanitarian work fitted well with Gorbachev's idea of a new and open Soviet Union.

In the Soviet press, aid from within was used to create a sense of unity as often observed elsewhere after disasters.[28] However, the need for unity was especially pressing due to the ethnic tensions arising in almost every Soviet republic. When the earthquake struck, the Karabakh conflict between Armenia and Azerbaijan was intensifying. The aid influx from all over the Soviet Union was thus fostered by the Soviet leadership to bind the republics back to the Union and to peace. With newspaper headlines such as 'We do not leave our brothers alone in the hours of need' or 'Brotherly solidarity', Soviet journalists tried to convey a feeling of togetherness in the name of the government. By referring to other Soviet disasters such as the earthquakes in Ashgabat 1948 and Tashkent 1966 (interestingly not Armenia 1926), it was suggested that the Soviet people had already overcome difficulties by sticking together. Blood donations in particular proved to be a handy metaphor for Soviet unity, as a quotation from Soviet daily *Pravda* shows: 'whether it is the blood of a Tatar or of a Russian, of a Ukrainian or a Belarussian, is not important, because we have all got the same blood.'[29] From an exposure of the state's inadequacies before *perestroika*, aid was now used to boost the image of a strong, unified state.

The decision to allow humanitarian aid from abroad marked a turning point as the Soviet Union had last received aid from abroad to sustain war efforts until 1945. In 1988, the Politburo did not immediately decide to open the borders, although offers of humanitarian help and letters of condolences flooded in from abroad. After thorough consideration, most Western relief agencies were authorised to deploy their humanitarian interventions in Soviet Armenia thirty-three hours after the earth had trembled.[30] Little is known about the process that led to this decision, but the time-lapse of thirty-three hours between the earthquake and the Soviet greenlighting of foreign aid is indicative of the difficulties. Nevertheless, in the following weeks the airports in Yerevan and Leninakan turned into international hubs. The United Nations Disaster Relief Organization (UNDRO) report of January 1989 sums up that Soviet Armenia received 348 flights with relief from at least forty-five countries. Most international support to Armenia was in kind and in service, for example about 300 rescue workers and doctors from eighteen countries arrived within the first four weeks. The majority of governmental and non-governmental aid was channelled through either the League of Red Cross and Red Crescent Societies or national Red Cross societies, which helped either directly or through the Soviet Alliance of Red Cross and Red Crescent Societies.[31] Furthermore, the report stresses that 'a large portion of help came from local communities, Armenian groups, private citizens and religious groups abroad'.[32]

Mounting a broad international response to a disaster happening anywhere in the world was part of the zeitgeist of the 1980s and of an aid sector reaching an 'industrial' phase as non-governmental organisations proliferated and agencies began to engage in competition over funds and projects, accompanied by intense media involvement.[33] The famine in Ethiopia, for instance, triggered wide-ranging media attention all over the world and has been recognised as the 'archetypal media famine'.[34] In response to the 1985 earthquake in Mexico, during which 5,000 people died, a total of 177 international flights from thirty-one countries were registered.[35] But the Armenian case was different again, because this time it was the Soviet Union that opened its borders to humanitarian aid workers, waiving visa restrictions regardless of origins or ideological commitments.

Humanitarian cooperation across the Iron Curtain provided a perfect opportunity for the General Secretary Mikhail Gorbachev to improve his image at home and in the West as the reformer eager to end the Cold War. On the very day of the earthquake, Gorbachev had just given his speech in New York at the General Assembly of the United Nations in which he had announced a significant reduction of Soviet troops. Part of his *perestroika* reforms were to change the image of the Soviet Union. The Politburo wanted the Soviet Union to become 'in the eyes of the world community a completely new country'.[36] Allowing humanitarian aid was intended to boost Western trust in the willingness of the Soviet government to end the Cold War, which would have stimulated the suffering Soviet economy. At home, Soviet journalists praised Gorbachev in their articles, saying that it was only thanks to him that Soviet citizens did not have to 'cringe anymore at the sight of a French soldier with a dog'.[37]

For this national and international reshaping of the Soviet image to work, appropriate reporting in the Soviet press was required. Up until 1987, Soviet newspapers were filled with negative descriptions of the West as wealthy, racist, violent and ignorant towards human rights abuses – the opposite of the Soviet Union.[38] But coinciding with the nuclear disarmament discussions of 1986 and 1987, which smoothed the relationship between both superpowers, there was a change. As the newspaper *Izvestiia* reported in an article from March 1987, 'It's time to learn mutual understanding!', the tone changed in order to 'improve the international psychological atmosphere'.[39] Henceforth, the Soviet press portrayed the United States increasingly as a country the Soviets could learn from. Writing about the international humanitarian aid was a tightrope walk for Soviet journalists. While the Western press often used reporting about relief in Armenia to boost the image of the West and to illustrate the supposed backwardness of the Soviet Union, the Soviet journalists had to tread more carefully in their descriptions of the relief work. Inasmuch as the temporary opening of the Soviet borders offered an opportunity to convey messages of a new and friendlier foreign policy, the news articles could not depict the changes as a sign of inability of the Soviet government to take care of its people on its own. At the same time, they also needed to portray the aid as something positive and gratefully received in order not to disgruntle Western donors. In consequence, Soviet news articles emphasised the fact that the help was offered by the West and not demanded by the East. Headlines in *Izvestiia* such as '... we grieve, we condole, we ask you to accept our help – this is how the planet reacted to the calamity' or statements by US-American aid workers, who apparently thanked the Soviet government for the opportunity to 'reduce the suffering of thousands of people' portrayed the West as the petitioner and the Soviet Union as the generous granter.[40]

The Armenian diaspora: shaping local politics through humanitarian aid

The Soviet donor campaign tailored for Western countries targeted one group especially: the Armenian diaspora. One can actually argue that an earthquake happening in a different Soviet Republic, with weaker diasporic connections – Georgia for example – would have triggered a much smaller international reaction. And as the diaspora became entangled in local politics, its motives and actions quickly altered the power dynamics in an illustration of the complex, unforeseen and often unintended impact of humanitarian interventions on the social fabric and on power structures.

The involvement of the Armenian diaspora in Soviet politics was not a new phenomenon in the 1980s. As Vahé Tachjian has discussed in the previous chapter, during the 1920s and 1930s they were deeply engaged with the resettlement in newly established Soviet Armenia of Armenians fleeing the Genocide.[41] In order to manage its own relations with the diaspora, the Hayastani Ognutian Komite (HOK, Committee for Armenian Assistance) was created in September 1921. According to historian Razmik Panossian, the HOK had the sole purpose of securing material support for Soviet Armenia from diaspora communities.[42] The Armenian General Benevolent Union (AGBU), an Armenian charity organisation founded in 1906, acted as a major representative of the diaspora and provided in cooperation with the Soviet government relief for refugees and contributed to infrastructure projects.[43] These efforts through the Armenian diaspora continued after 1945 and helped them frame Armenia as a national homeland. In the Soviet Union it shaped the perceptions of 'the diaspora as a resource for social and economic development' as historian Jo Laycock argues.[44]

These perceptions were rearticulated in the 1980s and gained new momentum with Gorbachev's economic reforms. Reports and letters exchanged between the Soviet Armenian and the central Soviet ministries of Foreign Affairs from the years 1985 to 1988 reveal that the Soviet government aimed to increasingly tap into the financial potential of the Armenian diaspora. The foreign ministry of Soviet Armenia intended to 'observe the developments in the foreign Armenian communities, with the aim of a possible utilisation of the political and economic potential' in order to enable the 'import of foreign capital and technology'.[45] From 1987, the Soviet Armenian Ministry of Foreign Affairs received numerous proposals from Armenian diaspora businessmen and companies to form joint ventures and joint-stock companies. Considering the state of the Soviet economy, the authorities in Moscow wanted these proposals to be followed 'vigorously', as stated in their response to the 1987 report from the Soviet Armenian Ministry of Foreign Affairs.[46]

The Armenian diaspora actively involved itself in the relief operation for different reasons than those of other Western groups. As diaspora Armenians were present all over the world and had trans- and intra-state networks, they were able to respond both with speed and volume. Armenian diaspora charity organisations such as the AGBU, the Armenian Assembly of America (AAA) and the Armenian Missionary Associations of America provided three airlifts with eighty tonnes of medical supplies and forty to fifty physicians. AGBU airlifted forty-nine patients to US American hospitals and provided $2 million for stone-cutting equipment to expedite house construction, while the AAA raised $4 million for relief. The Armenian Relief Society (ARS), active since the beginning of the twentieth century like AGBU, provided another fifty-six tonnes of medicines and twenty hemodialysis machines.[47]

The ethnic affiliation added to the motives behind diaspora involvement in the response to the earthquake. Helping Soviet Armenians mitigated some diaspora Armenians' perception of their own victimhood, which had been shaped by the Genocide and its aftermaths. As one young French Armenian explained, rushing to Armenia helped him to abandon 'his victimhood to make himself a relief worker' instead.[48] Many diaspora Armenians donated because they identified with the suffering of the victims, even if they neither had close connections to Armenia nor spoke Armenian. The majority of the diaspora were from the former Ottoman Empire and did not have roots in the territory of the Soviet Republic but donated out of grief for the past stemming from a transgenerational traumatic experience:[49] 'I went because it made me think of the losses the Armenian people suffered in the Genocide. As if that wasn't enough, nature was adding her bit', recounted an Armenian psychiatrist working for *Médecins sans frontières*.[50] As the sociologist and anthropologist Didier Fassin suggests, a current trauma reactivated an old one, people were recognising a debt.[51] Thus, the images of the earthquake area generated heavy feelings of guilt for their own current life conditions among diaspora Armenians, as one woman explained in an interview: 'I associate [the earthquake with] what my parents had gone through as children. The genocide. Every Armenian has a complex, they have a guilt feeling in a way. Why have my mother and my father gone through that? And now I am living in this wonderful land and I enjoy all these wonderful things. Why is it? You see? You don't verbalize that. But it is in the back of your head. Always.'[52]

The second generation of the Armenian diaspora in the United States spoke 'of its gratitude for the parents' sacrifices, [...] and of their rebellion against and eventual acceptance of the guilt of survival'.[53] Similar findings exist for the third generation: young diaspora Armenians in a Los Angeles high school surveyed just after the earthquake, for instance, expressed a sense of conflict between their comfortable lives and 'the contrasting deprivation of their Soviet-dominated brethren'.[54] This contrast increased their enthusiasm for helping and 'strongly motivated them to want to share their wealth with their less fortunate nationals'.[55] In an interview a woman explained her urge to help: 'Everybody [from the diaspora] has this guilt feeling. A friend just came this morning. We said we had to do something. In some schools they have no water, no heating. We feel guilty. We should be doing something. This is the Armenian feeling and it is there. Every morning, when we get up, we have an argument. And it will be about Armenia.'[56]

Doing something gave her and her friends the opportunity to break the re-enactment of their perceived victimhood. Interestingly, some diaspora Armenians projected guilt as a motivation onto other, non-diaspora organisations and communities who provided aid. A French Armenian wondered thus 'whether this [humanitarian] response does not originate from the unconscious desire of the international community to redeem itself of having abandoned the Armenians at the time of the genocide as well as later for the recognition of it'.[57] Another was sure, that 'the genocide belongs to the bad conscience of the world'.[58]

Diaspora Armenians also expressed other motivations. These same teenagers, for example, acted out of group pressure 'to render as much help as possible' and found that 'everyone should be willing to sacrifice to the utmost for the common cause'.[59] Other American Armenians such as the physician Vartiter went to Soviet Armenia after the earthquake to preserve the Armenian nation: 'This is the last place that Armenians are living together. [...] there is no other foothold than this little Armenia. Squeezed. No Sea. No boundary with France.'[60] Going to Armenia meant for her to save her 'homeland' from more devastation and destruction. Similarly, when asked about what should happen to orphaned children, the teenagers agreed that the 'national and religious character of the Armenians' was to be preserved. To bring Soviet Armenian orphans to the United States was considered by them as a loss to the Armenian people and therefore not acceptable.[61]

While many survivors complained about the insufficiency of state support in the aftermath of the disaster, they had high expectations of the Armenian diaspora whose aid was even considered 'normal' if not taken for granted from such wealthy brothers.[62] As Carolann Najarian, a US physician of Armenian origin who facilitated medical relief to Armenia for many years through an NGO, put it in her memoirs: 'People held us to a standard much more exacting than the one for non-Armenian relief workers. They assumed we could do anything we wanted; we simply had to want to do it. [...] When we said that we could not help with something, it was sometimes interpreted as not caring.'[63] However, these expectations were perhaps produced by the Armenian diaspora themselves. The long-lasting involvement of the Armenian diaspora in Soviet Armenian affairs over several decades had already shaped perceptions of the diaspora as a financial resource, which could be tapped into any time.

Many considered the earthquake to inaugurate a new relationship between homeland and the diaspora. According to Ronald Suny, there were three ways to live Armenian identity until the earthquake struck: forgetting about it or wishing to do so, because it was laden with too many painful memories and stigma; cultivating it relentlessly decade after decade; or constantly oscillating between the two – as was the case for the majority of diaspora Armenians.[64] This made it acceptable for them to integrate while, at the same time, maintaining their Armenian identity. The earthquake helped many to remember that there was an Armenia, to which they often did not have any personal relationship, because the Soviet Armenia was not the one their ancestors escaped from, but it recovered a feeling of Armenian identity, as the US historian of Armenian origin Richard Hovannisian stated in an interview: '[...] People, who had not felt or been Armenian for 50 years suddenly discovered that they were Armenians. [...] Everybody who had given up being identified ethnically, suddenly wanted to be identified as an Armenian.'[65] In fact, the suffering they perceived through the images on TV and its accounts helped some to feel Armenian. As an Armenian French physician explained: 'Until then, I had not suffered like an Armenian, but I needed to suffer to feel Armenian.'[66]

The humanitarian involvement of the diaspora soon morphed into a desire to permanently impact social and political developments in Soviet Armenia. When, in spring 1988, up to one million Soviet Armenians demonstrated for the integration of Nagorny Karabakh to Soviet Armenia, most Armenians outside of the Soviet Union remained silent or even officially asked for these protests to stop.[67] The protests in Yerevan and Stepanakert [Xankəndi] had come as a surprise to Armenians who had almost no knowledge of the developments inside the Soviet Armenian society.[68] Many in the diaspora were afraid that Soviet Armenia would lose its protection from the central government in Moscow if the protests continued with an increasingly anti-Soviet approach. Moscow's protection seemed like the best compromise to the majority.

The idea of an independent Armenia outside of the USSR felt uncomfortable to many in the diaspora communities. All three diaspora parties, including the Armenian Revolutionary Federation (ARF, Dashnaktsutiun), which had for decades been fighting for Armenia's independence and had been extremely anti-Soviet, agreed that Soviet Armenia should remain within the Soviet Union as the most efficient protection from Turkey. The humanitarian aid influx gave the Armenian diaspora the chance to shape the political dynamics in the republic. Or so they thought. Each diaspora party did so first by establishing offices of its diaspora charity organisations. In winter 1989 the Armenian Assembly of America (which officially belonged to the ARF) opened an office in Yerevan. A few months later, in the summer of 1990, the Armenian Revolutionary Party followed with an office. Around the same time, the AGBU (linked to the liberal Ramkavar Party) and the Armenian Relief Society of the Hunchakian Party also opened offices.[69]

In doing so, the Armenian diaspora tried to shape trajectories of change from Soviet Armenia to an independent state by reconnecting with the Soviet Armenian people and (successfully) aiming for impact in local decision-making processes. Indeed, just as the Communist government before had intended to use the financial resources of the diaspora, the leaders of the new government under Levon Ter-Petrosyan based Armenia's future on expected diaspora aid. In his famous article 'It's time to jump off the train', written in May 1990, Vazgen Manukian, at the time a political partner of Levon Ter-Petrosyan, explained why Armenia could not be part of the Soviet Union any more. The Soviet economy, he reasoned, 'will continue to roll down this economical abyss for a long time to come, pulling us [Armenians] with it and offering no prospect of development. [...] When on our own, we could also pull out much faster. Here, our sovereignty, our spirit of initiative, and our diaspora will play important roles.'[70] In order to create 'new guarantees for the existence' of an independent Armenia, Levon Ter-Petrosyan, in a speech in October 1990, referred to 'the diaspora, whose material, political, and intellectual capabilities can be of essential help to the welfare of Armenia'.[71]

Armenians took these ideas to the street. Between 1988 and 1990, demonstrations in Yerevan were accompanied by the slogan 'Together with the diaspora'.[72] Like their leaders, the people on the street assumed that 'the Armenian diaspora and the foreign capital' would help to rebuild a country that would then 'base itself on the help of the foreign Armenian diaspora'.[73] Many Armenians believed that Armenia could later live off selling the 'Jermuk' mineral water or minerals with the diaspora acting as cooperation and trading partner.[74] In addition, Armenia was to be declared a 'free trade zone' in which the Armenian diaspora could invest as much as it pleased, an idea that was first developed by Suren Arutyunyan, the former head of the Armenian Communist Party.[75] These high expectations were based not only on the experiences of the humanitarian aid Soviet Armenians had received from the diaspora, but also on fantasised ideas about the life enjoyed by Armenians living abroad.

The declaration of Armenia's sovereignty dated 23 August 1990 made two explicit references to the diaspora. First, it stated that diaspora Armenians had the right to Armenian citizenship, something previously unthinkable under Soviet rule, which confirmed to the diaspora its full-fledged belonging to the Armenian nation.[76] Second, the document emphasised genocide recognition as a key objective for the sovereign Armenian nation – an idea that was more important to diaspora

Armenians. Also, diaspora Armenians soon became part of the new government. Already in 1990, some were allowed to speak in the Armenian Parliament and to express their ideas about the nation.[77] In January 1991, the Armenian American historian Gerard Libaridian became Levon Ter-Petrosyan's closest political advisor. A year later, Levon Ter-Petrosyan nominated Sebough Tashjian, the manager of a Californian energy company, as his Minister for Energy.[78] The most far-reaching decision though was to make Raffi Hovannisian the new Minister of Foreign Affairs. He was a young California-based lawyer, had named his children after towns in eastern Turkey (western Armenia) and was considered an 'original model of the Armenian repatriate: a successful citizen of the diaspora who gives up the good life in pursuit of the meaningful one'.[79] All of these men brought with them a range of foreign employees into the Armenian government. Their numbers may have been small in comparison to Soviet Armenian employees, but it still shows the significant influence the diaspora was able to establish on local politics as a consequence of their humanitarian intervention in 1988.

The relationship between Armenia and its diaspora could not, however, withstand the realities of the post-Soviet period. More and more diaspora politicians had to leave the scene, and the influx of foreign aid decreased quite quickly within a year or two of the earthquake. The dream of an Armenian nation united across continents through the disaster response did not last long. People donated what they had, but many diaspora Armenians went back to their normal lives, keeping loose ties with Armenia for lack of a structure to keep them strongly bound.[80] At the same time the technical and economic cooperation between Armenians in the diaspora and in Armenia very often came to a halt. This was due to the conditions under which Soviet joint ventures could exist, which were not attractive for Western investors and usually came along with heavy corruption.[81]

What had initially fascinated both sides about each other, separated them increasingly to the point that they came to regard each other as strangers. As much as many Armenians were grateful for the aid they had received, they were not always automatically happy about it. When the American University of Armenia for instance opened its doors in Yerevan in September 1991, a substitute for the polytechnic school in Leninakan (today Gyumri) destroyed by the earthquake, some Armenians voiced their dislike of the fact that the classes were going to be taught in English. For some it meant only a repetition and prolongation of the external colonial power, only now it was humanitarianism and not communism that enforced on them its state-(re)building ideology. The writer Rafael Ishkanian lamented in an article that 'Armenian had been second to Russian for 70 years, now it is going to be second after English'. He considered the American university to be a 'mortal blow to Armenia'.[82] He was not the only opponent. Some parliamentarians also questioned the legality of English as a language of instruction even in such foreign institutions.[83]

The Armenian diaspora had aimed at connecting Armenia with the outside world through education in English, but Soviet Armenians, who were about to build a new independent state, seemed to fear the loss of Armenian identity – a fear that should have been familiar for diaspora Armenians. This seemingly small disagreement over language among Armenians in fact perfectly illustrates the difficulty of uniting Armenian with different social, political and cultural traditions, even in the aftermath of a humanitarian disaster.

Conclusion

This chapter has explored how Soviet and diasporic actors implemented, utilised and framed humanitarian aid to Armenia after the 1988 earthquake. It argued that, through humanitarian aid, the people in Soviet Armenia found a new political reference point in the Armenian diaspora, despite the fact that Soviet aid formed 90 per cent of the overall aid contributed. This was due to three reasons. First, the new Soviet humanitarianism that emerged with this earthquake not only gave the Soviet state an opportunity to improve its relationships with Western governments and to increase its credibility. It also provided opportunities for forming new networks or refreshing old ones between Soviet Armenians and people in the West. Soviet press campaigns that aimed to unite the East with the West and to shape a transnational nationhood contributed unintentionally to the construction of a global Armenian nation state, which included Soviet Armenians as well as diaspora Armenians. Second, the earthquake revealed the lack of security and state care felt at the time by Soviet Armenians. The way the Politburo of the Communist Party in Moscow dealt with the sharpening Karabakh conflict and the violence towards Armenians in Soviet Azerbaijan led Armenians to seek an alternative outside of the Soviet Union, which presented itself in the shape of foreign relief workers. Armenians turning away from the Soviet Union, despite the destruction and the Soviet aid received, illustrates how low the trust in the state's ability to provide security was. And third, the dedication to relief work of the Armenian diaspora, who had a very strong personal and historical connection to the tragedy, stemming from their own experience of the Genocide and associated feelings of guilt. Their engagement in earthquake relief gave them the opportunity to break the re-enactment of their perceived victimhood. As a result of this unusually tight connection in comparison to the wider humanitarian aid community, Soviet Armenians based their hopes on the financial and political support of the diaspora for the time after their possible independence. But the duality of the Armenian diaspora's position in the Armenian nation-building process contributed rather to instability in the new country as it sparked conflicts over the politics of the recognition of the Genocide and, later, over the solution to the Karabakh conflict. The compounded effects of both the earthquake and the conflict shaped perceptions of the Armenian diaspora as both a benevolent humanitarian donor and a force that would continue to influence Armenian politics in years to come.

Notes

1 Y. Aysan, S. Kilde, E. Ricci, T. Schorr and R. Stephenson, *An Evaluation of Red Cross and Red Crescent Federation Response to the Armenian Earthquake of 7 December 1988*, prepared by the Armenia Earthquake Evaluation Team for the International Federation of Red Cross and Red Crescent Societies (Geneva, 1992), p. 3.
2 K. Watenpaugh, 'Between Communal Survival and National Aspiration: Armenian Genocide Refugees, the League of Nations and the Practices of Interwar Humanitarianism', in C. Schayegh and A. Arsan (eds), *The Routledge Handbook of the History of the Middle East Mandates* (London: Routledge, 2015), pp. 41–61, p. 67; M. Barnett, *Empire of Humanity: A History of Humanitarianism* (Ithaca, NY: Cornell University Press, 2011), p. 29.
3 D. Fassin and R. Rechtman, *The Empire of Trauma: An Inquiry into the Condition of Victimhood* (Princeton, NJ: Princeton University Press, 2009), p. 164.
4 D. Hilhorst and B. J. Jansen, 'Humanitarian Space as Arena: A Perspective on the Everyday Politics of Aid', *Development and Change* 41:6 (2010), 1117–39.
5 F. Terry, *Condemned to Repeat: Paradox of Humanitarian Action* (Ithaca, NY: Cornell University Press, 2002); Hilhorst and Jansen, 'Humanitarian Spaces as Arena'.
6 Barnett, *Empire of Humanity*; J. Paulmann (ed.), *Dilemmas of Humanitarian Aid in the Twentieth Century* (Oxford: Oxford University Press, 2016); A. De Waal, *Famine Crimes: Politics and the Disaster Relief Industry in Africa* (Bloomington, IN: Indiana University Press, 1999); J. R. Wedel, *Collision and Collusion: The Strange Case of Western Aid to Eastern Europe* (New York: Palgrave, 1999).
7 For the UK: L. Mahood and V. Satzewich, 'The Save the Children Fund and the Russian Famine of 1921–23: Claims and Counter-Claims about Feeding "Bolshevik" Children', *Historical Sociology* 22:1 (2009), 55–83; for the US: B. Patenaude, *The Big Show in Bololand: The American Relief Expedition to Soviet Russia in the Famine of 1921* (Stanford, CA: Stanford University Press, 2002); for Germany: P. Weindling, *Epidemics and Genocide in Eastern Europe, 1890–1945* (Oxford: Oxford University Press, 2000).
8 Patenaude, *The Big Show in Bololand*.
9 Weindling, *Epidemics and Genocide in Eastern Europe*, p. 165; H. F. Dahl, *Quisling: A Study in Treachery* (New York: Cambridge University Press, 1999), p. 67.
10 J. Laycock, 'Saving the Remnant or Building Socialism? Transnational Humanitarian Relief in Early Soviet Armenia', *Moving the Social* 57 (2017), 77–96, 94; I. M. Okkenhaug, 'Refugees, Relief and the Restoration of a Nation: Norwegian Mission in the Armenian Republic, 1922–1925', in H. Nielssen, I. M. Okkenhaug and K. Hestad-Skeie (eds), *Protestant Missions and Local Encounters in the Nineteenth and Twentieth Centuries* (Leiden: Brill, 2011), pp. 207–32, p. 231.
11 B. Stöver, *Der Kalte Krieg, 1947–1991: Geschichte eines radikalen Zeitalters* (Munich: C. H. Beck, 2007), p. 315.
12 G. Miterev, *The Soviet Red Cross* (Moscow: Novosty Press Agency, 1964), p. 13.
13 Interview with Boris Ionov (Russian Red Cross), Moscow, 15 June 2013.
14 G. Miterev, *40 let sovetskogo krasnogo kresta 1918–1958* (Moscow: Medgiz, 1959), p. 154; Miterev, *The Soviet Red Cross*, p. 17. Further details on these missions are still missing.
15 See also T. Nunan, *Humanitarian Invasion: Global Development in Cold War Afghanistan* (Cambridge: Cambridge University Press, 2016); A. M. Kalinovsky, *Laboratory of Socialist Development: Cold War Politics and Decolonization in Soviet Tajikistan* (Ithaca, NY: Cornell University Press, 2018).

16 J. Paulmann, 'Conjunctures in the History of International Humanitarian Aid during the Twentieth Century', *Humanity: An International Journal of Human Rights, Humanitarianism, and Development* 4:2 (2013), 215–38, 220.

17 K. Doose, *Tektonik der Perestroika: Das Erdbeben und die Neuordnung Armeniens, 1988–1998* (Cologne: Böhlau Verlag, 2019).

18 J. Gibbs, *Gorbachev's Glasnost: The Soviet Media in the First Phase of Perestroika* (College Station, TX: Texas A&M University Press, 1999); B. McNair, *Glasnost, Perestroika and the Soviet Media* (London: Routledge, 1991).

19 E. Mickewicz, *Split Signals: Television and Politics in the Soviet Union* (New York: Oxford University Press, 1988), p. 136.

20 A. Brown, *Seven Years that Changed the World: Perestroika in Perspective* (Oxford: Oxford University Press, 2007).

21 League of Red Cross and Red Crescent Societies, *Les secours aux victimes du tremblement de terre d'Arménie en octobre 1926* (Berne, Jungfraustr. 22: Édition de la Délégation auprès du Comité international de la Croix-Rouge, 1927), p. 32, 36; *Pravda*, 11 October 1948, p. 2. *Pravda*, 28 April 1966, p. 4; on the reconstruction of Tashkent through volunteers see N. Raab, *All Shook Up: The Shifting Soviet Response to Catastrophes, 1917–1991* (Montreal: McGill University Press, 2017), pp. 84–121.

22 Office of the UN Disaster Relief Coordinator, *Report on International Relief Assistance for the Earthquake of 7 December 1988 in the SSR of Armenia*, UNDRO/89/6 (Geneva, 1989), p. 2; F. Krimgold, 'Economic and Social Impacts of Armenia Earthquake', in World Conference on Earthquake Engineering, *Proceedings of the Tenth World Conference on Earthquake Engineering* (Rotterdam: Balkema, 1992), p. 7012.

23 On Chernobyl, see M. Arndt (ed.), *Politik und Gesellschaft nach Tschernobyl: (Ost-) Europäische Perspektiven* (Berlin: Ch. Links Verlag, 2016); E. Geist, 'Political Fallout: The Failure of Emergency Management at Chernobyl', *Slavic Review* 74:1 (2015), 104–26.

24 *Ogonek*, no. 4, 1989, p. 2; E. B. Urdang, *The Armenian Earthquake Disaster* (Madison, WI: Sphinx Press, 1989), p. 6.

25 R. Sartorti, '"Du sollst deinen Nächsten lieben wie dich selbst": Caritas und Philanthropie im neuen Russland', in K. Kucher, G. Thum and S. Urbansky (eds), *Stille Revolutionen: Die Neuformierung der Welt seit 1989* (Frankfurt: Campus Verlag, 2013), pp. 45–56, p. 46.

26 Interview with Boris Ionov, Moscow, 15 June 2013.

27 Sartorti, '"Du sollst deinen Nächsten lieben wie dich selbst"', p. 47; F. Barringer 'Soviet Communism Lets Private Charity Revive a Tradition', *New York Times* (25 December 1987), p. 7.

28 C. Pfister, 'Von Goldau nach Gondo. Naturkatastrophen als identitätsstiftende Ereignisse in der Schweiz des 19. Jahrhunderts', in C. Pfister and S. Summermatter (eds), *Katastrophen und ihre Bewältigung. Perspektiven und Positionen* (Bern: P. Haupt Verlag, 2004), pp. 53–73; C. J. Schencking, *The Great Kanto Earthquake and the Chimera of National Reconstruction in Japan* (New York: Columbia University Press, 2013).

29 A. Sarkisyan and V. Khatuncev, 'Salvation and Hope' [Spasenie i nadezhda], *Pravda* (10 December 1988), p. 6.

30 P. Verluise, *Armenia in Crisis: The 1988 Earthquake* (Detroit, MI: Wayne State University Press, 1995), p. 41.

31 Office of the UN Disaster Relief Coordinator, *Report on International Relief Assistance*, pp. 3, 5.

32 *Ibid.*, p. 6.

33 De Waal, *Famine Crimes*, p. 65; Paulmann, 'Conjunctures', 219.

34 S. D. Moeller, *Compassion Fatigue. How the Media Sell Disease, Famine, War and Death* (New York: Routledge, 1999), pp. 111–24.
35 Pan-American Health Organization, *Disaster Chronicles Number 3: Earthquake in Mexico, September 19 and 20, 1985* (Washington DC, 1985), p. 52.
36 Arkhiv Prezidenta, 'Zasedanie Politbiuro CK KPSS, 27–28 dekabria 1988 goda' (excerpt), in *Istochnik. Dokumenty russkoĭ istorii* (Moscow: Rodina, 1993), p. 134.
37 M. Sturua, 'Solidarity' [Solidarnost'], *Izvestiia* (12 December 1988), p. 1.
38 J. Becker, *Soviet and Russian Press Coverage of the United States: Press, Politics and Identity in Transition* (Basingstoke: Macmillan, 1999), p. 67–71.
39 A. Bobin, 'It's time to learn mutual understanding!' [Net, uchit' vzaimoponimaniiu!], *Izvestiia* (14 March 1987), p. 7.
40 Press service 'Izvestii', '… we grieve, we condole, we ask you to accept our help – this is how the planet reacted to the calamity' [… skorbim, soboleznuem, prosim priniat nashu pomoshch' – tak otkliknulis' narody planet na bedu], *Izvestiia* (9 December 1988), p. 4 and A. Ivan'ko, 'American rescuers return home' [Amerikanskie spasateli vozvrashchaiutsia domoĭ], *Izvestiia* (16 December 1988), p. 5.
41 J. Laycock, 'Belongings: People and Possessions in the Armenian Repatriations 1945–1949', *Kritika: Explorations in Russian and Eurasian History* 18:3 (2017), 511–37, 521.
42 R. Panossian, *The Armenians: From Kings and Priests to Merchants and Commissars* (London: Hurst, 2006), p. 367.
43 Laycock, 'Belongings', 522.
44 J. Laycock, 'Armenian Homelands and Homecomings, 1945–9: The Repatriation of Diaspora Armenians to the Soviet Union', *Cultural and Social History* 9:1 (2012), 103–23, 110; Laycock, 'Belongings', 522.
45 National Archives of Armenia, Hayastani Azgayin Arkhivi (HAA), f. 326, op. 8, d. 60, l. 3, report of the Soviet Armenian Ministry of the Interior for 1988.
46 HAA, f. 326, op. 8, d. 48, l. 22, report of the Soviet Armenian Ministry of the Interior for 1987.
47 Office of U.S. Foreign Disaster Assistance, *Annual Report FY 1989* (Washington DC, 1989), pp. 29–30.
48 P. Verluise, *Arménie: La Fracture* (Paris: Stock, 1989), p. 62.
49 G. Lingelbach, *Spenden und Sammeln: der westdeutsche Spendenmarkt bis in die 1980er Jahre* (Göttingen: Wallstein, 2009), p. 402.
50 Fassin and Rechtman, *The Empire of Trauma*, p. 165.
51 *Ibid.*
52 Interview with Mary N., Los Angeles, 5 August 2014.
53 S. Pattie, 'At Home in Diaspora: Armenians in America', *Diaspora: A Journal of Transnational Studies* 3:2 (1994), 185–98, 187.
54 V. V. Yacoubian and F. J. Hacker, 'Reactions to Disaster at a Distance: The First Week after the Earthquake in Soviet Armenia', *Bulletin of the Menninger Clinic* 53:4 (1989), 331–9, 335.
55 *Ibid.*
56 *Ibid.*
57 Verluise, *Arménie*, p. 58.
58 *Ibid.*
59 Yacoubian and Hacker, 'Reactions to Disaster at a Distance', p. 335.
60 Interview with H. Vartiter, Los Angeles, 27 July 2014.
61 Yacoubian and Hacker, 'Reactions to Disaster at a Distance', p. 336.
62 Verluise, *Armenia in Crisis*, p. 61.

63 C. S. Najarian, *A Call from Home: Armenia and Karabagh. My Journal* (Cambridge, MA: Arpen Press, 1999), p. 175.
64 R. Suny, *Looking Toward Ararat: Armenia in Modern History* (Bloomington, IN: Indiana University Press, 1993), p. 216–17.
65 Interview with Richard Hovannisian, Los Angeles, 27 July 2014.
66 Verluise, *Arménie*, p. 62.
67 G. J. Libaridian, *Armenia at the Crossroads. Democracy and Nationhood in the Post-Soviet Era: Essays, Interviews, and Speeches by the Leaders of the National Democratic Movement in Armenia* (Watertown, NY: Blue Crane Books, 1999), p. 129.
68 G. J. Libaridian, *The Challenge of Statehood: Armenian Political Thinking Since Independence* (Watertown, NY: Blue Crane Books, 1999), p. 136.
69 Interview with Richard Hovannisian, Los Angeles, 27 July 2014; G. Hovannisian, *Family of Shadows: A Century of Murder, Memory, and the American Dream* (New York: Harper, 2010), p. 157; AGBU, 'History Of The Armenian General Benevolent Union', www.agbu.am/en/about-2/agbu-history-1 (accessed 15 September 2018).
70 V. Manukian, 'It's Time to Jump Off the Train', in Libaridian, *Armenia at the Crossroads*, p. 66.
71 Levon Ter-Petrosyan, speech in front of the Soviet Armenian parliament on 22 October 1990, in Libaridian, *Armenia at the Crossroads*, p. 116.
72 V. Dyatlov and E. Melkonyan, *Armyanskaya diaspora: otcherki sotsiokul'turnoy tipologii* (Erevan: Caucasus Institute, 2009), p. 170.
73 HAA, f. 1159, op. 3, d. 29, l. 46, speech given on 28 May 1989 in Erevan; HAA, f. 1159, op. 3, d. 29, l. 93 speech given on 24 September 1989 in Erevan.
74 Interview with K. Vachik, Gyumri, 27 October 2013.
75 Gosudarstvennyĭ Arkhiv Rossiĭskoĭ Federatsii (GARF), f. 9654, op. 1, d. 31, l. 45, speech of S. Arutyunyan at the Congress of People's Deputies, Moscow, 31 May 1989.
76 Suny, *Looking Towards Ararat*, p. 230.
77 Interview with Gerard Libaridian, telephone, 7 October 2016.
78 M. Fischer and S. Grigorian, 'Six to Eight Characters in Search of Armenian Civil Society Admits the Carnivalization of History', in G. E. Marcus (ed.), *Perilous States: Conversations on Culture, Politics, and Nation* (Chicago, IL: University of Chicago Press, 1993), pp. 81–130, p. 117.
79 Hovannisian, *Family of Shadows*, p. 161.
80 Interview with Richard Hovannisian, Los Angeles, 27 July 2014.
81 P. Hanson, *The Rise and Fall of the Soviet Economy: An Economic History of the USSR from 1945* (London: Longman, 2003), pp. 200–9; Interview with Mihran S. Agbabian, Los Angeles, 29 July 2014.
82 M. Agbabian, *American University of Armenia. A New Beginning for a New Generation: Recollections* (Oakland, CA: American University of Armenia, 2002), p. 155.
83 *Ibid.*, p. 156.

Humanitarian intervention meets a de facto state: International peacebuilding consortiums in Nagorny Karabakh, 2003–16

Laurence Broers

In the early 1990s the appearance of a small, war-ravaged and unrecognised Armenian republic in the South Caucasus created a new context in the history of international interventions in Armenian crises.[1] The Nagorno-Karabakh Republic (NKR), proclaimed on 2 September 1991, was one of several cases of unilateral secession challenging Soviet successor states, in this case Azerbaijan.[2] These secessions were contested in small but often vicious wars, characterised on all sides by violations of the human rights of civilian populations on a massive scale. Their modal outcome was the formation of a 'de facto state', entities to varying extents fulfilling the Montevideo criteria for statehood but not recognised as such by other states, least of all by the 'parent state' from which they seceded.[3]

The NKR framed itself as a successor entity to the Nagorno-Karabakh Autonomous Oblast' (NKAO), a territorial autonomy established by the young Bolshevik regime in 1923 inside Soviet Azerbaijan, but featuring an ethnic Armenian majority. Beginning in late 1987, a movement for the unification of the NKAO with Soviet Armenia emerged as the founding idea of an Armenian national revival. The movement was almost immediately overtaken by violence and mass displacements of Armenians from Azerbaijan and Azerbaijanis from Armenia followed. Successive efforts to contain conflict in the terminal Soviet period failed, and a large-scale Armenian–Azerbaijani war followed the dissolution of the Soviet Union on 26 December 1991. The two-and-half-year war ended with an Armenian military victory, as Armenian forces retained control over almost all of the NKAO, in addition to occupying in whole or in part seven adjacent Azerbaijani regions that had not formed part of the original dispute. A Russian-brokered ceasefire came into force on 12 May 1994. Despite unbroken Armenian–Azerbaijani negotiations since that time, no viable approach to a resolution of the conflict has emerged. The NKR consolidated as an unrecognised yet sustainable de facto state, characterised by tactical performances of separate sovereignty and a deep strategic integration with its 'patron state' Armenia.[4]

De facto states straddle the dilemmas of humanitarian intervention in multiple ways. They typically appear as a result of wars fought on the territories they claim, and the legacies of violence make them prime candidates for intervention. Their political institutions are weak, their economies ravaged by war, and their populations are generally vulnerable and impoverished. Yet as claimants to sovereignty they violate the territorial integrity of their parent states, invoking a collective responsibility among other states not to recognise them. In post-communist Eurasia, de facto states also violated the legal norm of *uti possidetis juris* ('as you possess'), mandating the recognition of former internal administrative boundaries as new international state boundaries. And in some cases, the insurgent military campaigns that brought them into being resulted in large-scale displacements of communities belonging to the parent state nationality. This breach of peremptory norms of international law (*jus cogens*) further politicises the image of de facto states as transgressive entities founded on ethnic cleansing, even when their parent states have similarly violated the same norms.

These tensions were all present in the NKR. As a lower-level autonomous unit in the former Soviet Union, a right to secessionist self-determination was not recognised by the international community, and Azerbaijan entered the United Nations in March 1992 with its Soviet boundaries inclusive of Nagorny Karabakh. Moreover, while massacres, dispossession and displacement marked the experiences of Armenians in 1988–94, these were juxtaposed with similar experiences among Azerbaijanis at the hands of Armenians, which in terms of scale were in fact worse. More than any other de facto state resulting from conflict in the former USSR, the NKR was enlarged by wartime operations involving the conquest of adjacent regions and the expulsion of their almost exclusively Azerbaijani inhabitants. These realities meant that Armenians could not be represented simply as victims, and further restricted possibilities for international intervention, as aid could be seen as consolidating the conquest, occupation and ethnic cleansing of the territory.

De facto states consequently emerged as small, yet enduring zones of exception to the complex post-Cold War conjuncture. Across post-socialist Eurasia, recognised successor states became theatres for multifaceted interventions that sought to transform polities through democratic transition, and, where present, to resolve conflicts through the 'liberal peace': a post-Cold War iteration of liberal internationalism predicated on inclusive and interventionist peace processes.[5] Post-Soviet de facto states, however, remained off-limits for the vast majority of humanitarian organisations and aid agencies, who could neither secure funding for activities targeting their populations, nor establish a physical presence within them. Moreover, parent states increasingly pursued counter-recognition strategies targeting de facto states as not only exceptional, but also aberrant spaces. A key element of these strategies was to promote a singular, hegemonic narrative defining de facto states as occupied territories, invoking further legal proscriptions on international engagement with them. Outside the bounds of legitimate development, democratisation or capacity-building assistance, de facto states appeared on the international humanitarian horizon only as minor actors in protracted conflicts. As political subjects, they were visible only to a peacebuilding gaze.

This conjuncture of factors resulted in forms of international intervention that differed sharply from those described in the previous chapters of this volume but which raise related questions regarding the relationship between 'neutral' interventions, national agendas and state-building. Apart from emergency relief and initiatives funded by the Armenian diaspora, the only interventions over the NKR's first twenty-five years of existence came in the form of peacebuilding initiatives facilitated by international non-governmental organisations (NGOs). This chapter focuses on two such interventions. Between 2003 and 2009 Britain funded a consortium of mainly British-based NGOs to implement a multi-level intervention aimed at 'improving the prospects for a permanent settlement' of the Armenian–Azerbaijani conflict.[6] In 2010 this initiative was succeeded by a larger consortium funded by the European Union (EU), featuring three organisations from the original group plus two others based in Finland and Sweden respectively. This consortium aimed to 'enact initiatives which will cumulatively contribute to a peaceful settlement over Nagorno-Karabakh', and continued to operate in the same configuration through to 2019.[7]

Both interventions reflected contemporary research findings emphasising comprehensive, multi-scalar and multi-actor interventions as the most effective route to conflict transformation.[8] Post-conflict peacebuilding, so this thinking went, needed to reach beyond peacekeeping interventions or transitional measures such as elections, and to address the structural conditions underlying conflict. The activities undertaken by the two consortiums were not limited to Nagorny Karabakh, but covered Armenia and Azerbaijan in their entirety. But while a multitude of other international civil society organisations and networks were present in sovereign Armenia and Azerbaijan, only those mandated to provide emergency relief (such as the International Committee of the Red Cross (ICRC) and the mine clearance organisation Halo Trust) or similarly acting on peacebuilding remits were engaged in the NKR. In the context of this de facto state, multiple agendas and interests were consequently refracted through the prism of peacebuilding due to the stark reality that international funding for intervention in the NKR was available only for activities framed as supporting 'peace'.

This chapter offers a practitioner's retrospective drawing on the author's experience as a project manager for Conciliation Resources, a London-based peacebuilding NGO and member-organisation of both the UK- and EU-funded consortiums. Working with Armenian and Azerbaijani partners, I managed a series of initiatives between 2005 and 2013, some of them implemented directly in Nagorny Karabakh. This chapter draws heavily on my notes, correspondence and conversations during that time. It proceeds by first considering the formation and trajectory of the UK-funded consortium, before discussing the contradictory impacts of the nexus between 'peace' and 'democracy' in the local context of the NKR. I then turn to the formation and trajectory of the EU-funded consortium. As a direct participant in the activities covered here, my impartiality in reflecting on them can certainly be questioned. It is not my intention to present a rose-tinted view of peacebuilding, however, but to critically explore with the benefit of hindsight some of the problems I encountered as a practitioner.

The Consortium Initiative (2003–9)

Coming nearly a decade after the ceasefire of May 1994, the British intervention in the Armenian–Azerbaijani conflict followed an intense but ultimately fruitless phase of negotiations between the parties. That Britain sought to address the challenge of Armenian–Azerbaijani conflict resolution was conditioned in part by its presence in Azerbaijan as that country's largest single foreign investor, and British Petroleum's significant stake in the Azerbaijan International Operating Company responsible for developing the Baku–Tbilisi–Ceyhan oil pipeline. British interests were consequently directly implicated in the resolution (or at least non-resumption) of the Armenian–Azerbaijani conflict, and perhaps no less importantly, Britain's image would benefit if its material interests in the Caspian could be juxtaposed with investment in the public good of regional peace. The British initiative was not purely instrumental, however, but owed also to the fact that several peacebuilding organisations already active in the Georgian–Abkhaz and Georgian–South Ossetian conflicts were based in London.

In January 2001 the Department for International Development (DfID), the UK's overseas aid agency, commissioned a study of the Armenian–Azerbaijani conflict. One of this study's main findings concerned the lack of coordination among Western donor governments: 'Interventions tend to be quite ad hoc and piece meal and in many respects are less than the sum of their parts. The challenge is to move from isolated encounters to sustained links on concrete issues of concern.'[9] Based on these findings, the DfID expressed its interest in funding a single intervention by a consortium of NGOs working together. Over six months in 2002 three London-based organisations, Conciliation Resources, International Alert and the London Information Network on Conflicts and State-Building (Links) devised a concept for a collective intervention. A fourth NGO, Catholic Relief Services, joined the discussion late in the year.

The concept was explicitly multi-level in approach. It proposed a programme arranged across four strands, each led by one of the four organisations: 1) a political dialogue strand led by Links involved work with national parliaments and research institutes; 2) a civil society development strand led by International Alert aimed to institutionalise networks of local NGOs; 3) a media strand led by Conciliation Resources sought to raise public awareness about the peace process and to challenge stereotypes in new media production; and 4) a strand led by Catholic Relief Services addressed sensitivity in the practices of aid agencies to the context of conflict. The result came to be known as the 'Consortium Initiative' (CI), an attempt to put synchronised, multi-actor peacebuilding into practice by interweaving engagement with politicians, civic and community actors, the media and development organisations. In July 2003 the DfID awarded the CI a tender for a grant initially scheduled at £2.6 million over three years. It was the largest single intervention to date for peacebuilding in the South Caucasus, and the largest grant in the UK's Global Conflict Prevention Pool. Following consultations with the Armenian and Azerbaijani governments, the project was formally named the 'Project Underpinning the Nagorno-Karabakh Conflict Resolution Process', yielding the unlovely acronym PUNKCRP, and began work on 1 September 2003.

Even the best-laid plans to build peace often fail at first contact with their putative beneficiaries. The CI entered a context where peacebuilding interventions had hitherto – as the DfID's study had found – been sporadic and scattered. In its aspiration to comprehensiveness, the CI's structure was easily interpreted as a key to what the international community believed the conflict was about. This perception was exacerbated by initial reports in the local press, which to the alarm of British embassies in Baku and Yerevan, presented the consortium as 'London's proposal to politically solve the conflict'. Ruffled feathers in the Foreign Office were the least of the consortium's problems, however. Local audiences read its activities through the prisms of two rival interpretations of the Armenian–Azerbaijani conflict. They looked for the replication of their own readings of the conflict in the consortium's programme of activities and saw bias when they did not find it.

In Azerbaijan, the conflict is seen as irredentist in nature, initiated and waged by Armenia. By this reasoning the Armenians of Karabakh have no separate agency of their own; their rights and status are paired with those of the 40,000-strong Azerbaijani minority expelled from the territory in 1992. Peacebuilding interventions should, in this perspective, reflect this by focusing on bilateral Armenia–Azerbaijan relations only; if peacebuilding is to engage society in Nagorny Karabakh itself, then this should also be bilateral in nature by bringing together the territory's two communities. In this view, 'there should be no peacebuilding without Karabakh Azerbaijanis'.[10] By contrast, the Armenian narrative parses the conflict as a self-determination struggle and depicts the Karabakh Armenians as a fully-fledged party to the conflict. They reject the 'communities' approach as a negation of both their claim to self-determination and democratic majority. By this view, Azerbaijan and the NKR are the conflict's protagonists, with Armenia in a secondary role. Peacebuilding should consequently embrace all three actors. In the light of this meta-conflict about what the actual conflict was really about, where the CI's activities emphasised interstate relations, such as Links' facilitation of parliamentary dialogue that did not include the NKR's de facto parliamentarians, they attracted Armenian criticism. Where activities assumed a trilateral structure, they attracted Azerbaijani censure, even if this was a practical rather than political choice – as was the case with International Alert's engagement with civil society in Baku, Yerevan and Stepanakert.[11]

Two of the consortium's strands explicitly sought to reach out to the population in the NKR. International Alert's civil society strand was directed at developing civil society organisations across the conflict. To this end three resource centres were established in 2004 in Baku, Yerevan and Stepanakert as hubs around which activities were organised. For many local observers, this trilateral format signalled a symbolic affirmation of the Armenian reading of the conflict. The activities of the Stepanakert resource centre were quickly picked up in the Azerbaijani press. Articles featuring sensational headlines such as 'In Karabakh International Alert discussed the topic of recognition for the "NKR"' prompted some urgent damage control stressing local ownership of Alert's activities rather than the conferral of legitimacy.[12] Perhaps the most visible single activity in the NKR was Conciliation Resources' support of a new newspaper, *Demo*, founded by the Stepanakert Press Club. Published bilingually in Armenian and Russian, the newspaper regularly reprinted articles about the Armenian–Azerbaijani conflict produced by journalists (including by Azerbaijanis) within the network of the Institute for War and Peace Reporting (also based in London).

The mere fact that international NGOs were operating in Nagorny Karabakh threw down a gauntlet to Azerbaijani sensitivities. In June 2004 the deputy executive secretary of the ruling New Azerbaijan Party, Mubariz Qurbanli, asked: 'Why is Nagorny Karabakh engaged in the project as a separate entity, not as part of Azerbaijan? ... Karabakh separatists are trying to come out of isolation in all possible ways. Projects of this kind help them in this issue.'[13] Several of the CI's early encounters with Azerbaijani officials were fraught. One CI representative was brought before an official from the Cabinet of Ministers six months into the project and instructed that the consortium was to cease all operations immediately. Yet as internal lines of communication within the Azerbaijani Ministry of Foreign Affairs were clarified, attitudes changed and Azerbaijani officials could be much more positive once 'on message'.

Despite teething difficulties and suspicion all-round, over the following three years the CI established effective working relationships with all the necessary parties. Cross-conflict contacts ceased to be news, and peacebuilding established itself as a legitimate and potentially influential political strategy. Yet the emphasis remained on 'potentially'. The consortium facilitated activities as diverse as political dialogue within the South Caucasus Parliamentary Initiative, humanising narratives of everyday lives broadcast across the region as 'radio diaries', and the institutionalisation of new civil society networks. But after three years no tipping points sufficient to trigger significant political change were reached. In the CI's own jargon, despite a substantial investment peacebuilding had not 'mainstreamed'. The consortium could claim credit for normalising contacts, expanding the peacebuilding space and sensitising development organisations to the impact of their work, yet a clear strategic vision for peace remained elusive.

The South Caucasus was in the meanwhile changing. A decade in the making, the Baku–Tbilisi–Ceyhan oil pipeline came online in 2005; two years later Azerbaijan doubled its military budget, and the Azerbaijani perspective on the utility of peacebuilding altered correspondingly. Eduard Nalbandian's appointment to the role of Armenian Foreign Minister in April 2008 also signified a cooler approach to Armenian–Azerbaijani peacebuilding. As it engaged in the politically fraught gambit of normalising Armenia–Turkey ties in 2008–10, Yerevan's preferences were for all Armenian–Azerbaijani contacts to be contained within the official mediation format of the Minsk Group, within the Organization for Security and Co-operation in Europe (OSCE). In the NKR, aspirations to the consolidation of statehood, with or without recognition, were signalled by the adoption of a new constitution in 2006. After the end of its first iteration in August 2007, the CI – now minus Catholic Relief Services – continued to work together as a platform rather than a unified project until 2009. By then once enthusiastic British officials were taking a more sanguine line: peacebuilding was long-term, painstaking and unglamorous work, and 'there has to be a realisation that we are in it for the long haul'.[14]

When 'peace' stands in for 'democracy'

The British intervention coincided with the dramatic onset of the post-Soviet 'colour revolutions'. Three months after it began work in 2003, Georgian opposition parties and civil society activists emulated tactics used against Slobodan Milošević in Serbia to eject President Eduard Shevardnadze from power. One year later Leonid Kuchma's regime fell in similar fashion to the Ukrainian opposition. Against the backdrop of President George W. Bush's 'Freedom Agenda', and Britain's short-lived flirtation with an 'ethical foreign policy', Western enthusiasm for democratic transition had never been higher. The post-Soviet de facto states also sought to harness this energy, by linking their struggle for statehood to the global receptivity to democratisation. In 1998, Freedom House, the influential Washington-based foundation founded in 1941 'to champion the advancement of freedom globally', included unrecognised entities in post-Soviet Eurasia in its *Freedom in the World* survey for the first time. This allowed direct comparison between the NKR and its parent state, Azerbaijan. In 2003 Nagorny Karabakh was rated 'partly free' for the first time, edging ahead of Azerbaijan—rated as 'not free'.

Secessionist enthusiasm for democratic forms was not purely instrumental, however, but originated also in pragmatic matters of state-building. Containing warlords empowered by victorious secessionist war is a challenge faced by all civil leaders in such contexts. To continue to survive in the margins of international politics, the leaders of Eurasia's unrecognised states needed to build popular legitimacy for the secessionist project. Popular legitimacy also held a specific resonance in the NKR because of the local image of the Karabakh movement as a broad-based movement that had led the South Caucasus in terms of democratic demand in the late 1980s.

Strengthening the republic's civil leadership had become imperative for its image, both at home and abroad, and in 2003 NKR President Ghukasyan 'declared the need for an opposition'.[15] But whereas several international donors and foundations were ready to support democratic transitions in recognised states, virtually none was prepared to support this process in contested de facto states in violation of multiple international norms.

This set the stage for a short-lived elective affinity between a local demand for visible democratisation as a source of regime legitimacy and an international project to build a 'liberal peace'. To be sure, the symbolism of the NKR's inclusion into the CI's programme of activities was hardly a substitute for Karabakh Armenians' absence from the OSCE-mediated talks (and nor was it intended to be). But the consortium's ability to work directly in the NKR, and its readiness to work with actors closely associated with democratic transition in civil society and the independent media, offered a rare conjunction of donor, regime and societal agendas. In this context, peacebuilding effectively 'stood in' for democratisation assistance, which as an unrecognised secessionist entity the NKR was not eligible to receive. The duality of peacebuilding and democratisation was hardwired into liberal perspectives on peace. The idea of the liberal peace, hegemonic in the late 1990s, assumes a plurality of voices, inclusive dialogues, and the empowerment of local stakeholders in broad-based movements. A Karabakh Armenian activist captured this duality in 2008: '[our objectives were] to stimulate the process of democratisation in Nagorny Karabakh, and second to increase the possibilities of a dialogue between the two conflicting parties. One would help the other.'[16] Over time, however, it became clear that when peace stands in for democracy, local actors on both sides of the government/opposition divide face some uncomfortable trade-offs.

From the perspective of the de facto authorities, the consortium's support for civil society and a new independent newspaper played well for an externally oriented narrative of democratisation. On the other hand, some local actors partnering with the consortium were vocal regime critics. This dilemma became more pressing in 2004 when, having declared the need for an opposition, the de facto authorities were shocked when one actually appeared. In April 2004 a new opposition party was founded, Movement-88; its name recalled the mass political participation with which the Karabakh movement had begun. Gegham Baghdasarian, President of the Stepanakert Press Club, parliamentarian and editor of the *Demo* newspaper – a CI project – was among the party's founders.[17] In a shock result, Movement-88 candidate Eduard Agabekyan won a municipal election in August 2004 to become mayor of the republic's capital, Stepanakert. Outward-facing representatives of the de facto authorities parsed the result in meetings with foreigners as evidence of the republic's democratisation.[18] Inside Karabakh, however, Agabekyan was hounded from office with accusations of embezzlement and forced to retire for health reasons.[19] By giving oxygen to opposition in an otherwise closed environment, peacebuilding had suddenly taken on a more subversive air. What was supposed to have been a controlled exercise in legitimacy for external audiences had become an unexpected conduit of domestic change.

Peacebuilding confronted civil society actors with a different problem: funding was only available for activities connected with Azerbaijan. Where peacebuilding activities were structured trilaterally, they could be seen locally as affirming the NKR's claim to be a fully-fledged party to the conflict. But any participation in projects involving Azerbaijanis was vulnerable to Azerbaijani counter-propaganda depicting activities as the meeting of two equal communities, Karabakh Armenians and Karabakh Azerbaijanis – thereby replicating an Azerbaijani parsing of the conflict. This is indeed how the consortium's activities were reported in the Azerbaijani press.[20] This exacerbated a long-term structural distortion in peacebuilding interventions: international partnerships could only be formed with those parts of local civil society willing to engage with Azerbaijanis. Yet local civil society in Nagorny Karabakh was composed of diverse actors and groups, some of whom rejected outright the premise of dialogue or contact with Azerbaijanis. Liberal peacebuilding was literally self-selecting, attracting like-minded partners but falling far short of the kind of comprehensive coalitions that theorists such as John Lederach proposed were crucial for liberal peacebuilding to succeed.[21]

By the last years of the CI's intervention, there was palpable disillusionment with peacebuilding in the NKR. It had become obvious that participation by Karabakh Armenians in the CI's activities was uneven. Much of the more political work, such as the parliamentarian dialogue facilitated by Links, remained off-limits to Karabakh Armenians – and with it the coveted parity in political status with Baku. The conflict sensitivity strand managed by Catholic Relief Services, targeting development agencies working in Armenia and Azerbaijan but not Karabakh, was all but invisible in the territory. De facto officials and civic activists alike continually expressed disappointment at the limited number and profile of consortium representatives visiting the territory. This could easily translate into frustration vented at those who did. After a two-hour meeting in October 2009, an exasperated Foreign Minister exploded: 'But are you now representing the Consortium Initiative, are you talking as Conciliation Resources, or are you speaking just for Broers?!'[22] The consortium, it transpired, only engaged with Nagorny Karabakh through the 'soft' prisms of civil society and the media. This had been tolerable for as long as demonstrable evidence of transition was useful in a wider game of competitive democratisation with Azerbaijan. But over the long-term, rather than countering the exclusion of the NKR from the formal peace process, the consortium's relegation of Karabakh Armenian participation to these spheres appeared to confirm it.

As international recognition continued to elude the NKR, and the power asymmetry with Azerbaijan grew more acute, attitudes towards peacebuilding hardened in the territory. De facto officials began to portray peacebuilding as motivated by a more sinister purpose of 'softening up' society for concessions. Standalone projects once cited as evidence of the NKR's 'standalone democracy' now attracted criticism as disproportionately inducing Karabakh Armenians to see compromise as inevitable. De facto officials cited the harder lines taken by their Azerbaijani counterparts, and asked why should they be different.[23] The inability of peacebuilding practitioners to guarantee that outputs, such as joint Armenian–Azerbaijani films, would be disseminated in the same way across the conflict led to accusations that peacebuilding NGOs were in fact complicit with Azerbaijan's strategy of containment vis-à-vis the NKR.

The year 2008 was an *annus horribilis* for the South Caucasus and the wider world. In March, post-electoral protest in Yerevan was violently dispersed, leading to ten deaths; within days the Armenian–Azerbaijani ceasefire was seriously violated for the first time in many years, auguring a long-term decline in the security situation along the Line of Contact. In August, the Georgian–Russian war in South Ossetia both demonstrated the risks to the region of unresolved conflicts and shattered many prevailing assumptions about how they might be resolved. In autumn, financial crisis swept through the world, shrinking humanitarian and peacebuilding budgets. Against this backdrop, practitioners in the South Caucasus confronted the groundhog day of peacebuilding objectives. Five years after the CI had started, the theories of change informing international peacebuilding efforts still stipulated the need for 'opening the peace process up to civil society engagement' or 'developing concrete ideas for confidence building measures'. There was a palpable sense that despite substantial funds, labour and the passage of time, peacebuilding was standing still. This provided the inauspicious backdrop for the formation of a second consortium, this time funded by the EU.

The European Partnership for the Peaceful Settlement of the Conflict over Nagorno-Karabakh (EPNK)

The absence of EU intervention in a major inter-state conflict in its neighbourhood had been a persistent theme in policy research about the EU's Eastern Neighbourhood Policy (ENP) for several years.[24] After the fiasco of the August 2008 war in South Ossetia, Russia sought to mitigate the damage to its regional reputation by inducing Presidents Ilham Aliyev and Serzh Sargsyan to sign the Moscow Declaration, affirming – rhetorically at least – commitments to a peaceful resolution and offering an opening for increased international engagement. While the EU was wary of supplanting the role of the OSCE's Minsk Group, there was little alternative but to mount some kind of intervention in the Armenian–Azerbaijani conflict.

As an external actor, the EU brought a complex array of strengths and weaknesses to a peacebuilding intervention. On the one hand, as a large, multilateral actor, the EU could be seen as less implicated in narrow national agendas. It had considerable experience in stabilising the Western Balkans, where it had been able to leverage membership aspirations among several Balkan states. Inaugurated in May 2009, the EU's Eastern Partnership also offered a new framework – and potential leverage through the negotiation of association agreements – for enacting policy in the Eastern Neighbourhood. On the other hand, the EU had no obvious political role in the Armenian–Azerbaijani peace process. Symbolically, the EU is present in the wider Minsk Group through the participation of France, Sweden, Finland, Italy and Germany. But although France is one of the permanent troika heading the Minsk Group since 1997 with Russia and the US, there is no sense that France acts as a conduit in this role for wider EU interests.

Responsible for politically fraught negotiations, the Minsk Group takes a very cautious attitude to inputs by other external actors, particularly parliamentary assemblies vulnerable to the lobbying efforts of the conflict parties. The fact that many individual parliamentarians in the European Parliament took openly pro-Armenian or pro-Azerbaijani views complicated prospects for an intervention complementary to OSCE mediation. Moreover, the EU's aspirations to normative power politicised its involvement in a conflict involving intractably contested issues, such as the standoff between self-determination and territorial integrity. In the past, the EU had fudged this issue, for example through differentiated language in Partnership and Cooperation Agreements with Armenia and Azerbaijan – much to the latter's irritation. Furthermore, prospects for the Eastern Partnership to offer leverage over Armenia and Azerbaijan were limited in the light of both states' lack of interest in long-term membership perspectives. In sum, the EU was in the unenviable position of having no choice but to field an intervention in a highly sensitive context, with no clear strategic perspective, and every reason to be concerned over political risk.

In planning an intervention, the EU also faced a trade-off between funding something new and not reinventing the wheel. There were concerns about not being seen to fund international peacebuilding NGOs to 'do what they always do'. EU officials stressed that they were looking for innovative initiatives that would reach beyond the circles of 'usual suspects' and engage wider constituencies. Inevitably, the CI was seen as a very British consortium; there was little desire in Brussels to fund a continuation. Yet like British officials in the DfID and the Foreign Office before them, officials at what was then still the Directorate-General for External Relations (DG RELEX) were looking to fund a large project with different components. This again implied a consortium, as a bureaucratically more viable alternative to multiple contracts with individual organisations. In autumn 2009 a group of European NGOs and their local partners hurriedly discussed the formation of a new consortium, which came to be known as the 'European Partnership for the Peaceful Settlement of the Conflict over Nagorno-Karabakh' (EPNK). Funded by a pilot €2 million grant, the EPNK began work in January 2010.

It was perhaps inevitable that the EPNK was neither a continuation of the British intervention nor an entirely new venture, but a sometimes awkward amalgam of the two. The EPNK consisted of the three organisations that had formed the CI

(Conciliation Resources, International Alert and Links), with the addition of the Finland-based Crisis Management Initiative and Sweden-based foundation Kvinna till Kvinna. The latter both had prior experience of working in the South Caucasus, with a focus on youth leadership development and women's participation in peacebuilding respectively. Like the CI, the EPNK was also structured across distinct 'strands' of work: 1) a media strand addressed public awareness through the training of journalists and the support of new outlets and production; 2) a strand focused on social inclusion targeted specific constituencies affected by conflict, such as youth, women and border communities; and 3) a public policy strand aimed to work with political parties and institutions. Unlike the CI, however, the EPNK's five members did not work on their 'own' strands; each strand featured more than one organisation. As before, engagement with Nagorny Karabakh was nested within the wider programme of activities. Karabakh Armenians participated along with peers from across the conflict in youth dialogue and leadership development, the training of young women, new media production and policy research. The EPNK's sole standalone project in the NKR was the publication of a monthly political journal, *Analitikon*, which replaced *Demo* as the Stepanakert Press Club's flagship publication, supported by Conciliation Resources.

The resulting consortium was large, diffuse and unwieldy. Locally in the South Caucasus, the EPNK was managed by staff at the EU delegation in Tbilisi, for whom Armenian–Azerbaijani issues had not previously been a focal point. This made the EU delegations in Baku and Yerevan, like the British embassies before them, particularly sensitive observers of peacebuilding activities that implicated them but over which they had no control. Overall, the volume of communication and liaison required to ensure that national governments, de facto authorities, EU delegations in Tbilisi, Yerevan and Baku, the renamed External Action Service (EEAS) in Brussels, interested member-states, the EU's Special Representative to the South Caucasus (EUSR) and the OSCE were all sufficiently briefed on the EPNK's activities was certainly under-estimated. Simply by virtue of its size and multiplicity of actors, the EU generated a constant supply of officials who were new-in-post and needed to get across the EPNK brief. Within the consortium, the fact that multiple organisations worked in each strand meant that none 'spoke for' a particular strand of work. This hindered efforts to communicate the logic of an already complex consortium to external audiences.

On the positive side, local reactions to the founding of an EU-funded consortium were generally calm. If anything, the reactions of Azerbaijani suspicion and Armenian welcome that had greeted the CI in 2003 were inverted. The EPNK aroused few concerns in Baku; according to one Azerbaijani official, 'we tell the population that peace isn't possible but we need you to play devil's advocate'.[25] Perhaps reflecting a learning curve that peacebuilding was of less utility to securing Armenian interests than originally thought, responses in Yerevan were more equivocal. The question of whether EU staff would visit the NKR was a persistent fly in the ointment. De facto officials in the NKR nevertheless welcomed the consortium and saw in it opportunities to connect with a wider range of political actors across the EU. Yet the broad seal of approval testifying to the fact that local officials had become used to international peacebuilding was not accompanied by a common strategic vision of peace even among peacebuilding practitioners. At 'stakeholder meetings' between EU officials and the EPNK's local partners, Armenian and Azerbaijani civil society activists proffered sharply contrasting recommendations and prescriptions as to the role that the EU might play.

The rapidly evolving political context in which the EPNK was operating was hardly conducive to defining a strategic vision for peace. The South Caucasus was still reeling from the fallout of the Georgian–Russian war. Russia's recognition of Abkhazia and South Ossetia as independent states in its aftermath and Western recognition of Kosovo in February 2008 established a new game of 'unipolar recognition' among Eurasia's de facto states. Karabakh Armenians pondered its implications, and in particular whether the effort to 'earn' recognition through democratisation was still relevant. Across Eurasia, the Georgian–Russian war augured a revived bipolarity, as the EU and Russia fielded competing projects in regional cooperation, the association agreements of the Eastern Partnership and the Eurasian Economic Union (EAEU) respectively. In the Middle East, the Arab Spring challenged authoritarian regimes and sent tremors through their post-Soviet counterparts. In 2011 Azerbaijan again doubled its military budget to \$3 billion, and was increasingly able to fund a loyal civil society. In June of that year, a fruitless summit between Presidents Ilham Aliyev and Serzh Sargsyan at Kazan signalled a definitive end to the largely fictive momentum associated with their Moscow Declaration of 2008. With no peace process to speak of, the meaning of peacebuilding became increasingly subject to question. Answers differed across the conflict: preventing violence, legitimating the status quo, the preservation of a narrowing space, or creating grassroots networks – albeit limited – of 'de-radicalised' individuals.

As practitioners increasingly struggled to define their role, the institutional logic of the EPNK rolled on. The pilot phase of the EPNK was followed in March 2012 by a €6 million grant over three years to 'EPNK-II'. EPNK-II was composed of the same five organisations, and both scaled up and developed many of the activities from the earlier phase. EPNK-II represented a significant increase in the resources made available to the consortium, but from 2013 a series of political events effectively overtook it. In September 2013 President Serzh Sargsyan renounced the three-year process of negotiating an association agreement within the framework of the EU's Eastern Partnership, announcing that Armenia would instead join Russia's EAEU. This dramatically reduced the EU's leverage in Armenia over the short-term. In February 2014, the Azerbaijani authorities introduced legislative amendments considerably complicating the receipt of foreign funding by local NGOs. Most independent Azerbaijani NGOs engaged in peacebuilding had their bank accounts frozen; local EPNK project partners could not receive transfers. EPNK activities that engaged individuals rather than organisations were able to continue, but many activities slowed down. Others continued to completion, yet their outputs could not be publicised. EPNK-II ended quietly in 2015.

Peacebuilding in consortium: Size as a sword of Damocles

On 2 April 2016 Presidents Aliyev and Sargsyan were returning from a nuclear security summit in Washington when intense fighting broke out at multiple locations along the Line of Contact between Armenian and Azerbaijani forces in Nagorny Karabakh. Over what would become known as the 'four-day war' more than 200 people were killed, and slivers of territory exchanged hands for the first time since 1994. Popular mobilisation in support of the armed forces was rapid and large-scale across the conflict, and many previous participants in peacebuilding programmes disavowed pacific sentiments in bitter online exchanges. Some observers saw the failure of peacebuilding at large – and the EPNK in particular – in these outcomes. According to analysts Cavid Ağa and Onnik Krikorian: 'For too long, projects such as EPNK – for those that actually know about it – have been plagued by a feeling that the "usual suspects" operate in "closed circles," always using the excuse of "security concerns" to justify doing nothing with projects voluntarily bid on and funded by international donors.'[26]

Although the CI and EPNK were not the only peacebuilding interventions in the Armenian–Azerbaijani conflict over the period being reviewed here, by virtue of their scale, they came to bear the brunt of criticism directed, as Ağa and Krikorian put it, at 'large, bloated, and ineffective projects'.[27] Ağa and Krikorian's perspective chimed with a wider interrogation of expansive humanitarianism, as Michael Barnett and Thomas Weiss observe: 'There is now agreement that good intentions are not enough ... Results matter.'[28] In assessments of their impact, size hung over both interventions as a sword of Damocles. Compared to international aid budgets, and in the cold light of what it costs to implement peacebuilding work 'off-shore', these interventions were in reality marginal in financial terms. But within the confines of peacebuilding, these were substantial grants awarded to complex, multi-actor projects. How, then, could they be seen as 'doing nothing'?

For both Britain and the EU, a single large contract was a bureaucratic convenience, but also promised high visibility. High visibility in turn generated high expectations of impact. These were evident in a joke circulating in 2004 that played on some poor translation in British embassy press releases about the CI: 'Since you won the competition for the prize of two million pounds for the best solution to the Karabakh conflict, can you tell us what the solution is?' Eight years later the figure of €6 million became a totemic figure mentioned in almost any discussion of the EPNK. In the mouths of critics, the figure stood for wasted resources, but in the mouths of EU officials it signalled seriousness and commitment. Albeit under different circumstances and with differing expectations, both London and Brussels wanted to be *seen* to be doing something. This dynamic reasserted itself in the aftermath of April's 'four-day war', when the EU committed a further €4.7 million to a third phase of the EPNK.

The scale of both interventions also gave the impression of constituting a monopoly on peacebuilding funds. As soon as the outcome of the DfID's tender was made public in August 2003, consortium members were inundated with requests for 'cooperation' from local NGOs; they came to be seen as gatekeepers to what was in funding terms the only show in town. The mere fact of establishing a consortium simultaneously also created a constituency of local NGOs who remained outside of it. Some of them would number among its most vocal critics, sowing further division among local civil societies already notoriously fractured by personal and political turf battles. Both the CI, through a 'Small Projects Initiative', and the EPNK, through a 'Regional Grants Initiative', attempted to address this problem by allocating funds for which non-affiliated local NGOs could apply. But this muddied perceptions of the consortium's proper role in each case: strategic counterpart to local actors in seeking political influence, or a re-granting benefactor and gateway to British/EU funds? Bureaucratically expedient, a single large grant both amplified local competition and gave those left outside of the consortium a powerful discursive yardstick with which to negatively frame its impact.

Impact itself is, of course, fluid, contextual and for the political work of post-conflict peacebuilding, notoriously difficult to pin down. Furthermore, the CI was conceived as a 'design and build' consortium founding several new processes and networks without established baselines. For the EPNK the conflict's escalatory dynamic shaped different conceptions as to the kind of impact that was seen as desirable. For EU officials in Baku, quiet, under-the-radar work with no surprises was ideal: for them, no news was good news. But their counterparts in Yerevan typically took a different view: 'we want more provocative, more visible work that can build up EU capacities to understand and react to the conflict, and we want learning that is specific to this conflict, not generic peacebuilding messages'.[29]

Impact, in the end, is about communication. While other aspects of their work can be debated, where there is consensus is on the failure of the CI and EPNK to develop effective communications strategies. Practitioners engaged in sensitive work or working with vulnerable constituents are often reluctant to see that work publicly explained by others. In the internal discussions of both the CI and the EPNK this modus operandi was expressed through the metaphor of the 'submarine' (an infelicitous one, to be sure, for a peacebuilding initiative). By consensual agreement no member had the right to speak about the others' work, or in the name of the consortium as a whole. Imagining the consortium as a submarine implied a safety mechanism that could lock down any troublesome compartments and allow the wider vessel to continue. But while the idea of compartmentalising risk was intended to act as a safety mechanism, it also resulted in a lack of mechanisms drawing different compartments into a single strategic direction, and communicating that direction to outsiders. Ironically, while both consortiums featured media strands addressing public awareness, they were ineffective in creating public awareness about themselves. The compartmentalisation of communication detracted from the brand recognition that donors were seeking, and the collective showcasing of impact that sceptics of peacebuilding were calling for. As a result, it was not only political risk but also peacebuilding itself that was locked down in sealed and inconspicuous compartments, with little diffusion of its message across wider audiences.

Size, then, was both a Damoclean and double-edged sword for the CI and the EPNK, creating both expectations and obstacles for impact. Critiques of these initiatives need to be weighed up against their capacity to work across de facto boundaries. Both consortiums featured individual projects structured in ways unacceptable to one or other party. They included bilateral, trilateral and, in the case of a small number of standalone projects in the NKR, unilateral activities. Standalone projects in de facto states encounter, as this chapter has described, a propensity to sticky entanglement in dissonant humanitarian and political agendas. Yet in the absence of wider development and democratisation assistance, standalone projects in de facto states are highly significant in contributing to a civic infrastructure within which political issues can be openly discussed. Without a civic domain capable of debating, weighing up and reconciling alternative policies and options – in other words, of institutionalising contested politics – it is difficult to imagine how de facto states can one day come to play a constructive role in wider peace processes. The consortium format allowed for these kinds of trade-off to occur, enabling activities that would otherwise run foul of political commitments to more exclusive formats. In this sense, their large size permitted the consortiums to manifest neutrality through comprehensiveness, and to embody – however imperfectly – the humanitarian aspiration to universality.

Notes

The views expressed in this chapter are solely those of the author and cannot be taken to reflect the views of Conciliation Resources or the European Union.

1 I thank Marc Behrendt, Jonathan Cohen, Craig Oliphant, Dennis Sammut and the editors of this volume for many useful comments on an earlier draft of this chapter. All errors of fact or judgement, of course, remain mine alone.
2 For ease of reading, I do not use the qualifiers 'de facto' and 'unrecognised' at every mention of the NKR. I emphasise here that no state or United Nations member, including Armenia, recognises the republic. I prefer the spelling 'Nagorny Karabakh' to 'Nagorno-Karabakh', but cite the latter when referring to secondary sources using this spelling. I use the terms 'NKR' and 'Nagorny Karabakh' interchangeably in this chapter.
3 See S. Pegg, 'Twenty Years of *de facto* State Studies: Progress, Problems and Prospects', *Oxford Research Encyclopedias* (2017), http://oxfordre.com/politics/view/10.1093/acrefore/9780190228637.001.0001/acrefore-9780190228637-e-516 (accessed 24 March 2020).

4 See L. Broers, *Armenia and Azerbaijan: Anatomy of a Rivalry* (Edinburgh: Edinburgh University Press, 2019), p. 251.
5 S. Campbell, D. Chandler and M. Sabaratnam (eds), *A Liberal Peace? The Problems and Practices of Peacebuilding* (London: Zed Books, 2011).
6 Project proposal, internal document, Conciliation Resources, 2003.
7 *Ibid.*
8 J. P. Lederach, *Building Peace: Sustainable Reconciliation in Divided Societies* (Washington, D.C.: United States Institute of Peace, 1997).
9 T. Vaux and J. Goodhand, *War and Peace in the Southern Caucasus: A Strategic Conflict Assessment of the Armenia–Azerbaijan Conflict* (Stonesfield: Humanitarian Initiatives, 2002), p. 32.
10 Author's notes, meeting with Bayram Safarov, Karabakh Azerbaijani community leader, Baku, 30 June 2011.
11 Stepanakert is referred to as Khankendi in Azerbaijani sources.
12 R. Orudzhev, 'International Alert – za dialog mezhdu liderami obshchestvennosti Azerbaydzhana, Armenii i Nagornogo Karabakha – Po mneniyu koordinatora britanskoy organizatsii Pola Lourensa, eto vykhod iz slozhivsheysya na segodnya tupikovoy situatsii v razreshenii konflikta', *Ekho*, August 2004.
13 'Azeri Official, Media Union Chief Against Joint Radio Project with Armenia', *Ekho*, 23 June 2004.
14 Personal communication, British official, October 2009.
15 Author's conversation, civil society activist, Stepanakert, 12 March 2005.
16 Internal document, Conciliation Resources, 2008.
17 The main newspaper distributor in Nagorny Karabakh refused to distribute *Demo*.
18 Author's notes, meeting with Arman Melikian, de facto Foreign Minister of the NKR, Yerevan, 9 March 2005.
19 Author's interview with Eduard Agabekyan, former mayor, Stepanakert, 11 September 2014.
20 R. Orudzhev, 'Karabakhskie separatisty iskazili sut' vstrechi NPO v Stambule. Predstaviteli nashey strany nazyvayut lozh'yu vyskazyvaniya "rukovoditelya" "delegatsii" "NKR"', *Ekho*, 10 May 2005.
21 For this argument, see V. Kopecek, T. Hoch and V. Baar, 'Conflict Transformation and Civil Society: The Case of Nagorno-Karabakh', *Europe-Asia Studies* 68:3 (2016), 441–59.
22 Author's notes, meeting with Georgi Petrossian, de facto Foreign Minister of the NKR, Stepanakert, 14 October 2009.
23 *Ibid.*
24 International Crisis Group, *Conflict Resolution in the South Caucasus: The EU's Role*, Europe Report No. 173, 20 March 2006.
25 Personal communication, January 2010.
26 C. Ağa and O. J. Krikorian, 'No Hope for NK peace? When Activists and Journalists Become Combatants', Meydan TV, 16 May 2016, www.meydan.tv/en/site/society/14489/ (accessed 24 March 2020).
27 *Ibid.*
28 M. Barnett and T. G. Weiss, 'Humanitarianism: A Brief History of the Present', in M. Barnett and T. G. Weiss (eds), *Humanitarianism in Question: Politics, Power, Ethics* (Ithaca, NY: Cornell University Press, 2008), pp. 1–48, p. 7.
29 Author's conversation, EU official, April 2015.

10

Refuge in the 'homeland': The Syrians in Armenia

Sossie Kasbarian

The Syrian Civil War has caused widespread devastation.[1] Syrian refugees now number in excess of 6.3 million.[2] Of these, an estimated 24,000 Syrians of Armenian origin have arrived in the Republic of Armenia since 2011. The United Nations High Commissioner for Refugees (UNHCR) estimates those who have stayed to number around 15,000.[3] In 2016 the departures from Armenia of Syrians exceeded the new arrivals. However, there are Syrians still arriving in Armenia every month, indicating that this is very much a fluid situation.[4] This suggests that Syrian Armenians' encounter with Armenia is a process of negotiation – Armenia is simultaneously a site of refuge, a historic or potential homeland, and a temporary transit zone in which to recover, recuperate and regroup. Local, diasporan and international actors all play a role in this process. Alongside this convergence of different actors – and their remits and agendas – is situated the refugee, not (just) as a victim of external forces, but as an active agent in negotiating his/her trajectory.

This chapter reflects on the role of a 'homeland', however complex in the Armenian diaspora case, in claiming refugees as part of its nation-building process, and in offering security and sanctuary in times of crisis.[5] Contemporary Diaspora Studies celebrates the privilege and creativity that comes with diaspora's mobility and adaptability, in contrast to more historical ideas of diaspora as exilic misfortune and victimhood. What has perhaps been neglected are the latent, deep-seated and enduring anxieties and complexities associated with being diasporan, which can surface at times of crisis – especially when painstakingly reconfigured attachments are attacked. In this particular case diasporans have been forcefully displaced from (an actively constructed, rooted and nurtured) home in diaspora and compelled to take refuge in a relatively unknown 'homeland'. In these respects, the Syrian Armenian case is one with great potential to challenge prevailing ideas about home, homeland and diaspora, and to further nuance narratives about multi-layered diasporan identities.

Armenian life in Syria can be traced back centuries, but the modern community was mostly composed of Genocide survivors from 1915 onwards. Aleppo was a hub during the time of the Genocide, and also a site of relief and rescue. The mandate authorities estimated that by 1923 over 200,000 Armenians had passed through Aleppo.[6] Refugee camps were set up which eventually became Armenian neighbourhoods. Western Armenian life, i.e. Ottoman Armenia, was 'reconstructed' in Syria and Lebanon.[7] At the same time, as noted by Razmik Panossian, modern Armenian diasporic identity was actively constructed here: 'Under the leadership of competing organisations, a heterogeneous group of people ... were moulded into a relatively coherent community with a collective consciousness as a diasporic nation'.[8]

Syria was a destination country for refugees who built the state and Syrian identity, and even helped establish its borders.[9] The modern Syrian state was constructed by complex historical processes and dynamics between the French mandate, the League of Nations, international humanitarian agencies, the Syrian nation (as articulated by Syrian Arab nationalists) and refugee settlement. Benjamin Thomas White makes the point that Syria's refugees in the inter-war period (Armenians and other Christians, as well as Kurds and Assyrians) were 'a site for the articulation of the national and international (a sphere which was itself in construction in the period)'. The newcomer Armenians were at first seen as a threat to the Syrian nation by Arab nationalists and a source of resentment, gradually becoming an important element in state-building.[10] Historians have written vividly about the survival and resilience, and renaissance of these communities, in the Syrian Armenian case, a 'transformation from abject poverty into an urban proto-middle class'.[11]

Syria became home to these Armenians, who, while treated as refugees, were granted Syrian citizenship by the French authorities after 1925. Syrian Arab attitudes towards the Armenians changed over time and they were upheld as a positive example of a Syrian community.[12] At its peak the Syrian Armenian community numbered 150,000 in the 1990s although emigration has been a constant theme. Before the Syrian Civil War, the estimated number of ethnic Armenians in Syria was about 100,000. More than 60,000 lived in Aleppo, with smaller communities in Damascus, Kessab, Qamishli, Yacubiyah and Kobane. Many in the western Armenian diaspora consider the Syrian Armenian community their 'mother community' from where they emigrated to the US, to Canada and to South America, and have maintained both emotional and material links to Syria.[13]

This chapter is based on a period of fieldwork interviews and participation/observation in Yerevan in November 2016, and is also informed by an earlier period of ethnographic research in 2001, as well as a short research trip in 2006.[14] It is situated within the interdisciplinary conceptual concerns of contemporary diaspora studies and refugee studies, and is framed by wider questions about homes and homelands, displacement, 'return' and belonging. This fieldwork does not include interviews with the most recent Syrian arrivals but more established ones, and those involved in NGO and civil society organisations. As recently discussed in scholarship, researchers studying refugee communities in their moment of crisis and vulnerability is problematic ethically, and potentially exploitative. The implications of treating traumatised displaced people as objects of study comes with a particular set of concerns that I have been mindful of in this research.[15] At the same time, I would not wish to reduce or objectify the lived human experience that lies at the heart of this study, so it is a question of balance and considered choices. I have drawn from personal testimonies in secondary sources, and from primary sources involved in working with refugees and arrivals.

Much of the history of humanitarianism research focuses on the narratives and policies of international organisations and their wider regimes. This universalising of diverse and distinct experiences of displacement under the legal status of 'refugee' with its accompanying infrastructures and nomenclature, risks dehistoricising and decontextualising the subjects, and potentially dehumanising them as well. 'Hearing' the unmediated, nuanced and disparate voices and experiences of refugees has been problematic, because as anthropologist Liisa Malkki has noted, 'humanitarian practices tend to silence refugees'.[16] Similarly, Peter Gatrell points out the 'absence of refugees from mainstream historiography' and argues for an approach that 'is attentive to connections between the circumstances, actions and trajectories of refugees through time and space'.[17]

This ethnographically informed chapter offers a 'way in' to giving a platform to the voices of those who have been more often objects rather than subjects of their plights. This chapter therefore also seeks to be true to the spirit of Gatrell's call to be mindful of the past as a resource for refugees and as a means by which to understand contemporary displacement experiences.[18] More specifically, it is situated in Gatrell's use of the concept of 'refugeedom' as 'acknowledging the world that refugees made, not just the world that has been made for them … It thus extends to categorical practices, legal frameworks, bureaucratic instruments and humanitarian relief work, whilst enabling us to relate to refugees' experience, conduct and responses to those prevailing institutions and norms'.[19]

As a case study, the experience of Syrians in Armenia opens up several important lines of inquiry: an investigation of a contemporary refugee experience on the ground; a study in how local, state, diaspora and global actors converge (and diverge) in their approach to the situation; as an experiment in 'emplacement' and 'homemaking'; an exploration of what constitutes Armenian identity and the Armenian nation.[20] This chapter is a preliminary study of each of these four aspects and their convergence. Underlying each of these concerns is the wider theoretical contribution of reconceptualising the refugee and his/her relationship with the homeland.

The Syrian experience of Armenia

The Syrians are the latest in a number of waves of ethnic Armenians who have had to take refuge in Armenia due to war in their home countries. Prior arrivals include Iraqi, Iranian and Lebanese Armenians, and the Armenians from Azerbaijan in the late 1980s and early 1990s. These waves of arrivals are distinct from the very small numbers of (western) diasporan Armenians who have, since the fall of the Soviet Union, chosen to 'return' to Armenia, for varying stretches of time, from a position of relative privilege, due to their commitment to a nationalist cause and/or the development of the country.[21] Decades before these post-Soviet arrivals Syrians were a substantial component of the *nerkaght* ('gathering in') 'repatriation' programme of Soviet Armenia from the 1920s to the 1960s (most in the period June 1946 to December 1947) as the Soviet authorities and certain diaspora organisations tried to refashion Armenia as a homeland for all Armenians, and also destabilise the diaspora.[22] The move from diaspora to 'step-homeland' was traumatic and disappointing for many of these migrants, such that many of them 'returned' to the diaspora when they could.

From the late 1990s there was also a different kind of movement between the diaspora and Armenia, a small-scale trend of diasporan Armenians forging connections with Armenia – for business, study or philanthropy/outreach. This included a number of Syrian and Lebanese individuals and families who were 'trying out' living in Armenia. During an earlier period of research in 2001, I encountered a number of Syrians who were going back and forth, connected and 'in between' the two homes, exploring options and planning to stay longer term depending on opportunities.[23] Therefore, when the civil war broke out in Syria, some Syrian Armenians had already established connections with Armenia, and were able to mobilise them – in the case of those with means – moving to the 'summer homes' they had already set up.

The contemporary Syrian experience in Armenia is a varied one, encompassing a range of experiences, differentiated by factors including: wealth and means; date and manner of arrival; class and connections; educational and professional background. All this constructs a multi-layered experience of displacement, interpreted variously as exile, displacement, migration or homecoming by refugees themselves and the state and non-state actors on the ground. The early wave of Syrians escaping the violence (from 2011) were in general better equipped, better prepared and better off than later arrivals. The wealthier Syrians set up home in Yerevan – although even here, some left or returned to Syria as they could not financially sustain themselves. The poorer ones were left little choice but to settle in Nagorny Karabakh, where they were given free housing and land to farm. Given the unresolved conflict between Armenia and Azerbaijan over Nagorny Karabakh, the de facto status of the Nagorny Karabakh Republic, and the fact that thousands of Azerbaijanis had been displaced from the territory less than three decades previously, Syrian Armenian resettlement in the region was a deeply sensitive issue.[24] However, the numbers of Syrians in Nagorny Karabakh have been greatly exaggerated and politicised. The reality is that there are about thirty Syrian families there, from rural Syrian backgrounds, and therefore suited to the lifestyle and setting. As the vast majority of Syrian Armenians are from cities, settling in Nagorny Karabakh is not an attractive or feasible option.[25] This example highlights again the diversity of the displacement experience – that multiple sites, destinations and trajectories are simultaneously present, at times converging, and at other times diverging, depending on context, external factors and actors.

Those who arrived from Syria during the earlier stages of the conflict are better integrated into the Armenian economy and society, and some of them are doing quite well. Some in the food industry are notable names already – like thousands of other Syrians 'spicing up' and enhancing the local cuisine all over the world.[26] The impact on the local food scene by refugee Syrians has many dimensions, among them the creation of a sense of home in a 'hostile environment' and the widespread belief that Syrian cuisine and hospitality are distinct and superior to others ('culinary pride').[27] This is not the first time that food has played a role in both differentiating and integrating diasporans who have sought to make their homes in Armenia. The importance of food 'as a marker of repatriates' transition from one world to another' is noted by Maike Lehmann with regard to the 1946–48 *nerkaght* wave of diasporans migrating to Soviet Armenia, but also as a divisive factor: 'this difference inscribed itself on the immigrants' bodies, through clothes and consumption, as they encountered not just the scarcities of postwar Soviet life, but a culture they felt to be essentially different from what they considered Armenian.'[28] Syrian Armenian arrivals are therefore understood as part of a longer tradition of diaspora contributing to and transforming the homeland.

A survey of the international and diaspora press up until 2013 reveals a recurring theme of Syrians torn between home and 'ancient homeland' (Armenia), their difficulties in embracing and settling in Armenia, and their desire to 'return home' to Syria. This theme is common throughout Armenian history, the dynamic present in every 'repatriation' to Armenia, whether forced or voluntary, and indeed is common in comparable cases too.[29] Armenia is the remnant site of eastern Armenia and as the modern day 'step-homeland' can lay claim to western Armenians from the former Ottoman lands – Ottoman Armenian life now relegated to memory, archive and dedicated cultural projects.[30] Eastern and western Armenia, the former influenced by Ottoman (and Arab) culture, the latter by Russian and Persian, were differentiated by language and culture more broadly. The Syrian Armenian culture is typical of Armenians in the Middle East, and the western, established diaspora more widely (many members of these communities have their roots in the Middle East). As such, the Syrian Armenians' encounter with Armenia is a meeting between western and eastern Armenian, to put it crudely. Obviously the past two decades have meant that these two 'representations' have met many times, and in many settings and their differences are more familiar than previously portrayed. Nonetheless, for many Syrian Armenians, being in Armenia is not a comfortable position, as they are caught between the home of attachment (Syria) and the new potential home of 'emplacement':

> If you ask Syrian-Armenians why they are so connected to Syria, they will reply that Syria gave them a lot. I want to add to this, that we also gave a lot to Syria. We built up

and developed its cities. My grandpa had a shop in the old Aleppo which has now been destroyed to the ground. I mean, a part of my home is lost there. My grandpa gave so much to Syria, my dad and I also gave a lot. Indeed, the Arab people supported us and we are grateful for that, but we also reciprocated for what we received. We feel pain for Syria not because we were welcome in that country, but because we were also the builders of the country.

The Arabs in Aleppo would ask me the same question as the Armenians ask me here in Yerevan: how is it possible to be both Syrian and Armenian? My parents were born there, I was born there, Aleppo is my city. I knew the architecture of all the buildings in Aleppo and had a feeling of belonging to them. At the same time, we were brought up like Armenians, we had our books and literature in Armenian. It's like we had two parallel identities. When in Armenia, it's natural that this identity will rise in me, but the longing for Syria will remain. These two identities are inseparable.[31]

The narrative of longing to go home seems to wane somewhat among the Syrian Armenians from 2014, probably as the war persists. Instead the focus seems to shift to whether and how Syrians will stay in Armenia. At the same time, some Syrians have indeed gone back to Syria, where they at least have homes (if not destroyed) and believe that they are better off there. Many have emigrated further afield, most notably to Canada.[32] In these cases Armenia has served as a temporary home, and perhaps a disappointing and frustrating 'homeland'. There are also Syrians, who like other Arabic speakers have found better jobs in the Gulf states and have stationed their families in Armenia while they send remittances and go back and forth. In these cases, Armenia serves as a safe and secure base and allows families to reconfigure and navigate their collective lives with a degree of agency, in time. From 2014, the prevailing narrative seems to be a resigned acceptance of the realities of being in Armenia, despite struggles and disappointments. In the words of one now successful Syrian jeweller: 'We have always been told of the motherland, dreamed about it and encouraged to move to our homeland. We made that big move and all we came up with was disappointment. Our motherland didn't receive us with open arms'. The article cites the attitudes of locals as being particularly provocative for Syrian newcomers, many of whom are struggling to survive and are highly critical of the state: 'I hear such things constantly, but to me everything else (in Armenia) is not that awful. No one denies that there are still many problems to deal with, but I believe many people are exaggerating the situation somehow. This is your motherland, you have to take it as it is.'[33]

There are wide ranging experiences and positions articulated by Syrian Armenians. These are perhaps so fluid because people are in the early stages of experiencing Armenia, looking into and weighing up their options and plotting their trajectories in time. Among my interviewees, there were those who expressed an intention to embrace Armenia as a new and long-term home, those who were 'out of place' and longing to return home to Syria and those who were thinking of Armenia as a home for the time being. The variation within the Syrian experience in Armenia is united by the thread of dual attachments and identities. In all cases Syrian Armenians are fully cognisant and reflective of their 'in between', hybrid or multiple orientations. The latter are actually a source of anxiety in terms of negotiating self and belonging, and also in 'choosing' a 'homeland'. Conversely being diasporan is also a kind of resource, in that one can activate one's Armenianness and lay claim to the Armenian state, whether temporarily or permanently.

Being a refugee diasporan Armenian in Armenia can therefore be both a source of stress and a source of strength. The stress is associated with the struggle to situate oneself in a new environment that is neither home nor entirely foreign; the strength and hope is associated with the opportunities that being diasporan can bring – return, relocation or settlement. This is augmented by the diasporan collective memory of past misfortunes, displacements, journeys and reconfigurations that act as a historical resource that one can delve into.

The Armenian state

A prevailing belief in the policy world is that refugees ideally are repatriated, and if that is not an option, that they are best off in countries close to home, in cultures similar to theirs, and especially among co-ethnics in a form of 'homeland'. In fact, despite having arrived in a country that bears their name, Syrian Armenians face similar integration problems as other refugees. Far from a smooth slotting in, Syrian Armenians have issues with language and understanding, cultural differences, difficulties in schooling and education, and in inserting themselves into a struggling and small economy. General concerns expressed by the Syrian Armenians included the high cost of living, the lack of decent affordable housing, the lack of opportunity and the poor economy. All of this plays out against the backdrop of a small post-Soviet state with a history of corruption.

Armenia's GDP is $3,500 per capita and its population less than three million. Therefore 15,000 is a high number of refugees relative to the population, making Armenia, per capita, the third highest host country of Syrian refugees.[34] These figures are even more significant when put in the context of high unemployment and a constant stream of labour emigration. It is therefore noteworthy that international organisations and governments have only given very modest support to Syrian refugees in Armenia, in contrast to recipient countries like Turkey, Lebanon and Jordan. In the summer of 2017, the European Union (EU) Regional Trust Fund in Response to the Syrian Crisis gave €3 million to Armenia, a relatively small and late contribution.[35]

The reasons for this lie in the special status of Syrian Armenians and their relationship to Armenia. Armenia, especially since the collapse of the Soviet Union, has been actively forging relations with its diaspora and rebranding itself as a 'homeland' for diasporans.[36] Therefore, the Syrian Armenians' cause was one that the state took on without hesitation, seeing this unfolding tragedy as an opportunity for

Armenia and a duty towards co-ethnic brethren. In this respect, the state has taken on a responsibility towards Syrian Armenians, redefining them not as refugees but as potential 'repatriates'. In this respect the Armenian state lays claim to the Syrians *as Armenians*, part of the global Armenian nation who have the right to expect refuge and to settle in Armenia. There are striking parallels here with the ways that the early Soviet Republic of Armenia sought to position itself as a homeland for Armenians displaced in the course of the First World War and the Armenian Genocide, as described in Vahé Tachjian's earlier chapter in this volume. Because of this articulation of 'national' responsibility, Syrians therefore cease to become the responsibility of Syria and crucially also that of international refugee regimes. In this way the Armenian state is at least partly responsible for making this an Armenian issue rather than a global humanitarian one. The peculiarity of the Syrian Armenian case means that they are not classed as refugees, as the Armenian government grants and facilitates their citizenship or residence permits. In this way this has 'become and remained an Armenian issue', because 'being an Armenian refugee in Armenia has different connotations'.[37]

The UNHCR presence in Armenia, though essential, is limited in terms of resources. The UNHCR considers the Syrian Armenians' status to be 'refugee-like' and the support offered is comparable to being internally displaced persons (IDPs).[38] Indeed the UNHCR head in Yerevan considers the Syrian Armenian refugees 'not just a humanitarian issue' but 'something close to the heart for Armenia'.[39] It would seem that diasporic identity and networks are being implicitly recognised by international refugee/humanitarian regimes not just as partners – and therefore complementary to their roles – but actually as alternative actors. In the context of international organisations being under immense pressure, diaspora regimes can be reconceived as local/transnational networks which can take on their role and remit.

As recognised by the UNHCR, 'Armenia has ... per capita, significantly contributed to the global response to displacement from Syria and has facilitated the entry and stay of more than 20,000 persons from Syria'. The government has 'in principle, taken a very generous approach in offering Syrian Armenians choice between three protection options': facilitated and simplified acquisition of citizenship; accelerated asylum procedures which resulted in a 100 per cent recognition of status; and privileged granting of short, mid-term residence permits.[40] The government has also granted privileges and protections to those coming from Syria, including: maintaining its consulate in Aleppo (one of the very few to have done so); facilitating bringing cars and personal belongings and in some cases machinery by waiving custom duties; free university or largely subsidised education; health care support (though basic); assistance in finding employment and micro-credit schemes; temporary accommodation for the most vulnerable. Such practices echoed the privileges granted to potential repatriates from the Armenian diaspora by the Soviet authorities in the aftermath of the Second World War.[41]

In official state rhetoric the Syrian Armenians' arrival has been portrayed as a homecoming. The government seems to be doing its utmost to facilitate the Syrians' refuge in Armenia and encouraging their long-term settlement, although it is limited by its lack of resources, and has to rely on partner and external organisations as well as international organisations like the UNHCR to fund its policies and initiatives. Bureaucratically, however, the state has extended its infrastructure to support the Syrians in every way. The state narrative also extends to claiming the allegiance of the Syrians *as Armenians* such that those who choose to leave Armenia are seen as ungrateful and unpatriotic. In this way, the Armenian state (however intentioned) is imposing a national(ist) identity on Syrian Armenians that is at odds with their own self-identification, attachments and feelings, contributing to the 'stress' discussed in the previous section. In addition, it is important to emphasise that this attempt to import and retain diasporans is not (only) an altruistic act but one of nation-building. The Syrians, with their personal, and in many cases, material resources, are regarded as a potential asset to the state, bringing in skills, experiences and networks that Armenia needs and can benefit from.[42]

The Armenian civil society landscape

The Armenian civil society landscape is vast and highly developed – composed of local initiatives, national, diaspora and international organisations, each with their own remit and mission but intersecting and cooperating with each other.[43] In the case of the Syrian arrivals, both new and established NGOs and related organisations are playing leading and expansive roles.[44] As in comparable cases of crisis, civil society steps in and in many ways does the job or supplements the role of a state – certainly in welfare and relief. Armenia has a non-camp approach to hosting refugees, although many people are living in very basic conditions, housed by the government in decommissioned Soviet barracks.[45] Civil society organisations are tackling all aspects of life for the Syrian arrivals, from housing to education to cash assistance upon arrival and trauma counselling. The UNHCR has urged the government to have a more 'joined up' strategy regarding the Refugee Integration Concept, particularly in the realm of economy and the socio-cultural sphere and to take on a leadership role with a clear policy and implementation procedures – for all Syrians regardless of their legal status (including crucially those who do not have refugee status or a residence permit).[46]

It is important to emphasise that Armenian life in Syria has continued throughout the war, with schools and churches still open and functioning. There are an estimated five to seven thousand Armenians still in Syria. Diasporan Armenian institutions have therefore had a two-pronged approach – supporting those who have stayed, and helping facilitate the exodus of those who choose to leave, although of course the element of 'choice' in these cases is qualified. Many diaspora organisations cannot countenance the idea of the end of Syrian Armenian life and are doing what they can to support it. For example, the IDeA foundation, a major diaspora funder in Armenia, distributes its funds to NGOs working on the ground to three distinct constituencies: 'This includes assistance for families still living in Syria, families who wish to leave Syria for Armenia, as well as those who have already resettled in Armenia'.[47] Some diaspora-focused organisations in Armenia, such as Repat Armenia have meanwhile shifted their focus since the Syrian crisis began and are now fully occupied with helping the Syrian arrivals integrate and settle.[48] These different approaches are typical of the diaspora, which is a broad church in every sense, including its accommodating attitudes towards notions of home, homeland and the Armenian state. For many diasporans living in diaspora is the fundamental core of Armenian identity, yet the reframing of the Armenian state as a potential 'step-homeland' can simultaneously be viewed as essential in safeguarding the futures of diaspora communities under (physical) threat.[49]

A key development on the ground in Armenia is Syrian refugee activism – Syrians organising and helping each other. This is aided by the fact that there are more established Syrians from the earlier wave of arrivals who are in positions where they can act as mediators and advocates with agencies and the government on the one hand; and set up their own initiatives on the other, supported by the fact that they are not, legally speaking, refugees but in most cases now Armenian citizens or official residents. Refugee activism is also important in terms of recognising the refugees' part in negotiating and shaping power relations both on the ground and in terms of knowledge production and narratives.

Interestingly it would appear that Syrian women are leading many of these initiatives, carrying on a gendered tradition of charity and philanthropic work in the diaspora community infrastructure. Lina Halajian, the President of the Centre for Coordination of Syrian Armenian Issues, an NGO established in October 2012, is herself a Syrian arrival. She and her extended family used to spend summer holidays in Armenia and like other Syrians were building a sense of material and emotional attachment to the country before the war forced their hand. The organisation has more than 10,000 beneficiaries and is run by AGBU salaried staff, and an army of full-time Syrian volunteers. Halajian is an advocate of 'refugees helping refugees', stressing that the Aleppo community was 'self-sufficient'.[50] By 2018 the centre was also functioning as a polyclinic with equipment provided by funding from the AGBU, and other funds from Syrian Armenians worldwide.

Aleppo Compatriotic Charitable Organization (Aleppo-NGO), another leading organisation, has the espoused objective 'to provide emergency relief assistance to the most vulnerable Syrian families and individuals, while at the same time, develop and implement durable solution projects to facilitate the local settlement and integration process of Syrians in Armenia'.[51] Alongside this is the focus on choice and agency for Syrian Armenians: 'To ensure welfare and decent living conditions for Syrians sheltered in Armenia, prohibiting urgent phenomenon of migration and giving them an opportunity to return and stand up for their own property at the end of the civil war of Syria, thus taking part in reconstruction activities of Syria'. Aleppo-NGO, founded in 2013, is run by an all-female executive board, and has a number of creative and constructive projects including an Arabic club for speakers to maintain and improve their Arabic language.[52] In recent years there has been a recognition of the important role played by local actors and local communities in responding to refugees.[53] This example highlights the need to also pay attention to diasporic activities as part of the wider humanitarianism framework, a neglected dimension of experiences of displacement.

Apart from trying to meet basic needs, NGOs are also focused on the integration of Syrians into the economy and society. At Repat Armenia, the team does a 'needs assessment' for every arrival, helping them with the CVs, and connecting them to potential employers and opportunities.[54] The goal is the successful integration of the arrivals, such that staying is economically sustainable. There are regular events to address the issues faced by Syrian arrivals and also to help them to make contact with the relevant organisations and individuals. These are sometimes billed as 'Meet and Greet' events, although the range of topics covered includes everyday advice to sharing traumatic and poignant experiences.[55] Alongside all the good will and efforts extended by organisations, there is also the perception that some Syrians are not exercising enough agency and initiative to make the best of their circumstances. They are not used to being 'pro-active', and 'marketing themselves' or 'networking', having come from a settled, secure and comfortable existence, where they often owned their own businesses.[56]

Armenia is a small market, and oftentimes the skills and experience that the Syrians are equipped with are not appropriate or in demand in such a different environment. There are also complaints that Syrians are reluctant to 'retrain' and to do what is necessary to 'adapt'; that they are full of expectations but when these are not quickly met they lack the drive, tenacity and the vision to plot their own trajectories. This underlying criticism is somewhat in tune with some historical representations of refugees as passive recipients of aid and, furthermore, unreliable articulators and spokespeople who need to have narratives imposed on them in order to be intelligible/palatable to the international community. Malkki exposes how 'their accounts are disqualified almost a priori, while the languages of refugee relief, policy science, and "development" claim the production of authoritative narratives about the refugees'.[57]

Diaspora organisations are often accused of being out of touch with Armenian realities and complicit with government corruption.[58] This would appear to be a case where they are playing a leading and much needed role in Armenia. The dense networks and operations working for the Syrian Armenian plight in Armenia suggest that this is an issue that unites the Armenian state and the diaspora. Despite differences in approach and ethos, there is a unified sense of concern and purpose evident – although each of these actors is positioned somewhat differently. Civil society actors and agencies, while cooperating with the government of Armenia, are not promoting the same narrative of 'Armenia as homeland'. Instead these organisations appear more ready to recognise the complexities of the Syrian case and of being a refugee diasporan. As such, these organisations, while tending to the situation on the ground in real and practical ways, are not imposing one trajectory on the Syrians, even though some like Repat Armenia are certainly encouraging settlement. The UNHCR along with diaspora institutions seem to be taking a more pragmatic approach, supporting the Syrians in Syria, and supporting the Syrians in Armenia as they go about making their choices about return, settlement or emigration elsewhere. This ideological gap between the state and the civil society is generally glossed over although it is a source of latent tension.

Conclusions: Reimagining the refugee and home

The discussion as to whether diasporans settling in Armenia can be identified as 'repatriates', 'refugees', 'newcomers', 'migrants' or 'sojourners' continues to be a salient one at the heart of what/who constitutes the Armenian transnation.[59] In the case of the Syrian refugee arrivals, Armenia takes on many meanings, and its 'step-homeland' quality can make it both easier and harder. On the one hand, the official welcoming line of the government, the historical and nationalist pull and cultural similarities, make Armenia an obvious choice. On the other hand, the latter can in fact make Armenia more complicated and alienating a site of refuge for Syrians who might never have even visited and have lived for generations as Syrians in Syria. Many of them suffer from 'mixed emotions' when confronted with the 'Armenia as homeland' narrative.[60] The inflated prevailing nationalist narratives from various sources that would seek to frame the Syrian's arrival as a homecoming can be a source of resentment and conflict for the Syrians themselves who are not the manufacturers of this narrative, although in many cases are taking or trying it on. In the Syrian case therefore, Armenia is best conceived as playing different overlapping roles – as land of refuge, transit site, step-homeland and national motherland – but it is not 'home', at least not yet. Syria is home and the destruction of Syrian Armenian life is a source of great sorrow, for both this community and the diaspora at large.

The case of the Syrian refugees in Armenia has clear theoretical relevance when considering questions of nation, home, homeland and belonging. A nuanced analysis of the situation reveals that there are multiple narratives and concerns co-existing. The state is reframing Armenia as a site of resettlement for Syrian Armenians, but it lacks the resources to make this an appealing prospect for many Syrians who are used to be a better standard of living. Civil society organisations are more circumspect in terms of recommendations, and more aware of the different pulls and pushes, orientations and attachments that the Syrian refugees are grappling with. The refugees themselves are active agents in exploring their potential trajectories, whether returning to Syria, settling in Armenia, migrating elsewhere, or choosing an in-between existence that is some form of these combinations.

The Syrian refugees are being reconceptualised as a resource by the state. New arrivals, including refugees, represent the potential to build and shape and transform a country. There is widespread awareness that the Syrians can contribute to the Armenian economy and society, with their distinct culture, connections with the Arab world and experience. The state is keen to capitalise on that. Beyond the material, though, there is also the long-term potential to build a more diverse and inclusive Armenian nation in the Armenian state, one that represents a more global range of Armenian identity. The mass arrival of Syrian and other Armenians also imbues dynamism into Armenian identity in the Republic, challenging narrow interpretations of Armenianness.

This example also demonstrates how refugees are not passive recipients of aid and relief but have rights and intrinsic value that go beyond rights-based humanitarianism. In this case, the Syrians are being 'claimed' by the Armenian state as an attractive acquisition. They are not just the objects of intervention of state and non-state actors but active agents in their trajectory, within the delineated limits of being refugees. They represent the criss-crossing lines of attachment and orientation that are articulated and forged by different actors (state, community, diaspora, international organisations and norms), which lay claim to the refugee – that he or she can activate, reject or use instrumentally with some degree of agency.

Prevailing diasporic theories stipulate that an essential part of being diasporic is being both sedentary and routed (rooted and routed).[61] The rupture of civil war at home means that the previously settled and well-established Syrian Armenian community is being reframed in a narrative of mobility and exile, with a degree of circularity that overturns and challenges notions of 'home' and rootedness.[62] Furthermore, as many of the Syrian refugees articulated, forced dispersion, exile and living in diaspora is a defining theme in the Armenian experience and identity.[63] Drawing from the past as a resource from which to decipher the present, and choose a future with some degree of agency, is a strong component in the reflections of Armenian Syrian refugees.

Notes

1 My sincere thanks to the editors for their incisive comments and steering, as well as to Irina Levin for her helpful feedback on a conference paper on this subject.
2 As at April 2019. There are also 6.6 million internally displaced. Figures from the UNHCR website: www.unhcr.org/uk/figures-at-a-glance.html (accessed 24 March 2020).
3 As at November 2016.
4 As at summer 2018.
5 Sossie Kasbarian 'The Myth and Reality of 'Return' – Diaspora in the Homeland', *Diaspora – A Journal of Transnational Studies* 18:3 (2015), 358–81.
6 K. D. Watenpaugh, *Being Modern in the Middle East* (Princeton, NJ: Princeton University Press, 2006), p. 281.

7 N. Migliorino, *(Re)Constructing Armenia in Lebanon and Syria: Ethno-Cultural Diversity and the State in the Aftermath of a Refugee Crisis* (New York: Berghahn: 2008).
8 R. Panossian, *The Armenians: From Kings and Priests to Merchants and Commissars* (London: Hurst, 2006), p. 292.
9 B. T. White, 'Refugees and the Definition of Syria, 1920–1939', *Past and Present* 235:1 (2017), 141–78.
10 White, 'Refugees and the Definition of Syria', 145. For the French, the Armenians were seen as potential useful 'collaborators' and part of their self-image as protectors of Ottoman Christians. See E.-M. Lust-Okar, 'Failure of Collaboration: Armenian Refugees in Syria', *Middle Eastern Studies* 1:58 (1996), 53–68.
11 Watenpaugh, *Being Modern*, p. 280. See also S. Payaslian, 'Diasporan Subalternities: The Armenian Community in Syria', *Diaspora* 16:1/2 (2007), 92–132; L. Robson, *States of Separation: Transfer, Partition and the Making of the Modern Middle East* (Oakland, CA: University of California Press, 2017); B. T. White, *The Emergence of Minorities in the Middle East: The Politics of Community in French Mandate Syria* (Edinburgh: Edinburgh University Press, 2011).
12 White, 'Refugees and the Definition of Syria', 170–4.
13 This is evident in the narratives and orientation of community organisations in diaspora (personal observation and research), as well as in recent findings by the Armenian Diaspora Survey, www.armeniandiasporasurvey.com/ (accessed 24 March 2020).
14 This chapter was written before Armenia's Velvet Revolution of 2018 – the impact of which is still unfolding. Therefore it does not take into account any policy or personnel changes regarding the Syrian arrivals in Armenia.
15 See for example, E. Pascucci, 'The Humanitarian Infrastructure and the Question of Over-research: Reflections on Fieldwork in the Refugee Crises in the Middle East and North Africa', *Area* 49:2 (2016), 249–55; S. Kabranian-Melkonian 'Ethical Concerns With Refugee Research', *Journal of Human Behavior in the Social Environment* 25:7 (2015), 714–22.
16 L. H. Malkki, 'Speechless Emissaries: Refugees, Humanitarianism, and Dehistoricization', *Cultural Anthropology* 11:3 (1996), 377–404, 378.
17 P. Gatrell 'Refugees – What's Wrong with History?', *Journal of Refugee Studies* 30:2 (2016), 170–89, 170.
18 P. Gatrell, *The Making of the Modern Refugee* (Oxford: Oxford University Press, 2013).
19 Gatrell, 'Refugees', 179.
20 L. Hammond, 'Tigranyan Returnees' Notions of Home: Five Variations on a Theme', in F. Markowitz and A. H. Stefansson (eds), *Homecomings: Unsettling Paths of Return* (Lanham, MD: Lexington Books, 2004), pp. 36–53.
21 Kasbarian, 'Myth and Reality', 358–81.
22 See A. Sanjian, 'Homeland–Diaspora Relations under Khrushchev and Brezhnev: Soviet Embassy Reports from Beirut on the Armenian Community in Lebanon, 1959–1982 (A Preliminary Study)' [in English], in M. Bruneau, I. Hassiotis, M. Hovanessian and C. Mouradian (eds), *Arméniens et Grecs en diaspora: approches comparatives* (Paris: Athènes, 2007), pp. 273–82; S. Pattie, 'From the Centres to the Periphery: "Repatriation" to an Armenian Homeland in the Twentieth Century', in Markowitz and Stefansson (eds), *Homecomings*, pp. 109–24; J. Laycock, 'Armenian Homeland and Homecomings, 1945–9: The Repatriation of Diaspora Armenians to the Soviet Union' *Cultural and Social History*, 9:1 (2012), 103–23.
23 Kasbarian, 'Myth and Reality'.
24 On the status of the Nagorny Karabakh conflict, see the previous chapter by Laurence Broers.

25 D. Vorobyeva, 'Forced Ethnic Migrants' Integration: Syrian Armenians in Armenia and Lebanon (2011–2016)' (PhD thesis, St Andrews University, 2017).
26 M. Grigoryan, 'The Syrian Refugee Restaurateurs Spicing Up Armenian Cuisine', *The Guardian* (7 March 2016), www.theguardian.com/world/2016/mar/07/the-syrian-refugee-restaurateurs-spicing-up-armenian-cuisine (accessed 20 October 2019). In the UK alone, from a tiny village in Essex: W. Lodge, 'Syrian Family Launch The Olive Branch Cafe in Wivenhoe Supporting Re-located Refugees', *East Anglian Daily Times* (29 December 2016), www.eadt.co.uk/news/syrian-family-launch-the-olive-branch-cafe-in-wivenhoe-supporting-re-located-refugees-1-4831888 (accessed 20 October 2019) to urban Glasgow: L. Johnstone, 'Damascene Street Food: Everything You Need to Know About Scotland's Delicious New Trend', *Daily Record* (16 February 2018), www.dailyrecord.co.uk/news/scottish-news/damascene-street-food-everything-you-12026417 (accessed 20 October 2019).
27 R. Vandevoordt, 'The Politics of Food and Hospitality: How Syrian Refugees in Belgium Create a Home in Hostile Environments', *Journal of Refugee Studies* 30:4 (2017), 605–21.
28 M. Lehmann, 'A Different Kind of Brothers: Exclusion and Partial Integration after Repatriation to a Soviet "Homeland"', *Ab Imperio* 3 (2012), 171–211.
29 See, for example, Pattie, 'From the Centres to the Periphery'; Laycock, 'Armenian Homelands and Homecomings'.
30 Kasbarian, 'Myth and Reality'; on memories of western Armenia see for example www.houshamadyan.org/home.html (accessed 20 October 2019).
31 Razmik Tirarian quoted in S. Jebejian, 'Syrian-Armenians: Reaffirming Identity', Repat Armenia (11 September 2013), http://repatarmenia.org/en/engage/inspiration/a/syrian-armenians-reaffirming-identity (accessed 20 October 2019).
32 Over 40,000 Syrian refugees were resettled in Canada since the start of the war, with 25,000 between November 2015 and March 2016, www.canada.ca/en/immigration-refugees-citizenship/services/refugees/welcome-syrian-refugees/looking-future.html (accessed 20 October 2019). As Canada has been a destination country for Armenian refugees from Iraq, Iran and Lebanon since the 1970s many families already had ties there. Armenian Canadian voluntary organisations helped to facilitate the refugees' applications and arrival, with many of the arrivals being privately sponsored. Armenian National Committee of America, 'Toronto Armenian Community Resettles Syrian Refugees', https://anca.org/toronto-armenian-community-resettles-syrian-refugees/ (accessed 20 October 2019).
33 George Shakarian, 'For Syrian Businessman Armenia Is a Paradise If He Succeeds', Repat Armenia (11 April 2014), http://repatarmenia.org/en/engage/inspiration/a/for-syrian-businessman-armenia-is-a-paradise-if-he-succeeds (accessed 20 October 2019).
34 *The Economist*, 'Where Syrians Find Their Refuge' (10 September 2015), www.economist.com/graphic-detail/2015/09/10/where-syrians-find-their-refuge (accessed 20 October 2019).
35 European Commission, 'EU Regional Trust Fund in Response to the Syrian Crisis, the "Madad Fund"', https://ec.europa.eu/neighbourhood-enlargement/sites/near/files/eutf_madad_action_document_armenia_30602017.pdf (accessed 20 October 2019).
36 R. Panossian, 'Between Ambivalence and Intrusion: Politics and Identity in Armenia-Diaspora Relations', *Diaspora: A Journal of Transnational Studies* 7:2 (1998), 149–96.
37 Interview with Christoph Bierwirth, UNHCR Representative in Armenia, Yerevan, November 2016.
38 *Ibid.*
39 *Ibid.*

40 'The protection of refugees, asylum-seekers and stateless persons and the prevention and education of stateless in Armenia – Protection recommendations for Armenia' UNHCR Armenian, September 2016.
41 J. Laycock, 'Belongings: People and Possessions in the Armenian Repatriations 1945–49', *Kritika* 18:3 (2017), 511–37, 519.
42 Fieldwork interviews, Yerevan 2016. Also, this is the official narrative coming from the state, e.g. the speech from the Prime Minister to Syrian Armenians, framing and appealing to them as diasporans, reported on 27 March 2017: 'The purpose of my call was to invite Diaspora Armenians – scientists, managers, doctors, cultural figures – to forward us the potential and the wealth of experience they had because it is extremely important in today's rapidly changing and developing world', www.gov.am/en/news/item/8838/ (accessed 20 October 2019).
43 On the local see, A. Ishkanian, 'Self-determined Citizens? A New Wave of Civic Activism in Armenia', Open Democracy (16 June 2015), www.opendemocracy.net/armine-ishkanian/selfdetermined-citizens-new-wave-of-civic-activism-in-armenia (accessed 24 March 2020). The diaspora itself is 'institutionally saturated' as described by K. Tölölyan, 'Elites and Institutions in the Armenian Transnation', *Diaspora* 9:1 (2000), 107–35.
44 See for example, the Armenian General Benevolent Union (AGBU), www.agbu.am/en/project-programs-2/humanitarian-13-eng/syrian-13-eng; SquareSpace, https://syrian-refugees.squarespace.com/about-us/; The Gulbenkian Trust, https://gulbenkian.pt/armenian-communities/2014/01/06/support-for-the-armenian-community-in-syria/; Aleppo NGO, https://aleppo-ngo.org/; Repat Armenia, http://repatarmenia.org/; Mission Armenia, www.mission.am/NEW/?iL=1 (all accessed 24 March 2020).
45 Concilliation Resources, *Forced Displacement in the Nagorny Karabakh Conflict: Return and its Alternatives* (August 2011), www.c-r.org/resources/forced-displacement-nagorny-karabakh-conflict-return-and-its-alternatives (accessed 20 October 2019).
46 'The protection of refugees, asylum-seekers and stateless persons and the prevention and reduction of statelessness in Armenia – Protection recommendations for Armenia', UNHCR Armenian, September 2016.
47 These are divided thus: aid to those who continue to remain in Syria (AGBU); aid to those who seek temporary refuge outside Syrian borders (Mission Armenia); aid to those who have decided to relocate to Armenia (Aleppo NGO); aid to those who want to work and live in Armenia (Repat Armenia), www.idea.am/syrian-armenian-aid-initiative (accessed 20 October 2019).
48 See http://repatarmenia.org/ (accessed 20 October 2019); Interview with Vartan Mrashlyan, Executive Director of Repat Armenia, Yerevan, November 2016.
49 Kasbarian, 'Myth and Reality'.
50 Interview with Lina Halajian, President of Center for Coordination of Syrian Armenian Issues, Yerevan, November 2016.
51 Aleppo-NGO, 'About Us', https://aleppo-ngo.org/about-us/ (accessed 20 October 2019).
52 Aleppo-NGO, 'Arabic Club', https://aleppo-ngo.org/projects/arabic-club/ (accessed 20 October 2019).
53 E. Fiddian-Qasmiyeh, 'Local Communities and Contextualizing the Localization of Aid Agenda', The Refugee Hosts, 15 January 2018, https://refugeehosts.org/blog/contextualising-the-localisation-of-aid-agenda/ (accessed 20 November 2019).
54 Another interesting initiative headed by Repat Armenian and Ayo! is Siramark, the Syrian Armenian Business network. This platform provides information about Syrian Armenian

businesses in Armenia: www.siramark.am/ and http://repatarmenia.org/en/events/a/launching-siramark-the-syrian-armenian-business-network (accessed 20 November 2019).
55 Personal observations, Yerevan, November 2016. http://repatarmenia.org/en/events/a/meet-greet-syrian-armenians-aid-initiative (accessed 20 November 2019).
56 Interview with Vartan Mrashlyan, Executive Director of Repat Armenia, Yerevan, November 2016.
57 Malkki, 'Speechless Emissaries', 386.
58 G. Atanesian, 'In Wake of Armenia's Peaceful Uprising, Diaspora's Clout Is Questioned', Eurasianet (24 April 2018), https://eurasianet.org/s/in-wake-of-armenias-peaceful-uprising-diasporas-clout-is-questioned (accessed 24 March 2020).
59 This discussion crosses media, popular and academic spheres, e.g. M. Zolyan, 'Refugees or Repatriates? Syrian Armenians Return to Armenia', Open Democracy (15 October 2015), www.opendemocracy.net/od-russia/mikayel-zolyan/refugees-or-repatriates-syrian-armenians-return-to-armenia (accessed 20 November 2019); Pattie, 'From the Centres to the Periphery'; Kasbarian, 'Myth and Reality'.
60 Interview with Talar Kazandjian, Armenian General Benevolent Union, Yerevan, November 2016.
61 K. Tölölyan, 'Restoring the Logic of the Sedentary to Diaspora Studies', in L. Anteby Yemeni, W. Berthomiere and G. Sheffer (eds), *Les Diasporas 2000 ans d'histoire* (Rennes: Presses de Universitaires, 2005), pp. 137–48; P. Gilroy, *The Black Atlantic: Modernity and Double Consciousness* (London: Verso Books, 1993).
62 E.g. A. Malek 'Enduring Exile: A Family's Journey from Armenian to Syria and Back Again', *Guernica* (15 October 2013), www.guernicamag.com/enduring-exile/ (accessed 20 November 2019).
63 S. Kasbarian, *Diasporizing the Modern Middle East: Armenian Remnants, Resilience and Reconfigurations* (forthcoming).

Afterword:
Displacement and the humanitarian response to suffering: Reflections on aiding Armenia

Peter Gatrell

A quick search of the term 'Armenia' on NGram Viewer throws up some surprises. There are five obvious 'peaks' from 1800 to the present day, four of them in the nineteenth century. The most dramatic peaks occur in connection with what came to be called 'the Eastern Question' (hence those in the late 1820s and the late 1870s) and as a result of international concern with the Hamidian massacres of 1894–96. Not surprisingly, another peak is reached during and immediately after the First World War. Thereafter, Armenia as a search term figures much less prominently, apart from a brief flurry of attention in the late 1980s, in connection with the earthquake in 1988, Armenia's independence from Soviet rule, and the ongoing Nagorny Karabakh conflict.[1]

This raises the questions: Why, when and for whom does Armenia matter? Fortunately, we can do better than to track these questions via NGram. The chapters in this book point to international concern and advocacy specifically on behalf of Armenians, whether as victims of war or of other catastrophes at different times. We learn here of the expression of concern by foreign actors in countries such as Australia, Brazil, Britain, Russia, Norway and the USA over the course of a century or more. In the early twentieth century, this was related to Armenian suffering at the hands of Ottoman oppressors, whereas by the end of the century Armenia figured as having emancipated itself from Soviet domination yet was exposed to fresh hazards and challenges. In each instance, Armenia served as a kind of touchstone for foreign governments and overseas aid agencies that could mobilise and lobby in defence of 'humanity' while serving their own political interests.

Obviously, these are also questions for Armenians, whose experiences were articulated particularly within the extensive diaspora as victims of genocide or natural disaster, and as people condemned to live without a sovereign 'homeland'. Where victimhood is concerned, under what circumstances was it possible to think beyond pure suffering? Some of the contributions to this book provide answers, such as the French aid worker of Armenian heritage who responded to the 1988 earthquake by renouncing the label of victim and affirming instead his expertise, or in the case of Syrian Armenians who emphasised the contribution they had made to the development of the country from which many of them were displaced as a result of the civil war and who can now position themselves as valuable human capital for modern Armenia in turn. Not all stories are about victimhood.[2]

Aid to Armenia nevertheless reflected genuine calamity and ordeal. Multiple institutional actors included the local, the national, the regional and the supra-national or diasporic, each with their own interests and each making a contribution to relief and reconstruction. As this book makes clear, there were different strands to follow in humanitarian endeavour, rather than a single thread. Even less convincing are teleological accounts of ever more sophisticated or developed humanitarianism. Fortunately, the authors of *Aid to Armenia* avoid this pitfall.

If it is not difficult to understand why Armenia dominated the humanitarian agenda at key moments, is it equally obvious why it vanished from the humanitarian landscape? Put another way, what are we to make of concern for Armenia as chronologically focused on the late nineteenth and early twentieth century, and on the late twentieth century? Perhaps the hiatus is self-evident, because Armenia remained hidden behind Soviet closed doors where Armenians suffered in silence. After 1920, many Armenians scattered in far-flung locations and got on with their lives. Although the Dashnaks remained deeply attached to the idea of restoring the country's independence, for the diaspora as a whole the vision became more remote. For their part, Soviet Armenians clung on to a sense of national distinctiveness while adhering to the political line determined by Moscow. To be sure, this tells only part of the story, because it ignores the evidence of tangible economic and social progress under Soviet rule. More important for our purposes, however, is that the binary division between Soviet-era isolation and an active but constrained diaspora was not rigid.[3] Some Armenians in the diaspora maintained links with Soviet Armenia, notably the Armenian General Benevolent Union (AGBU), whose efforts were directed towards Armenia's social and economic reconstruction after the upheaval of war and genocide. These efforts could, in the eyes of the AGBU, be regarded as maintaining the survivors' attachment to an Armenian 'homeland' of sorts. From the point of view of the League of Nations, these schemes had the added advantage of alleviating the pressure in host countries such as Greece, which was dealing with its own 'refugee crisis' as a result of the population exchange with Turkey. Nevertheless, this kind of cooperation was intermittent, much the same as the scheme to 'repatriate' Armenians to Soviet Armenia after the Second World War.[4]

This suggests that an apparently lengthy hiatus brought about by Soviet-era isolationism does not entirely capture the complexity of aid to Armenia. Humanitarian action may be prompted by immediate calamity, but humanitarianism has antecedents and it has an afterlife. Its impetus may draw on past episodes of engagement with sites of crisis, and it lives on in the archives of aid organisations and in the minds of many of its protagonists and recipients. Third-generation

Afterword

Armenians in the United States collected money on behalf of the victims of the 1988 earthquake, because of the scale of the disaster but specifically because they identified with Armenians in the 'homeland' who had suffered greatly from Ottoman genocide and Soviet totalitarianism. So the continuities do matter.

Retracing our steps chronologically, humanitarian aid to Armenian refugees in late imperial Russia involved multiple actors including elite organisations but also unobtrusive relief bodies that were modest in size and reach but which mattered as expressions of local initiative. During the First World War, villagers close to the front-line assisted refugees in humdrum but not futile fashion. Here, as in other instances, downplaying this unobtrusive relief went hand in hand with an insistence on elite energy, embodied in Tsarist organisations and patriotic Armenian bodies alike, and on generosity and efficacy. Although contemporary politics portrayed them as rivals, there was a good deal of cooperation between Armenian elites and Russian officialdom. The rules of the game changed in 1917, when Armenian national organisations asserted, albeit briefly, their leadership over refugee relief programmes, contributing to a sense that village and municipal initiatives were at best subsidiary to the patriotic humanitarian narrative. The emergence of the First Armenian Republic in 1918 created a national optic that obscured local, village-level intervention.[5]

Armenia's indeterminate status in the era of the First World War could also be instrumentalised by politicians overseas who pursued their own agenda. Heitor Loureiro describes the activities of the energetic and idiosyncratic pro-Armenian advocate in Rio de Janeiro, Etienne Brasil, who capitalised on Brazil's wish to gain international leverage at the League of Nations (there was even talk of handing Brazil the League's mandate over Armenia), and Brazil duly managed to secure a seat on the League's Council. Twenty years after the Genocide, however, Armenians together with Assyrian refugees forfeited their image as Christian victims of Ottoman barbarism, and were instead portrayed in Brazilian society as undesirable 'immigrants'. In Australia, too, compassion for suffering Armenia had to be mobilised rather than taken for granted; compassion fatigue could easily set in, unless one could turn stories of suffering into 'sensation', in the words of Mary Serle, or find new tactics such as 'Golden Rule Sunday', which would loosen Australian wallets. Here, opponents of humanitarian relief suggested that it was a zero-sum game: more financial aid for Armenia meant less money for impoverished Australians.

In the space remaining, I want to suggest that the contributions to this book enable us to follow three paths: to follow those who were forcibly displaced, to follow aid workers, and to follow the money.

Refugees fled to or were resettled in different destinations: to the new Soviet Armenian Republic, as well as to Greece, Palestine, Syria, Lebanon, France, Switzerland, Bulgaria, Romania, Egypt, Tunisia, the United States, Australia and elsewhere.[6] However, League of Nations High Commissioner for Refugees Fridtjof

Nansen observed that 'the authorities in Australia are unwilling to take our refugees as they had promised to take unemployed from England', and he was open to the suggestion of transferring some refugees to South-West Africa or Algeria.[7] More concerted efforts were made to move significant numbers of Armenian orphans from the Near East and Greece to Soviet Armenia to settle on land earmarked for that purpose. Soviet leaders criticised schemes of this kind, on the grounds that they benefited capitalist employers such as Gulbenkian rather than the Armenian workers whom he was accused of exploiting in order to build an oil pipeline in Syria.

Several chapters describe what became of Armenian refugees who were scattered far and wide. The role of the inter-war League of Nations is familiar to scholars, but less well known is that UNHCR became involved in discussions taking place in the 1950s. In one instance, Hans Wilbrandt, a leading figure in the post-war Refugee Service Committee, wrote from Istanbul to High Commissioner Gerrit Jan van Heuven Goedhart in 1952 to say that Armenians were being expelled from Romania, on the grounds that they held Iranian passports, which they had purchased after the First World War in order to escape further persecution. They had no wish to go to Iran, and were currently being held in Turkey, where they were doubly demonised as Armenians and as former residents of a Communist state. Perhaps they might go to Argentina? He added, 'Prior to the advent of Communism in Romania, all of these Armenians were highly productive citizens.'[8] The suffering of Armenian refugees in what are now called protracted situations was not easy to alleviate. UNHCR officials noted the 'extremely precarious economic situation in Jerusalem', adding that 'most of the Armenian refugees are living under conditions which are no better than those prevailing in refugee camps in Jordan and neighbouring countries'. Their latent energy was being lost.[9]

To follow aid agencies and aid workers is to trace personal trajectories within shifting personal, professional and institutional networks.[10] Some agencies formed networks that brought aid workers from different countries into contact with one another. The material in this book provides abundant evidence of the political claims asserted by well-connected non-governmental elite actors at different junctures. We see the creation of institutions that had a vested interest in cementing their authority, which included writing themselves as prominently as possible into humanitarian narratives, something that applies equally to the epoch of the 'greater war' and the late Soviet era.

The contributors to this book reaffirm the familiar point that individual humanitarians did not sing from the same hymn sheet. Aid agencies regularly differ over campaign tactics, for example, but also over fundamental strategy, such as whether to prioritise short-term relief or long-term reconstruction. Smith College women who worked in the field to assist female survivors and orphaned children positioned themselves as dedicated, dutiful, skilled and progressive professionals, belonging to a 'unit' in which they took pride. But they did not necessarily see eye to eye with the missionary ethos within the corridors of Near East Relief back home. However, Norwegian aid workers saw no contradiction in combining a sense of faithful mission with the pursuit of a scientific vocation. In each case, women claimed authority on the basis of many years' familiarity with Armenian society; indeed, they succeeded in re-establishing pre-war networks in peacetime.[11]

Following the money and other resources is about asking what sources of funding were significant, what new funds might be raised in the light of compassion fatigue, and about how money was used, by whom and to what extent, including whether it might be wasted or diverted to other purposes. During the First World War, aid to Armenian refugees in the Russian Caucasus was channelled by a variety of elite organisations, but much of their budget actually came from the Tsarist government. Aid workers relied in part on contributions from communities in North America, Australia and Europe, impressed by images of distressed and beleaguered victims. To whom were budget-holders accountable? Norwegian aid workers sent regular bulletins and personal letters back home to keep donors informed about the uses to which their money and their gifts of woollen clothing had been put, part of a strategy to support their claims to be effective as well as scrupulous and transparent. On the ground, things did not always work out as they wished, as the AGBU found out when some of its funds were diverted by Soviet authorities to other purposes. But it could do little to prevent this.

Looking beyond Ararat (to misquote the title of Ronald Grigor Suny's important book), this volume poses broader and important questions, such as: where does history belong in discussions of humanitarian outlook and practice, and what does the past illuminate about the present?[12] History can check any tendency to self-congratulation on the part of aid agencies; conversely, it can restrain any excessive hand-wringing on their part. History can subvert dominant pieties, for example about the distinctive 'characteristics' of the 'nation' that might be asserted in order to justify humanitarian intervention. History also invites us to think about shifting political and geopolitical contexts and conjunctures, and how these contributed together with economic and technological changes to influence humanitarian practices. Lastly, history is a resource on which refugees themselves can draw: a reminder of misfortune, persecution and hardship, but also a kind of memory bank in which personal stories of survival are stored. How those stories relate to grand projects, whether of state-building or humanitarianism, remains an ongoing issue for scholars and refugees alike.

Notes

1 Searching on NGram does not provide very stable results, however. I carried out a search at https://books.google.com/ngrams (accessed 17 October 2019).
2 For an overview, including a discussion of Armenian enterprise across a broad region, see D. Chatty, *Displacement and Dispossession in the Modern Middle East* (Cambridge: Cambridge University Press, 2010).

3 See, for example, A. Ter Minassian, *Histoires croisées: Diaspora, Arménie, Transcaucasie* (Marseilles: Editions Parenthèses, 1997).
4 J. Laycock, 'The Repatriation of Armenians to Soviet Armenia, 1945–49', in P. Gatrell and N. Baron (eds), *Warlands: Population Resettlement and State Reconstruction in the Soviet-East European Borderlands, 1945–1950* (Palgrave: Basingstoke, 2009), pp. 140–61.
5 P. Gatrell, *A Whole Empire Walking: Refugees in Russia During World War 1* (Bloomington, IN: Indiana University Press, 1999). On the post-1918 situation, see D. Rodogno, 'International Relief Operations in Palestine in the Aftermath of the First World War: The Discrepancy Between International Humanitarian Organizations' Vision, Ambitions, and Actions', *Journal of Migration History*, 6:1 (2020), 16–39.
6 See Sir John Hope Simpson, *The Refugee Problem: Report of a Survey* (London: Oxford University Press, 1939); M. S. Mandel, *In the Aftermath of Genocide: Armenians and Jews in Twentieth-Century France* (Durham, NC: Duke University Press, 2003); N. Migliorino, *(Re)constructing Armenia in Lebanon and Syria: Ethno-Cultural Diversity and the State in the Aftermath of a Refugee Crisis* (New York: Berghahn Books, 2008), as well as forthcoming work by Victoria Abrahamyan, Seda Altug, Ayşenur Korkmaz, and others.
7 Nansen to Marshall Fox, 1 February 1930, Box C1586, document 17729; see also Box R1763 document 39145, September 1924, Refugees Mixed Archival Group (Nansen Fonds), 1919–47, UN Archives, Geneva.
8 Fonds UNHCR 11, Records of the Central Registry, Series 1, Classified Subject Files, 1951–70, Folder 15/39 Armenian refugees from various countries (1952–63). The career of Wilbrandt (1903–88) as agronomist and supporter of refugees from Nazism is discussed in R. Ege and H. Hagemann, 'The Modernisation of the Turkish University after 1933: The Contributions of Refugees from Nazism', *European Journal of the History of Economic Thought*, 19:6 (2012), 944–75.
9 K. L. Essayon to James Read, 12 June 1958, Fonds UNHCR 11, as above, Folder 15/JOR/ARM Armenian refugees in Jordan (1958–67).
10 R. Kent, *The Anatomy of Disaster Relief: The International Network in Action* (London: Pinter, 1987); Peter Redfield, 'The Unbearable Lightness of Expats: Double Binds of Humanitarian Mobility', *Cultural Anthropology*, 27:2 (2012), 358–82; D. Rodogno, B. Struck and J. Vogel (eds), *Shaping the Transnational Sphere: The Transnational Networks of Experts (1840–1930)* (New York: Berghahn Books, 2014).
11 D. Rodogno, 'Non-state Actors' Humanitarian Operations in the Aftermath of the First World War: The Case of the Near East Relief', in F. Klose (ed.), *The Emergence of Humanitarian Intervention: Ideas and Practice from the Nineteenth Century to the Present* (Cambridge: Cambridge University Press, 2015), pp. 185–207.
12 A good starting point is B. Taithe and J. Borton, 'History, Memory and "Lessons Learnt" for Humanitarian Pactitioners', *European Review of History*, 23:1–2 (2016), 210–24.

Epilogue

Ronald Grigor Suny

Historians often refer to major events as 'turning points' or 'watersheds.' Revolutions, major wars, genocides, a struggle for independence, or the collapse of a great state – all might qualify as future-shaping events. Small states and nations are seldom awarded such appellations, even though a murder in Bosnia-Herzegovina was key to the cataclysm of a world war and a suicide in Tunisia launched the Arab Spring. Armenians, however, pride themselves as being a 'world historical nation', and in the forgetfulness of the last centuries they have insisted that the genocide of Ottoman Armenians and Assyrians was the tragic predecessor that enabled even greater mass killings later in the century. From Khorenatsi's disputed histories to present controversies over ethnogenesis and the events of 1915, historians writing about Armenia and Armenians have located that small place and people at the nexus of the local and the transnational. This volume adds to the literature that rejects isolation and oblivion and introduces significance, in both the sense of importance and meaning, to the experiences of Armenians and those who sought to help them. Armenians here are not simply victims but actors in their own drama.

The stance of humanitarianism is that it is not political, but chapter after chapter in this book demonstrates how even apolitical actors in political contexts were unable to avoid political entanglements. Aid to Armenians began in Britain with the horrors of the Hamidian massacres of 1895–96 and almost immediately was enmeshed within British politics and in the disputes between Britain and the United States. International cooperation prevailed, nevertheless, as well as joint efforts by state and non-state actors. Stéphanie Prévost relates how this humanitarian intervention that moved from providing relief to supporting emigration preceded the usually assumed origin date for such initiatives, that is the years of the First World War, and shows that the mid-1890s were the 'starting point' or 'pivotal point' for what has been called 'humanitarian diplomacy'. From its inception international humanitarianism faced serious obstacles from those with isolationist and nationalist impulses, both on the right and the left, who preferred domestic relief to foreign aid. A forceful individual like Etienne Brasil might cajole his government for personal ethnonational reasons, even when popular support for Armenian aid did not exist. Instead of sympathy for 'starving Armenians', a conservative Australian newspaper ran the headline: 'Australians Starve While Armenians Eat: Scandal of Overseas Philanthropy'.[1] The Australian authorities considered Armenians to be non-white and therefore excluded by the White Australia policy, even though they were Christians. Appeals by Armenophilic sympathisers were made, not against the state's racist policies, but by asserting that Armenians were 'as white and as intelligent, and as easy of assimilation into the community as English boys'.[2]

As the idea of a civilising mission by Christians gave way to the 'modern humanitarianism' of social reform and 'making good', women in particular used the opportunity offered by humanitarian work to move beyond domesticity and the enforced behaviours of their own society back home. Charity and philanthropic work had long been gendered female, and humanitarianism abroad provided a place for escaping the conventions of gender back home. Preferring sanitary engineers to clergymen, the five Smith girls took pride in their work with women and their ability to outpace men as they overcame odds and learned on the job. They moderated their sense of superiority over the locals and criticised those who were condescending to the Armenians. In a landscape of devastation during and after the First World War, relief workers provided the connections that had been torn asunder by mass murder. Norwegian nurse Bodil Biørn, operating in Soviet Armenia, organised a Christian-based relief operation in a country run by an avowedly atheistic regime and managed without the support of the state or a supervising organisation by relying on networks that she had built up earlier. The more secular AGBU had a much rougher road as the Soviets imposed harsh conditions on cooperation with Western donors. It would take the earthquake of 7 December 1988 to open the doors that the Soviets closed under Stalin. The diaspora, which had been shut out of the country for half a century, now became significant players in the recovery and regained independence of Armenia. Gorbachev's ill-founded reforms were another turning point, this time overdetermined by their lateness, their lack of planning and the loss of control by the state. Whether Armenia benefited from the collapse of the Soviet Union and the subsequent suffering or has been placed in permanent peril as a consequence remains an open question.

Impressive throughout this volume is the revelation of the motives of these caregivers far from home, working under harsh, dangerous and unpredictable conditions. The aftermath of the Genocide required, and found, people ready to risk their lives for others. Instead of a model of human nature as economically rational or naturally acquisitive – the kinds of human behaviour promoted by capitalism – the drives of Biørn or Karen Jeppe, Maria Jacobsen or Karen Marie Petersen were based in faith, love for humanity, a 'need for attachment', and fulfilment in reaching out to help others. Resentment, envy, pride, anger, hatred, certainly fear also existed in an environment saturated with death and suffering. But love, empathy and generosity not only coexisted but more often than not triumphed. Without those powerful emotions, survival would have been even less possible.

Seventy years later the earthquake in Spitak ended the Soviet practices of regulating 'the feelings of private good will', and the authorities encouraged the sense of solidarity of Soviet citizens to mobilize aid for Armenia. For the first time in decades international aid was accepted, and in the Yerevan and Leninakan airlifts hundreds of foreign planes from dozens of countries helped feed and house the destitute. The diaspora rediscovered Soviet Armenia as a 'homeland' and came to its aid expressing its guilt for its relative privilege vis-à-vis their compatriots. Nature had awakened a dormant feeling that the pain of parents demanded that those who could bring relief had to help those in need.

Of course, good intentions are never enough. Conditions and desires of principal actors determine outcomes. As Laurence Broers demonstrates in his careful reconstruction of the efforts by international agents to deal with the Nagorny Karabakh conflict, frustration rather than achievement of peace has left exposed people on the edge of a volcano. Here interests overwhelm good will; suspicions of the other wear away the needed trust between parties. Yet even here the fragile effects of years of interventions have created possibilities for solution. Civic infrastructures have been established, and between and behind the lines there remains 'the humanitarian aspiration to universality' as well as the anticipated benefits of a purported 'homeland'.

'Armenia', writes Sossie Kasbarian, 'is simultaneously a site of refuge, a historic or potential homeland, and a temporary transit zone in which to recover, recuperate and regroup'. Armenia might be a transnation, a space that includes both homeland and diaspora, but it is also a place to which refugees, repatriates, the lost and homeless can belong in some way. Perhaps that is ultimately what a nation is about: a haven in a heartless world, a place of potential security and peace where the vicissitudes of global processes – war, state collapse and neoliberal capitalism – can at least be mediated,– even when it is not quite home. Perhaps Salman Rushdie said it best: 'the real secret of the ruby slippers is not that "there's no place like home," but rather that there is no longer such a place as home: except, of course, for the homes we make, or the homes that are made for us, in Oz, which is anywhere and everywhere, except the place from which we began'.[3]

Notes

1 *Smith's Weekly* (27 September 1924), p. 11.
2 *Daily Examiner* (Grafton) (15 September 1924), p. 5.
3 Salman Rushdie, *Step Across This Line: Collected Nonfiction 1992–2002* (New York: Random House, 2002), p. 30.

Index

ABCFM *see* American Board of Commissioners for Foreign Missions
Abdul Hamid II 17
accountability 2, 17, 18, 19, 26, 28
Adana 93
   massacres 35
adoption 39–40, 109
AGBU *see* Armenian General Benevolent Union
Aharonian, Avetis 39, 41, 43, 44
Aleppo 59–61, 87, 88, 90, 110, 164–5, 169
   NGO (Aleppo Compatriotic Charitable Organisation) 173–4
Alexandropol 69, 72, 100, 104, 105, 106, 108
   see also Leninakan
Aliyev, Ilham 156, 159, 160
All-Russian Union of Towns 67–8, 71, 72–3, 76, 77
All-Russian Union of *Zemstvos* 73, 74–6
American Board of Commissioners for Foreign Missions 8, 21–2, 23–4, 25–6, 27, 28, 83, 102
American Relief Administration 84, 89, 100
American University of Armenia 141
Anglo-Armenian Association 18, 19
Antilias 51, 59
ARA *see* Armenian Relief Association
Ararat 87
ARF *see* Armenian Relief Fund
Argentina 34, 38, 39, 184
   and mandate 40, 41
Argyll, 8th Duke of, (George J. D. Campbell) 19, 21

Armenian–Azerbaijani conflict 147, 149, 150, 152
   intervention in 156–7, 160
   rival interpretations of 151
   see also Karabakh conflict
Armenian Benevolent Society 67, 70, 71, 74
Armenian General Benevolent Union 115–26, 136–7, 140, 182
Armenian Genocide 11, 15–16n
   centennial 1, 4, 34
   and humanitarianism 36, 42, 54, 101
   history of 3–4, 36, 67, 118
   and refugees 104, 115
Armenian National Delegation 38, 117, 120
Armenian Question 18, 21, 23, 28, 35
Armenian Relief Association 22–3, 25, 26, 27
Armenian Relief Fund 17–28
   Australian 55, 56, 60
   Irish 20
   Scottish 20
Armenian Republic
   and Armenian National Delegation 38
   famine in 107
   independent 11
   recognition of 34, 37, 38–9, 43, 45
   refugees in 87, 100, 103, 104, 183
   Sovietisation of 44
   see also First Republic of Armenia; Independent Republic of Armenia
Armenian Revolutionary Federation (ARF) *see* Dashnaksutiun
Aurora Humanitarian Initiative 1–3

Index

Aurora Prize 1–2
Australasian orphanage 51, 61
Ayntab 22, 27
Azerbaijan
   and Britain 149, 150–1
   and EU 156–9
   and Nagorno Karabakh Republic (NKR) 151–2, 153, 155–6, 160
   and Nagorny Karabakh 1, 12, 134, 142, 148, 151, 167
   Soviet 134, 142, 147–8

Baku 151, 152, 158,
Barton, Clara 23–4, 25
Beirut 103, 117, 119, 121
Berlin Treaty (1878) 18, 24
Bible Land Missions Aid Society, 21
Biørn, Bodil 100–11, 188
Bird's Nest (orphanage) 103
Brasil, Etienne 34–46, 183, 187–8
Brazil
   and Armenian Genocide 34
   and Armenian mandate 40–2
   and Armenian Republic 39, 43–4
   and First World War 36
   and Paris Peace Conference 37, 38
British Empire 53, 58
Bryce, Mary 60–1, 62
Bryce, 1st Viscount (James Bryce) 18, 19, 38, 40

Catholic Relief Services 150, 153, 155
Caucasus front 36, 66–7
   and refugees 71, 73, 74, 104
Chamberlain, Joseph 23
Cleveland, Stephen Grover 22, 23
Cold War
   and Armenian diaspora 115
   history of 3, 5
   and humanitarianism 5, 116, 131, 132–3, 135
Committee of Brotherly Aid 72, 77
Communist Party of Armenia 117, 125, 131, 140
compassion 50–1, 56, 57, 61
   fatigue 183, 185
   organised 36
compatriotic associations 120
   see also Aleppo, NGO

Conciliation Resources 149, 150, 152, 155, 158
Consortium Initiative 150–5
Constantinople 19, 20–4, 44
   Armenian Patriarch of 26
   Smith College Relief Unit and 83, 86, 87, 93, 94
   see also Istanbul
Currie, Philip 19, 24, 25, 27, 28

Dashnaksutiun (Dashnaks) 44, 115, 118, 126, 127n, 139–40, 182
de facto state 4, 147
   and democratisation 153–5
   and humanitarianism 147–9, 162
   recognition of 159
Demo 152, 154, 158
democratisation 148, 153, 154, 155, 159, 162
denial 7, 8, 12
Department for International Development (DfID) 150
development
   and AGBU 116
   and Cold War 132, 133
   of Soviet Armenia 116, 118–20, 126, 136–7, 139, 140
diaspora
   and the Armenian Republic 39, 44
   and history writing 7
   and homeland 164, 167–8, 170, 173, 189
   and humanitarianism/relief 9, 116, 131, 136–40, 142, 149, 171
   and Soviet Armenia 115, 122–3, 125, 131, 136–7, 139, 141–2, 167, 182
   and Syria 165, 168
   and Syrian Armenians 172–5, 176
displacement 166
   and Armenian Genocide 11
   of Azerbaijanis, 148, 167
   in Russian Empire, 75
   of Syrian Armenians 167, 171

'Eastern Question' 6, 181
Elliott, Mabel E. 106
embroidery 61
emigration 25, 26–7, 28, 165, 170, 185
Epitácio Pessoa 34, 37–9, 41–5

EPNK *see* European Partnership for the Peaceful Settlement of the Conflict over Nagorno-Karabagh
Erivan
  famine in 104
  refugees 68–9, 70, 72, 73, 87
  see also Yerevan
Etchmiadzin 26, 66, 72, 73, 88
EU *see* European Union
European Partnership for the Peaceful Settlement of the Conflict over Nagorno-Karabagh 156–7
European Union 149–50, 156–60, 161, 170

faith 106, 188
famine 22, 25, 52, 100, 104, 107, 132
FARC *see* Friends' Armenian Relief Committee
First Republic of Armenia 115
  see also Armenian Republic
  see also Independent Republic of Armenia
foster mother 108–9
'four day war' 160, 161
Fox, Marshall 59
Freedom House 153
Friends' Armenian Relief Committee 20

gender 84–5, 89, 94, 173, 188
Gladstone, William E. 21, 38, 40
Glanville, Edith 59–60
Glasnost 133
Golden Rule Sunday 50, 54–5, 183
Gorbachev, Mikhail 133, 137, 188
  and humanitarian cooperation 134–5
Greece 27, 58, 117, 119, 120–1, 124, 182, 184
Greene, Frederick D. 23, 25
Grosvenor House Committee 18, 21
Grosvenor, Hugh Lupus, Duke of Westminster 18–21, 22, 27, 28
Gulbenkian, Calouste 121, 124–5, 126
Gyumri *see* Alexandropol; Leninakan

Halo Trust 149
Hamidian massacres 6, 28–9, 102, 181, 187
Harput 24, 27, 86, 87, 88–90
Harris, Helen B. 24, 27
Harris, James Rendel 20

Hayastani Ognutian Komite 119, 120, 122–3, 125, 126, 136
HOK *see* Hayastani Ognutian Komite
homeland 25, 115, 126, 182, 183, 189
  diaspora and 136, 138–9
  Soviet Armenia as 117, 167, 171
  Syrian Armenians and 164, 168–70, 173, 175
Howard, Willard W. 25
humanitarian diplomacy 29, 187
humanitarianism
  exotic 59–62
  faith-based 101, 104
  history of 5–6, 8, 11, 17, 51, 67, 166
  modern 5–6, 36, 42, 109, 188
  professionalisation of 84
  secular 5–6, 61, 101
human rights 4, 135, 147
Hunchakian Party 25, 140

ICRC *see* International Committee of the Red Cross
ILO *see* International Labour Organisation
immigration 24, 46, 51, 57–8, 119
Independent Republic of Armenia 12, 87, 104
  see also Armenian Republic; First Republic of Armenia
Internally Displaced Persons (IDPs) 171
International Committee at Constantinople 20, 22, 23, 27
International Committee of the Red Cross 23, 149
International Labour Organisation 9
Istanbul 35, 102–3, 121, 184

Jacobsen, Maria 87, 88, 102–3, 188
Jeppe, Karen 59, 60, 103, 188
Johansson, Alma 102–3

Karabakh conflict 134, 142, 151, 160, 181, 189
  see also Armenian–Azerbaijani conflict
Kerr, Stanley 90
Khanjian, Aghasi 125, 126
Khatisyan, Aleksandr 73, 74, 76
Kimball, Grace M. 26
Kiretchjian, Herant M. 22, 25
KMA *see* Kvinnelige misjonsarbeidere
knitting 108–9, 111

Kvinnelige misjonsarbeidere 100–3, 107, 111
   and volunteers 108–9

Lausanne Treaty 54
League of Nations
   and Armenian mandate 40, 42
   and Armenian refugees 9, 58, 120–1, 182
   and Armenian women 54, 59, 103
   and Brazil 34, 37–8, 43–4, 46, 183
   and Syria 165
League of Nations High Commission for Refugees 121
League of Red Cross and Red Crescent Societies 135
Lebanon 103, 107, 124, 165
Leninakan 100, 105, 134, 141, 189
   see also Alexandropol
liberal peace 148, 154
LON see League of Nations
Lukashin (Sargis Sraponian) 117, 118

MacColl, Malcom 19, 21
Malatya 88–93
Manchester 19, 20, 21
Mandate
   over Armenia 41–4, 90, 165, 183
   French (Syria & Lebanon) 165
Mansion House Fund 20
Mardiganian, Aurora 2, 55
Marsovan 26
Miliukov, Pavel 71
Minsk Group 153, 156–7
missionaries
   ABCFM 21–8
   and NER 54–5, 86, 89–90, 92–3, 105, 111
   Scandinavian 101–3
Moscow 117
   Armenian community 72
   Declaration (2008) 156, 159
Moscow Armenian Committee 72, 77
Movement-88 154
Mush
   Bodil Biørn in 101–2
   refugees from 103, 105, 108, 110–11

Nagorno-Karabakh Autonomous Oblast' 147
Nagorny Karabakh 7, 139, 147–67, 189

Nakhichevan 72
Nansen, Fridtjof 105–6, 107, 121, 184
Nansen International Office for Refugees 46, 121
   see also League of Nations High Commission for Refugees
'Nansen passport' 9
Near East Relief 9, 14n 24, 54
   in Australia 57, 59–60
   and Golden Rule Sunday 54–5
   and Smith College Relief Unit 4, 10, 83, 86–95, 184
   and Soviet Armenia 104–7, 110, 132
needlework 52, 61, 93, 101, 108
NER see Near East Relief
nerkaght 167, 168
   see also repatriation
NKAO see Nagorno-Karabakh Autonomous Oblast'
Nubarashen 119–24
Nubar, Boghos 38, 119–24

Organization for Security and Co-operation in Europe 153
orphans 1, 87–9, 90, 92, 103–9, 138
   adoption of 39–40
   Armenian General Benevolent Union and 115, 117–19, 125
   resettlement of 58, 117, 119, 121
OSCE see Organization for Security and Co-operation in Europe

Papadjanian, M. (Papadjanov) 70–1, 117–18
Perestroika 133–5
Petersen, Karen 102–3, 188
philanthropy 10, 22, 71, 132, 134, 167
professional experience 85
progressive era 84–6, 90, 94
Protestant
   Armenians 27, 110
   Armenophiles 28
   missions 102

Ramkavar Party 140
Ravished Armenia 2
reconstruction 5, 84–5, 89, 90–2, 116, 123, 126, 182

Red Cross
    American 8, 23–4, 108
    Armenian 87
    Soviet 132, 135
refugees
    Armenian 11, 115
        in the Armenian Republic 100, 103–4
        Australia and 58–60, 62, 184
        on Caucasus front 67–74
        registration of 75–6
        repatriation of 119–22
        resettlement of 26–7, 32–3, 59, 117
        and Romania 184
    Assyrian 46, 183
    biography 101, 109–11
    experiences of 54–5, 166
    and food 107
    and history 166, 185
    representations of 174
    and Syria 165
    Syrian Armenian 164, 170–1, 175–6
        activism 173–4
Repat Armenia 173, 174, 175
repatriation
    to Soviet Armenia 117, 119–22
    see also Nerkaght, resettlement
resettlement
    in Armenia 119, 136, 175
    in Australia 58–9
    in Nagorny Karabakh 167
    of orphans 119
    of refugees 27
    see also repatriation
Russian Empire 8, 11, 66, 67, 68, 70, 71, 73, 74–5, 77

Sargsyan, Serzh 156, 159, 160
Sassouni, Karo 68, 69
Sazonov, Sergei 70
Scandinavian Women's Mission Organisation
    see Kvinnelige misjonsarbeidere
Serle, Mary 52–4, 56, 62, 183
Smith College 83, 85–6
Smith College Relief Unit 83, 86
Source of Light (Lyskilden) 106–9
Sovetakan Hayastan (Soviet Armenia) 118, 124–5

Soviet Armenia
    corruption 124
    and diaspora relations 115–16, 122–3, 136–42, 182, 189
    and Gulbenkian, Calouste 125
    and history writing 7
    humanitarian intervention in 134–5
    national revival 147
    purges 126
    refugees 111
    repatriation to 167–8, 182
    resettlement in 117, 119, 121
Special Council for Refugees 75–7
Spitak 189
Stalin, Joseph 125, 132, 188
Stepanakert 139, 152, 154, 158
Sydney 55–6, 59, 61

Tasmania 52, 53, 57
Tatiana Committee 67, 71–3, 76–7
Tbilisi 158
    see also Tiflis
Ter-Petrosyan, Levon 140–1
Tiflis 67, 71, 73, 74
    see also Tbilisi
Treaty of Sèvres 42–4
Treaty of Versailles 37
Tumanyan, Hovhannes 66–7

UNDRO see United Nations Disaster Relief Organisation
United Nations Disaster Relief Organisation 134–5
United Nations High Commission for Refugees
    and Armenian refugees 184
    and Syrian Armenians 164, 171–2, 175
UNHCR see United Nations High Commission for Refugees
uti possidetis juris 148

Van
    refugees from 69, 79, 102–3
    relief at 26
Vickrey, Charles 54–5
volunteers 83–4, 89, 108, 173

Index

VSG (*Vserossiiskii Soiuz Gorodov*) *see* All-Russian Union of Towns
VZS (*Vserossiskii Zemskii Soiuz*) *see* All-Russian Union of Zemstvos

western Armenians 165, 168
White Australia Policy 58–9, 62, 188
Wilson, Woodrow 37, 40–4

Wirt, Loyal L. 57–8
Women's Armenian Relief Fund 26

Yerevan 87–8, 118–19, 120, 122, 126, 134, 158
 protest in 139, 140, 156
 Syrians in 167, 169
 see also Erivan

EU authorised representative for GPSR:
Easy Access System Europe, Mustamäe tee 50,
10621 Tallinn, Estonia
gpsr.requests@easproject.com

www.ingramcontent.com/pod-product-compliance
Lightning Source LLC
Chambersburg PA
CBHW070355240426
43671CB00013BA/2514